THINKING BLUE | WRITING RED

Thinking Blue | Writing Red

Marxism and the (Post)Human

Stephen Tumino

OpenBook
Publishers

https://www.openbookpublishers.com
©2024 Stephen Tumino

Any digital material and resources associated with this volume will be available at https://doi.org/10.11647/OBP.#resources.0324

ISBN Paperback: 978-1-80064-877-7
ISBN Hardback: 978-1-80064-878-4
ISBN Digital (PDF): 978-1-80064-879-1
ISBN Digital eBook (EPUB): 978-1-80064-880-7
ISBN HTML: 978-1-80064-883-8

DOI: 10.11647/OBP.0324

Cover concept by Stephen Tumino.
Cover design by Katy Saunders and Jeevanjot Kaur Nagpal

Acknowledgements

Several chapters are based on previously published essays in various online and print journals/books. Chapter 1 is based on 'What is Orthodox Marxism and Why it Matters Now More Than Ever Before', which appeared in the inaugural edition of *The Red Critique* (No. 1, 2001), and also draws in part from *Cultural Theory After the Contemporary* (Palgrave Macmillan 2011). Chapter 2 is drawn from 'Animal Matters, Sublime Pets, and Other Posthumanist Stories', which appeared in *The Red Critique* (No. 14, 2012), and also in part from *Cultural Theory After the Contemporary*. Chapter 3 has previously appeared as 'Contesting the Empire-al Imaginary: The Truth of Democracy as Class', in *The Red Critique* (No. 4, 2002), and also as 'Stylizing Global Protest: Latin America and the Media' in *Nature, Society, and Thought* (17. 2, 2004). Chapter 4 is based on 'The Affective Turn in Pedagogy' from *Rethinking Marxism* (23.4, 2011). Chapter 5 is taken from 'The Day Beyoncé Turned Black' in *The Inquirer* (Vol. 23, 2016). Chapter 8 is based on 'Is Occupy Wall Street Communist?', which appeared online as part of #OccupyThought, The New Everyday: A Media Commons Project (22 Feb. 2012). Chapter 10 is based on 'Trump Speak and its Discontents', which appeared online in *New Politics* (28 July 2020). Chapter 11 reworks 'Pierre Bourdieu as New Global Intellectual for Capital' from *The Red Critique* (No. 6, 2002). Chapter 13 is in part based on 'The War against the Virus is a Class War' in *The Red Critique* (No. 16, 2020), and in part from a review of 'Why Donald Trump will never admit defeat' by Judith Butler in *Marx & Philosophy Review of Books* online (23 Feb. 2021). An earlier version of Chapter 14 previously appeared as 'Speaking of Communism: How Badiou Subtracts Class from Marx's Speeches on the Paris Commune to Produce a New (Infantile) Communism', in a special issue of *Nineteenth-Century Prose* (*Talking Revolution Marx's Speeches*, 45. 2, 2018).

To: The Red Collective

Contents

A Class(ical) Preface

The triumphalist capitalism of the neoliberal period has ended in 'a miserable fit of the blues'.[1] As in all mourning periods, it is mixed with melancholic recriminations that speak a desire for its return. It is mourned not as itself, but as a series of 'ends' — the end of democracy, the end of the middle-class, the end of unipolarity, the end of geo-political stability, the end of peace and security, the end of humans and the biosphere, the end of the future,... — which all express the secret hope for a new capitalism to-come, a capitalism beyond capitalism, with a renewed sense of justice and possibility. In the gap between the triumphalist 'idea' and its miserable 'reality', newer 'indirect apologetics' of capitalism are endlessly produced in the idioms of left theory, which, while focusing on 'the atrocities of capitalism', explains them as 'attributes not of capitalism but of all human existence and existence in general'.[2] It is the task of these (post)humanist ontologies to spiritualize the existing class relations, and, in doing so, block explanations of the 'polycrisis' that uncover its cause in the social ontology of market relations. In this way, they seek to prevent any movement beyond the existing property relations in which the left apologists are recognized and rewarded for their service to capital.

Because the mystification of the materialist roots of the crises only defers coming to terms with what is required to change it, a host of 'morbid symptoms' (Gramsci) have emerged in left cultural theory that exhibit all the progressive stages of grief: from the 'elegiac' mourning of (post)marxism, which seeks a substitute for the revolutionary proletariat in 'cognitive workers' (Negri, Berardi), to the 'melancholic' resentment at the failure of (post)marxism to articulate a true Marxism beyond Marxism worthy of the name (Badiou, Zizek), and, finally, an 'endless' mourning that oscillates between 'remain[ing] faithful to a

---

1   Karl Marx and Frederick Engels, 'The Manifesto of the Communist Party', *Karl Marx/Frederick Engels: Collected Works*, 50 vols (Moscow: Progress Publishers, 1976), 6, pp. 477–519 (p. 510).

2   Georg Lukács, *The Destruction of Reason* (London: The Merlin Press, 1980), pp. 202–3.

   https://doi.org/10.11647/OBP.0324.00

certain spirit of Marxism', while making its peace with capitalism as a 'phantomatic mode of production' without the concept of 'social class' (Derrida, Butler).[3] From Berardi's affirmation of 'depression' in place of the 'identification with socialism' as the 'positive possibility of changing social relations', to Žižek's missives on ontological 'despair' and calls for a 'modest realist left which has positive proposals of what to do' because it fundamentally accepts 'we cannot obviously step out of capitalism', and, Butler's embracing a 'politics of mourning' while bemoaning the 'resurgence of left orthodoxy' and a 'materialism based in an objective analysis of class', the transpatriotic left is busy manufacturing a timeless capitalism that is immune to critique so as to make their own allegiance to capital appear like a principled opposition.[4]

The left's mourning politics are annotations of Derrida's late theory of 'general economy', which is itself a reiteration of Bataille, in which 'the work of mourning' is made a figure of 'work in general' and thus the basis of a new 'phantomatic mode of production' beyond capitalism.[5] The new 'phantomatic' capitalism, unlike the old terrestrial capitalism, is based not on the materialist appropriation of surplus-value from unpaid labor, but the 'exappropriation' of immaterial values by the 'spectral spiritualization that is at work in any *tekhnē*'.[6] In this technological determinism, Marx's concept of the capitalist mode of production is rejected for being a 'restricted economy' because, as it is centered on the 'destructive consuming' of surplus-value, it 'would only reorganize the world of work' and leave the 'sovereignty' of the concept of value as capital intact.[7] By contrast, what is truly

---

3   *Selections from the Prison Notebooks of Antonio Gramsci*, ed. and trans. by Quintin Hoare and Geoffrey Nowell-Smith (London: Lawrence & Wishart, 1971), p. 276; Jacques Derrida, *Specters of Marx: The State of the Debt, the Work of Mourning and the New International* (London: Taylor and Francis, 2012), pp. 69, 95, 110, 120. On the 'elegaic', 'melancholic', and 'endless' as stages of Freud's mourning theory, see, Tammy Clewell, 'Mourning Beyond Melancholia: Freud's Psychoanalysis of Loss', *Journal of the American Psychoanalytic Association*, 52.1 (2004), pp. 43–67.

4   Franco 'Bifo' Berardi, 'Sabotage and Self-Organization', *Ill Will*, 6 May 2024; Charlie Nash, 'What I like about coronavirus by Slavoj Žižek'. *Spectator, USA* (2020); Judith Butler, *Precarious Life: The Powers of Mourning and Violence* (New York: Verso, 2020); 'Merely Cultural'. *New Left Review* (1998), pp. 33–44 (p. 36).

5   Georges Bataille, *The Accursed Share: An Essay on General Economy*, Zone, 1991. Derrida, *Specters*, pp. 120–21.

6   Ibid. pp. 120–21.

7   Jacques Derrida, *Writing and Difference*, trans. by Alan Bass (Chicago: University of Chicago Press, 2017), pp. 342, 439.

'revolutionary', according to Derrida, is the 'general economy' in which the 'exappropriation' of values by teletechnology makes possible the 'significative reappropriation of surplus value' in culture and in turn reveals how 'there is no sovereignty itself' in 'relation to the loss of meaning' in general.[8] Because the decentering of 'sovereignty' by teletechnological exappropriation and its discursive reappropriation 'dissolves the values of meaning', sovereignty represents 'the impossible' that Derrida equates with an 'undeconstructible justice' to come.[9] The 'phantomatic' mode of production, in other words, 'is not capitalism anymore; it is something worse' — what Derrida calls 'teletechnology', and others call 'technofeudalism' — in comparison with which the normal capitalism of daily wage-slavery seems better because at least it affirms the sovereign value of 'free speech'.[10] Any critique-al opposition to capitalism based on the contradictory antagonism between capital and labor in production is dissolved in the left's mourning and melancholia over the loss of linguistic freedom in the market, so as to make their own brand of affirmative leftism for a more deregulated capitalism appear as a more 'revolutionary' Marxism beyond Marxism.

The left's mourning politics, which hypercynically oppose market domination while making peace with class exploitation, also replace the proletariat with the 'precariat' on the premise that 'the only thing worse than being exploited is not being exploited' (i.e., deprived of one's 'human rights').[11] Thus, for Butler, a truly radical politics 'begins

---

8   Ibid., pp. 342, 439.

9   Ibid., pp. 342, 439; Derrida, *Specters*, p. 33.

10   Mackenzie Wark, *Capital Is Dead: Is This Something Worse?* (New York: Verso, 2019), p. 5; Jacques Derrida and Bernard Stiegler, *Echographies of Television: Filmed Interviews* (Boston and New York: Polity Press/Blackwell Publishers, 2002). p. 37.
Resistance to 'technofeudalism', which is really a version of Baran and Sweezy's revisionist theory of 'monopoly capitalism' for the terminally online, has replaced the critique of capitalism on the North Atlantic left: see, Brenner, Dean, Hudson, Mazzucato, and Varoufakis. Technofeudalism is an example of 'phantomatic' economics in how it defines value as an outcome of the technological domination of the market to appropriate monopoly 'rent', rather than the exploitation of labor that produces surplus-value in production, which is the source of value that circulates in the market as wages, profits, and rent. Technology is not a posthuman source of value: it is 'dead labor' that transfers value, it does not create it (Karl Marx, *Capital, A Critique of Political Economy*, vol. I, *Karl Marx/Frederick Engels: Collected Works*, 50 vols [Moscow: Progress Publishers, 1983], 35, pp. 374–508 [p. 426]).

11   Guy Standing, *The Precariat: The New Dangerous Class* (London: Bloomsbury Academic, 2011); Michael Denning, 'Wageless Life', *New Left Review*, 66.6 (2010),

with the precarious life of the Other', following Levinas' argument
that the 'more persecuted' a people are 'than the proletariat itself,
which is exploited but not persecuted', the more they represent 'a
universality higher than that of a class exploited and struggling'.[12]
According to Butler, the precariat, who have replaced the proletariat
and made capitalism other than itself, are 'the collective for whom
work is elusive, temporary, and debt has become unpayable'.[13] By
saying farewell to the working class, Butler says goodbye to Mr.
Socialism as well.[14] They argue that more 'radical forms' of social
organization beyond capitalism are by definition impossible because
'no final control can be secured' in a world in which 'my life [of First
World privilege] depends [...] on anonymous others' who lack such
privilege.[15] Communism, a class-less and therefore state-less society,
'cannot be an ultimate value', in other words, because as the State as
such is necessarily constituted 'by virtue of the social vulnerability of
our bodies', in a world in which one is constantly 'at risk of losing those
attachments' due to 'larger global processes', 'no final control can be
secured'.[16] In this geospatial imaginary, Butler is effectively aligned
with the evangelist in concluding that, 'you always have the poor with
you' (Matthew 26:11).[17] While claiming 'not knowing how to theorize
[...] the basis for global political community', Butler is clearly recycling
the sociology of 'risk society' to divide the social according to 'bodies
that matter' because they are 'protected' by State power from those
that are vulnerable to the risks of the global market, so as to affirm the
contradictions of capitalism as the ontological fate of the 'inoperative
community'.[18] And yet, despite 'not knowing' how to theorize the

     pp. 79–97 (p. 79).

12   Butler, *Precarious Life*, p. xviii; Emmanuel Lévinas, *Nine Talmudic Readings*, trans. by
     Annette Aronowicz (Bloomington: Indiana University Press, 2019), pp. 98, 113.
13   Judith Butler, ‹The Inorganic Body in the Early Marx: A Limit-Concept of
     Anthropocentrism›, *Radical Philosophy*, 2.06, Winter (2019), n. pag.
14   André Gorz, *Farewell to the Working Class: An Essay on Post-Industrial Socialism*
     (London, Pluto Press, 1997); Antonio Negri, Raf Valvola Scelsi, and Peter Thomas,
     Goodbye Mr. Socialism (New York: Seven Stories Press, 2008).
15   *Precarious Life*, pp. xii, 20.
16   Ibid., pp. xii, 20.
17   Brettler, Marc Zvi, Carol A. Newsom, and Pheme Perkins, eds, *The New Oxford
     Annotated Bible with Apocrypha: New Revised Standard Version*, 5th edn (New York:
     Oxford University Press, 2018).
18   Ibid., p. xii; Ulrich Beck, *Risk Society: Towards a New Modernity* (Los Angeles: Sage

social, Butler is quite certain nonetheless that a 'materialism based in an objective analysis of class' is impossible.[19]

Butler's ethics of precarity demonstrates the 'hypercynicism' of mourning politics. Hypercynicism, as Teresa Ebert explains, is not merely a personal attitude (cynicism/kynicism), but represents itself as 'a response to the more complex processes in the material base of an increasingly more global capitalism', while occulting its basis in class exploitation by using the language of the affective as the 'limit of critique'.[20] Despite dissolving the basis of social theory in bodily feelings of vulnerability and precarity, according to which there can be no determination as to its cause as the body and its affects are thought to exceed the conceptual, in Butler's left orthodoxy there can be no critique-al questioning of the 'politics of mourning' as class ideology because the 'precarity of life' constitutes the 'limit of the arguable' beyond which any other 'way[ ] of figuring these conditions within the sphere of politics' such as to 'rid the world of this fact' would necessarily perpetuate 'violence' toward the other.[21] Violence is always already local and causeless in Butler's politics as an ontological real that belies history, rather than caused by the existing class structure, so as to put an end to the red critique of capitalism.

The hypercynicism of Butler's mourning politics is clear in their response to the 'war' in Gaza.[22] Butler frames their response as a critique of the contemporary *Denkverbot* of media representations that only allows 'hopeless moral outrage' so that 'we cannot even stage the debate over whether Israeli military rule of the region is racial apartheid or colonialism'.[23] Without 'making clear a moral and political position' on the nature of the State of Israel, Butler argues, it is impossible

---

Publications, 1992); Jane Franklin, (ed), *The Politics of Risk Society* (London: Polity Press), 1998; Jean-Luc Nancy, *The Inoperative Community*, ed. by Peter Connor, trans. by Lisa Garbus et al. (Minneapolis: University of Minnesota Press, 1991).

19 'Merely Cultural,' p. 36.
20 Teresa L. Ebert, *The Task of Cultural Critique* (University of Illinois Press, 2009), p. 160; Rita Felski, *The Limits of Critique* (Chicago: The University of Chicago Press, 2015).
21 *Precarious Life*, pp. xii, 19.
22 Judith Butler, 'The Compass of Mourning', *London Review of Books*, 45.20, 19 Oct. 2023, n. pag. The following analysis of Butler's essay is based on 'The Left Travesty on Gaza', *The Red Critique*, 17, 2024.
23 'Compass of Mourning', n. pag.

to arrive at 'a normative aspiration that goes beyond momentary condemnation' as to the question 'what form of life would release the region from violence such as this?'[24] On Butler's framing, the question of the political and the nature of the State hangs entirely on how best to represent the 'violence, the present violence, the history of violence and its many forms' if we are 'to create a future in which violence [...] came to an end'.[25] In this way, Butler conflates a State that would allow its voiceless victims to be heard with the arrival of a future in which violence comes to an end without the need to end capitalism. In other words, Butler's highest normative political aspiration is a future form of State that would not be violent, despite the fact that the existence of the State itself testifies to an unresolvable class contradiction in the relations of production.

The statist solution Butler imagines may politically put an end to violence through more freedom of speech, while maintaining the structural violence of class, and is a direct result of their theory of the social as divided 'forms of life' that differ in their relation to the State: between 'bodies that matter' because they are symbolically valued members of existing nation States, and the precariat, who is excluded from representation in any State. Butler's social theory denies the existence of the proletariat as 'a class of civil society which is not a class of civil society' at the center of capitalism, and thus denies the conditions of life of the majority of Palestinians in Gaza whose lives they are mourning.[26] In this way Butler also ignores that what the Palestinians need is not merely political freedom, but what all workers need: economic freedom from need. It is not the Palestinians' 'exclusion' from the nation-State that explains the conditions of life in Gaza as well as what may politically be achieved, but the opposite: it is the nature of their inclusion in the class relations as a part of the proletariat (which is not the part that is directly productive of value), that determines the authoritarian form of the State and the political horizon of possibility for socialism there. This is because, as Marx explains:

---

24   Ibid., n. pag.
25   Ibid., n. pag.
26   Karl Marx, 'Contribution to the Critique of Hegel's *Philosophy of Law*. Introduction', *Karl Marx / Frederick Engels: Collected Works*, 50 vols (Moscow: Progress Publishers, 1976), 3, pp. 175–87 (p. 186).

The specific economic form in which unpaid surplus labour is pumped out of the direct producers determines the relationship of domination and servitude, as this grows directly out of production itself and reacts back on it in turn as a determinant. On this is based the entire configuration of the economic community arising from the actual relations of production, and hence also its specific political form.[27]

It is their separation from ownership of the means of production that makes the Palestinians in Gaza subject to the law of value as a 'reserve army of labor' to be used to cheapen the cost of productive labor in the region, not their unjust 'exclusion' from cultural representation.[28]

The war(s) over Gaza between Israel and the US versus Hamas, with support from the Islamic Republic (formerly known as Iran), 'are economic and are ultimately about controlling resources in the interests of controlling the price of labor'.[29] These nation-states and their proxies all use nationalism, which divides workers into 'us' and 'them' categories of (il)legality and (il)legitimacy, to keep the workers exploited. Racism, in short, is 'the secret by which the capitalist class maintains its power' because '[l]abour cannot emancipate itself in the white skin where in the black it is branded'.[30] What is mystified by the mourning left is that even without the occupation, whether in their own nation-state or a reformed state of Israel, the Palestinians of Gaza, like the workers in South Africa after the official end of apartheid, would remain a source of exploited cheap labor in the region because '[r]ight can never be higher than the economic structure of society'.[31] Possessing 'equal rights', or what are called 'human rights', means having the freedom to be equally exploited by capital. The North Atlantic left, however, reads the class politics of Gaza, which exposes 'human rights' as the freedom to trade in the market, as a mark of being insufficiently attuned to otherness and thus a sign of 'incivility'. Class analysis of Gaza is taken to be disrespectful

---

27 Karl Marx, *Capital, Volume III*, *Karl Marx/Frederick Engels: Collected Works*, 50 vols (Moscow: Progress Publishers, 1983), 37, p. 777–78.

28 Marx, *Capital*, vol. I, p. 626.

29 Rob Wilkie, 'In the Case of Gaza', *The Red Critique*, 17, 2024, http://redcritique.org/WinterSpring2024/inthecaseofgaza.htm.

30 Karl Marx, 'Letter to Sigfrid Meyer and August Vogt', London, 9 April 1870, *Karl Marx/Frederick Engels: Collected Works*, 50 vols (Moscow: Progress Publishers, 1988), 43, pp. 471–76 (p. 475); *Capital*, vol. I, p. 305.

31 Karl Marx, 'Critique of the Gotha Programme', *Karl Marx/Frederick Engels: Collected Works*, 50 vols (Moscow: Progress Publishers, 1984), 24, p. 87.

of the cultural other on the left because it denies the need for a cultural politics for those subject to racialist violence. Class critique is silenced as a lack of civility so as to present the allegiance of the left to capital as the limit of the radical.

Butler, in the name of a 'different political morality' that would acknowledge 'all the horror there is to represent', maintains the bourgeois framing of events in Gaza by arguing that 'the history of violence, mourning and outrage as it is lived by Palestinians' is part of 'the history of colonial violence' rather than contemporary capitalism.[32] Leaving aside the allusion to the history of colonialism as a story of racialized violence — it is actually the history of capital accumulation — which Butler invokes not to explain but to mystify in the manner of Joseph Conrad by placing this 'horror' outside history ('where does this horror begin and where does it end?'), the root of the conflict in Gaza here is made affective (lived experience, mourning, outrage), and the goal of politics is therefore also immaterial: to recognize the horror of Gaza and, in so doing, symbolically value those whose lives have been devalued by racialist violence.[33]

It is not racial violence that explains the war(s) in Gaza, however, but the structural violence of class that daily through its inhuman economic logic determines who lives and who dies without the need for any overt political violence and despite any racial/moral justification or condemnation. The violence used against the Palestinians in Gaza — by Israel and Hamas — is wielded to regulate the cost of labor in the region as the Palestinians there constitute an 'industrial reserve army of labor' — 'a disposable mass of human material always ready for exploitation' that is 'a necessary product of accumulation or of the development of wealth on a capitalist basis'.[34] By making Gaza a 'symbol of European oppression and colonialism', the North Atlantic left conflates the actual conditions of life of the Palestinians in Gaza as a cheap source of labor power for borderless capital with the metaphysics of racial violence, so as to affirm market relations as the limit of the possible.[35]

---

32   'Compass of Mourning', n. pag.
33   Ibid., n. pag.
34   Marx, *Capital*, vol. I, p. 626.
35   Slavoj Žižek, 'Jews and Palestinians are both Victims of Western Racism', *Haaretz*, 12 Dec. 2023. For more on the class politics of Gaza, see, 'Dossier on Gaza' in *The Red Critique*, 17, 2024.

Butler takes a 'matterist' or 'object-al' orientation to Palestinians lives, rather than a materialist one, by assuming that the root of the crisis in Gaza is the lack of estimation that 'Palestinian lives matter', which reduces them to a condition of 'bare life' as so many bodies traumatized by State violence, rather than a source of labor power that is opportunistically used to increase the value of borderless capital.[36] As in nationalist discourse, what is thought to be lacking is the freedom for Palestinians to express their cultural identity and thereby acquire the self-esteem necessary for self-determination. The politics of class that comes out of the social conflicts over material resources are thus displaced with the 'politics of recognition', which relies on the concept of the political as an autonomous cultural realm where the rule of capital as a real abstraction is subsumed in the affective concrete, where an 'undeconstructible justice' stages its 'infinite vigilance' against the 'violence of metaphysics'.[37] As in Hegel's master/slave dialectic, here the problem of the political becomes how to invent a novel symbolic context where the proper recognition and self-estimation of others may take place beyond the contest to the death demanded by the existing order. Butler adopts the left Hegelian solution and imagines the inversion of ideology from within, the transvaluation of values, to be the only true solution, rather than the class critique of ideology from its outside.

Butler's mourning politics is cynical in how the justification for opposing the dominant 'contextualization' of what is happening in Gaza relies on the recognition that since any 'framework' would have to 'consider some lives to be more grievable than others' it must necessarily defer the arrival of 'true equality and justice'.[38] But, as Butler's affective framing in mourning the loss of politically non-violent others in Gaza equally does so, their mourning politics is actually hypercynical because what it means in the end is that 'no future of true peace can be imagined', and all that can be done is to mourn the loss of any truly emancipatory

---

36   Giorgio Agamben, *Homo Sacer: Sovereign Power and Bare Life* (Stanford: Stanford University Press, 2020).

37   Nancy Fraser, and Axel Honneth. *Redistribution or Recognition?: A Political-Philosophical Exchange* (New York: Verso, 2003); Jacques Derrida, 'Force of Law: The "Mystical Foundation of Authority"', in *Acts of Religion*, trans. and intro. by Gil Anidjar (London and New York: Routledge, 2002), pp. 228–98 (pp. 234, 243).

38   'Compass of Mourning', n. pag.

goal.[39] By marking any explanation of violence that goes beyond their affective framing as equally violent in its silencing of the suffering of others, Butler reveals that the 'true' goal of their 'politics' is sentimental and reactionary, rather than materialist and transformative. The affective is deployed, in other words, not to intervene into the existing conditions with an explanation of their root cause, which is necessary to change it, but to deflect awareness away from the class outside (exploitation) onto the psychological 'inside' (mourning), where 'desire and its object are one and the same thing' and the intensity of feelings defines the limits of the possible.[40] Butler's writings on Gaza as a result, give a 'picture thinking' (Hegel) of events that, as in the mainstream commentary, depicts the 'horror' and 'violence' as occasions for empathy, but that refuses to explain its abstract causality with the 'force of abstraction'.[41] Because such an explanation requires 'conceiv[ing] the sensuous world as the total living sensuous *activity* of the individuals composing it', by failing to conceptualize the class politics of Gaza, Butler is therefore

> compelled to take refuge in the 'higher perception' and in the ideal [...]
> and thus to relapse into idealism at the very point where the communist
> materialist sees the necessity, and at the same time the condition, of a
> transformation [...] of the social structure.[42]

In Butler's moralizing leftism it is only those who 'deplore violence and express our horror' who 'help to create the non-violent world' to come, which must always remain a spiritual center ('true equality and justice') rather than a material reality (the abolition of class).[43] The spiritual ideal of non-violence is thus made into the most infallible means for the realization of 'true' or 'ethical socialism' ('a normative aspiration' of 'a future in which violence comes to an end'), while ignoring the

---

39   Ibid., n. pag.
40   Gilles Deleuze and Félix Guattari, *Anti-Oedipus: Capitalism and Schizophrenia* (Minneapolis: University of Minnesota Press, 1983), p. 26.
41   G.W.F. Hegel, *Phenomenology of Spirit*, trans. by A.V. Miller (New York: Oxford University Press, 1977), pp. 35, 463; Karl Marx, 'Preface to the First German Edition of *Capital*', *Karl Marx/Frederick Engels: Collected Works*, 50 vols (Moscow: Progress Publishers, 1983), 35, pp. 7–11 (p. 8).
42   Karl Marx and Frederick Engels, 'The German Ideology', *Karl Marx/Frederick Engels: Collected Works*, 50 vols (Moscow: Progress Publishers, 1976), 5, p. 41.
43   'Compass of Mourning', n. pag.

materialist violence of class which is necessary to change it.[44] The true radical in this political morality tale is one who obscures the structural violence of class society with the metaphysics of violence, but whose 'heart goes out' to all non-violent victims of politically 'violent' speech.[45]

Not only is Butler's framing of events in Gaza not a 'different political morality' as they claim, but because it cynically immunizes the class relations from critique while deploring violence in general, it also spiritualizes the goal of politics into an impossible 'justice to come'.[46] This spiritualization of the conflicts is why despite denying that what is happening in Gaza 'is not simply a failure of political empathy', this is precisely what Butler ends up affirming by making 'mourning' the imaginary basis for realizing a non-violent world. For Butler, 'true equality and justice' is only realized in an affective commons that banishes materialist class consciousness.

The left's mourning politics is hypercynical in how it gives a knowing wink to the audience of their textual performances that signals that although they 'know' that the affective has always been used to undermine radical critique, they also un-know it by making 'the work of mourning' the basis of a 'phantomatic' capitalism without social classes, in order to make their own brand of cultural reformism appear to be the limit of the political. Their mourning politics has all the signs of what Hegel calls the 'Unhappy Consciousness' as a result.[47] Caught between the necessity of revolutionary class politics and opportunistic adjustment to going along to get along in the market, they make 'what should be' appear indistinguishable from 'what is'. In this way, they deny the materialist connection between 'the most radical rupture with traditional ideas' and 'the most radical rupture with traditional property relations'.[48] This book is the exact opposite: in its analyses it opposes to the *blue thinking* of leftist hypercynicism the principled politics of *writing red*, which reconnects cultural theory to its class basis.

---

44   Marx and Engels, *Manifesto*, pp. 510–13; V. I. Lenin, *Materialism and Empirio-Criticism, V. I. Lenin Collected Works*, 45 vols (Moscow: Progress Publishers, 1977), 14, p. 368.
45   'Compass of Mourning', n. pag.
46   Derrida, 'Force of Law', p. 243.
47   G. W. F. Hegel, *Phenomenology of Mind*, trans. by James Black Baillie (Harper Torchbooks, 1967), pp. 189–219.
48   Marx and Engels, *Manifesto*, p. 504.

Thinking Blue Versus Writing Red

In its chromatic spectralysis of cultural texts, *Thinking Blue/Writing Red* is, despite appearances, a 'classical' text. It is classical not in its subject matter — which is diverse and ranges in its readings from texts of literary modernism (Melville's narratives, Pauline materialism,...) and high theory (Marxism, (post)humanism, new communism,...), to popular culture (*Twin Peaks*, Beyoncé's performances,) and 'current events' (Trump, Covid,...) — but in its analytical mode. In its analyses it argues that there is no agency (change) without reflection (critique), no concrete realization of freedom (the new), without the abstract recognition of necessity (theory). In this it echoes the etymological origins of critique in ancient Greek (*kritikos*: discernment, judgment) and its medical associations with crisis (*krisis*: turning point) and *kairos* (opportunity) in the diagnosis and treatment of disease, in both the physical body as well as in the body politic.[49] In this classical tradition, there is no *kritik* without *krisis*, no *kairos* without *kritik*, as critique is necessary to discern the causes behind 'what is' to effectuate the concrete realization of what 'ought to be'.

Besides being classical in this philosophical sense, the analytical mode featured here is also, and more importantly, class-ical in the modern sense of 'radical' in that 'critique represents a class'.[50] As radical (i.e., root) knowledge, critique 'includes in its comprehension and affirmative recognition of the existing state of things, at the same time also, the recognition of the negation of that state, of its inevitable breaking up', and, therefore, 'exceeds', as Derrida puts it, the scholastic containment of critique as 'self-critique' that is 'most proper in the philosophical as such' because it foregrounds 'the mode of production

---

49   See, *Corpus Hippocraticum*, and, Aristotle's *Politics* (1289b). Because 'in classical Greek the subsequent separation into two domains of meaning –that of a 'subjective crisis' and an 'objective crisis' — were still covered by the same term', the subjective diagnosis of disease that uncovered its 'is-ness' (critique) was also understood to be the means for its objective prognosis (crisis) in terms of its becoming (Reinhart Koselleck, 'Crisis', trans. by Michaela W. Richter, *Journal of the History of Ideas*, 67. 2 (April 2006), pp. 357–400 [p. 359]).

50   Karl Marx, 'Afterword to the Second German Edition of *Capital*', *Karl Marx/Frederick Engels: Collected Works*, 50 vols (Moscow: Progress Publishers, 1996), 35, pp. 2–20 (p. 16).

and reproduction of the philosophical'.[51] Derrida's recognition of the institutional containment of 'outside' (radical) critique to 'immanent' (philosophical) critique is not contested but reinscribed in his theory of writing as *différance* (with an a), which he understands as suspending the 'logic of the decidable, in other words, of opposition, whether dialectical or not, whether an idealist or materialist dialectics'.[52] Such a move of suspending the dialectic of history in the writerly imaginary is symptomatic of what I am here calling *thinking blue*. By 'thinking blue' what I mean is the institutionalized mode of immanent critique that undoes the dialectic of the conceptual from within to produce an intellectual impasse that accepts what is as what ought to be, and thus, which must always end in 'a fit of the blues'.[53] Through cultural mediations that defer and delay the implication of knowledge in the social totality, blue thinking displaces the 'outside' knowledge that workers need for their emancipation from capital to instead construct a virtual commons that oscillates with surface differences and emotional intensities, but that resists fundamental 'change', which requires the overcoming of differences with sober senses to produce the new — international communism.

Derrida's understanding of critique as suspending the dialectic of 'inside' and 'outside' reinscribes the binaries of culture; it does not 'exceed' them. What it marks as the 'outside' is the *nonconceptual*, which it considers 'material', as in the scholastic sense of matter as the (sensual) other of the conceptual. Différance is 'neither a word nor a concept', and like Derrida's other neologisms such as the 'trace', 'supplement', 'pharmakon', etc., it represents a 'materiality without materialism', insofar as its being is dependent on its effects upon 'thought', which makes it legible as 'text'.[54] As in scholastic materialism, the material here is 'matterist': it is concerned with what is 'real' in

---

51 Marx, *Capital*, vol. I, p. 20; Jacques Derrida, 'The Crisis in the Teaching of Philosophy: Right to Philosophy 1', *Who's Afraid of Philosophy?* (Stanford: Stanford University Press, 2002), pp. 99–116 (p. 102).

52 Ibid., p. 101.

53 Marx and Engels, *Manifesto*, p. 510.

54 Jacques Derrida, *Margins of Philosophy* (Chicago: University of Chicago Press, 1986), p. 3; 'Typewriter Ribbon: Limited Ink (2) ("within such limits")', *Material Events: Paul de Man and the Afterlife of Theory*, ed. by Tom Cohen (Minneapolis: University of Minnesota Press), pp. 277–360 (p. 281).

itself separate from social 'praxis'.[55] The concept of matter, however, is itself determined historically and in its abstract form, is a reflection in thought of the commodity-form within the social relations in which labor-power is commodified and made into a thing that only exists so long as it produces profit in the market. In its cultural analyses, *Thinking Blue/Writing Red* argues that the 'outside' of critique is not the excess of thought or the extra-discursive, whether as the opacity of 'matter' or the self-difference of thought from within, but the class antagonism that produces 'what is' as well as its negation, and thus explains the phenomenal and discursive as sites of class antagonism that inform conflicting ideas of what 'ought to be'.

Knowledge of the outside, rather than its undoing ('thinking blue'), is necessary for side-taking in the agora over the shape of the social — 'writing red'.[56] Red writing is an intervention into the reinscription of the outside to the terms of the inside authorized by thinking blue that implicates writing in the 'constant/resistant critique' (*kritisieren beständig*) of capital/wage-labor relations, the dialectics of which is inscribed in the ratio of exploitation in 'the working day'.[57] The deconstruction of the dialectic of the concept in blue thinking leaves the material logic of the dialectic in the workday intact, it does not exceed nor escape it. Red writing goes beyond the metaphysics of writing as separate from the dialectic of class relations that shape writing and explain its alienated effects as owning to contradictions in the social relations of production. Writing, on this materialist account, is not merely a 'tool' nor is it 'agential' in-itself in its self-differing, but rather a necessary relay of the 'collective worker', as writing is 'the concrete concentration of many determinations' and the 'unity of the diverse'.[58] Writing is a

---

55   Karl Marx, 'Theses on Feurebach', *Karl Marx/Frederick Engels: Collected Works*, 50 vols (Moscow: Progress Publishers, 1975), 5, pp. 3–8 (p. 3).

56   Red writing is 'side-taking' not in the immediate 'spontaneous' activist sense of taking sides in the cultural conflicts over 'values' in ideology by taking up predetermined 'choices' in the market, but in the materialist sense that in class society 'polemics aimed against the ruling class are transformed at a certain moment into revolution' (Leon Trotsky, *Terrorism and Communism: A Reply to Karl Kautsky* [Ann Arbor: University of Michigan Press, 1961], p. xix).

57   Karl Marx, 'The Eighteenth Brumaire of Louis Bonaparte', *Karl Marx/Frederick Engels: Collected Works*, 50 vols (Moscow: Progress Publishers, 1979), 11, pp. 99–197 (p. 106); *Capital*, vol. I, pp. 239–243.

58   Karl Marx, *Grundrisse: Foundations of the Critique of Political Economy* (*Rough Draft*) (London: Penguin Books, 1993), p. 101.

diverse unity of social praxis because, it is, (1) always 'practical, real consciousness' of the life activity of humans that provides the means to coordinate and transform their diverse labor practices, (2) an archive of knowledge for-itself that connects the present moment of labor with its past and thus makes possible the differentiation of scientific advances from ideological false paths, and, (3) the medium for 'social-teleological positing' that guides transformative praxis through the never-ending critique of ideology in the historical series of humans' laboring activity.[59]

Outside Critique in the Teaching Machine

Blue thinking has been both instrumental in the construction of the (post)humanities as well as the current 'post-truth' culture and has also been used to teach the high-tech workforce educated in the academy to blur the 'inside' and the 'outside' so that everything is thought to be a matter of differing values and marks of taste. Among other things, what this has done to the concept of social class is to make it is 'a sort of affinity' or 'congeniality', rather than something as crude as 'property and ownership'.[60] Class, in other words, is made over into a delectable sign of cultural difference to be affirmed in localities as a mark of distinction, rather than the ruthless and systemic deprivation that determines who will be well housed and educated, medically cared for and nutritionally fed — and who will not — and that explains *why* such disparities continue to exist in the midst of abundance. Class, in short, is made casual, rather than causal, and thus naturalized. This 'post-al' view of a capitalism beyond capitalism in which the ruthless binary of class is translated into market differences and the cultural semiotics of distinction ('classy'), is underwritten by Derrida by his reification of writing as having 'exceeded [the] logic of the decidable' such that we take part 'in a completely different historical necessity': a 'phantomatic mode of production' that requires a new sense of justice that does not subscribe to the concept of 'social class' that is foundational for the 'Marxist critique' of capitalism.[61]

---

59 Marx and Engels, *German Ideology*, p. 44; György Lukács, *The Ontology of Social Being: 3. Labour* (London: Merlin Press, 1978), p. 3.
60 Jacques Derrida, et al., *A Taste for the Secret* (London: Polity, 2001), pp. 84–85.
61 Derrida, 'Crisis', p. 101; *Specters*, pp. 69, 120.

The semiotic pluralization of 'class', authorized by Derrida's deconstruction of Marx's binary class theory as rooted in exploitation, is facing serious challenges. This occurs at a time when the 'middle class' — which is another spectral effect as their professional salaries come from the hidden unpaid surplus labor of workers — is losing the cultural markers of distinction and awakening to the reality that class is, in fact, binary. Recently a video rant posted to Tik Tok went viral that posed the question: 'Where did the American dream go? What happened to the middle class?'[62] 'Middle class', as Ebert and Zavarzadeh have explained, is that privileged signifier in bourgeois social commentary meant to signal that Americans live in a 'post-class' society that has left the class binary of exploiters/exploited behind because class has become plural and is now an index of cultural taste pegged to an 'inventory of objects' (lifestyles), rather than an economic reality.[63] In the viral Tik Tok video, however, 'middle class' signals an out of touch refusal to grasp the reality that 'the world has fucking changed' and while 'there used to be upper class, middle class, lower class. It's literally turning into the ultra-wealthy and then everybody else is just poor'. The secret of Derrida's 'taste for the secret' that makes him 'prefer the secret to the non-secret' is a class denial of the class reality of 'everybody else is just poor'.

What in Derrida's allusive philosophical writings is announced in the abstract idioms of high theory as a new order of being that has surpassed class as the basis of social critique has since been fully integrated in the corporate university as 'postcritique'. In the postcritique-al academy, it is the reactionary side of deconstruction in which concepts are thought to be 'oppressive' of difference that is preserved, while its critique of writing as a sign of personal and individual freedom is placed under a discursive ban by returning to an aesthetic reading of texts based on one's singularly affective response. In the 'affective turn' of the (post) humanities, as I discuss in Chapter 4, even the immanent critique

---

62   Alanah Khosla, 'Mother causes a storm with rant about her adult children who are struggling to pay the bills', *Daily Mail*, 7 August 2023 https://www.dailymail.co.uk/femail/article-12380023/My-hard-working-children-struggling-pay-bills-Im-tired-feeling-helpless-did-American-dream-Mother-causes-storm-rant-adult-children-struggling-bay-bills.html [accessed 8 June 2024].

63   Teresa L. Ebert and Mas'ud Zavarzadeh. *Class in Culture* (London and New York: Routledge, 2016), p. 90.

of textuality is no longer to be tolerated but dismissed — at least rhetorically as it is secretly preserved — along with Marxist ideology critique for its pathological 'neglect of emotion' and 'chronic negativity', which are taken to be sure signs of critique as such being 'insufficiently attuned to [...] otherness' because of its singular focus on uncovering ideology.[64] Critique, by exposing ideology, is taken to be 'the dominant metalanguage' in how it fails 'to do [...] justice' to 'the distinctive agency of art works' and 'what literature does' as 'a coactor' that helps 'make a difference'.[65] The 'other' as text whose affective performance is to be 'appreciated' matters more in the postcritique-al (post)humanities than how texts construct the obviousness of social relations that maintains exploitative social differences.

Felski echoes Latour in arguing that the radical project of critique has failed because not only has critique become a culturally normative metalanguage and is therefore no longer 'outside' and oppositional, but also because its singular focus on exposing ideology fails to consider how the affective value of texts may help bring about more inclusive and just social practices. However, what this argument reveals is that 'postcritique' is not a 'new' inquiry into the agency of texts as is claimed, but a re-branding of the familiar post-al theory that makes the 'de-hierarchization' of cultural values the limit of social justice by separating the text from its roots in class exploitation. Felski is not opposing the 'dominant' mode of critique of 'the last four decades', as she claims.[66] She has no problem with equating the culturally normative with the oppression of difference, which is the libertarian dogma that the dominant immanent and reformist criticism of post-al cultural theory teaches. Such a rhetorical distancing from the dominant is necessary for left intellectuals to maintain their appearance of radicality while providing the high-tech workforce with the affective make-up required in the cyber-economy by limiting the concept of agency to the merely surface innovation of cultural appearances. However, because the market for such skills in beginning to wear thin and the workforce is demanding more radical changes in social

---

64   Elizabeth S. Anker and Rita Felski, eds., *Critique and Postcritique* (Durham: Duke University Press, 2017), pp. 8, 11–12.

65   Felski, *Limits of Critique*, pp. 5, 12–13.

66   Ibid., pp. 3–4.

relations, Felski is forced to diffuse the real object of her postcritique, which is to justify the exclusion from the (post)humanities of 'critique as outside', i.e., critique as a 'mode of militant reading' that is 'engaged in some kind of radical intellectual and/or political work' against 'oppressive social forces'.[67] Postcritique, like deconstructive immanent critique, opposes 'outside' critique by refusing to 'look[ ] behind the text — for its hidden causes, [and] determining conditions' and thereby reifies the surfaces of culture as an 'immanent [...] weightless, disembodied, freewheeling dance'.[68] Where Felski introduces a 'difference' to distinguish her own brand of culturalism from the many other brands on offer in the academic marketplace is by using a less-alienating language than the old discourse theory previously required. Instead, she adopts the 'new materialist' language of Latour's actor-network theory and talks about texts as a 'coproduction between actors'.[69] Of course the 'lesson' here teaches the future workforce that exploiter/exploited relations are overcome through the aesthetic: when we learn to appreciate exploitative differences as merely cultural differences that fuel the feeling that life is worth living and give 'hope' in market society. Felski is not opposed to 'critique'; she is in fact quite eager to critique the 'radical' critique for that which she, following arch-reactionaries like Nietzsche, considers its 'nay-saying' rather than 'yay-saying'.[70] In other words, critique that is non-affirmative of the existing has no place in Felski's version of the (post)humanities because its 'sadly depleted language of value' will not serve to sell, or, to use her word, 'legitimate', the university at a time of crisis.[71] The idea that 'the demand to give up illusions' is 'sad', however, is only displaced mourning over the *state of affairs which needs illusions*'.[72]

The negativity of critique that Felski dismisses is not, as she claims, an expression of a 'bad' affect or a pathological 'disposition', nor is it

---

67   Ibid., pp. 1–2, 7.
68   Ibid., pp. 11–12.
69   Ibid., p. 12.
70   Ibid., p. 9.
71   Ibid., p. 5.
72   Karl Marx, 'Contribution to the Critique of Hegel's *Philosophy of Law. Introduction*', *Karl Marx/Frederick Engels: Collected Works*, 50 vols (Moscow: Progress Publishers, 1976), 3, pp. 175–87 (p. 176).

a matter of 'style'. These are all tropes of a reformist cultural criticism to submerge critique in the affective and to affirm its own moody cultural politics as what someone once called 'capitalist realism': the inability to even imagine an alternative to capitalism.[73] As I will explain, the 'negativity' of critique has nothing to do with a subjective attitude, as in the oft-quoted and hollowed out fragment of Gramsci about the 'pessimism of the intellect' and its philosophical elaboration in Adornian negative dialectics and Žižek's negative ontology.[74] Critique is the negation of negation in the totality: a surfacing of class antagonism, for example, that explains why capitalism now can only be affirmed by denial of the self-negation at the root of its social ontology — the exploitation (and increasing abolition) of social labor for private profit.

It is ironic that Felski who does everything to deny 'critique as outside' and deprive it of any 'specialness' is herself denying the place and role of critique in the exploitative class relations. She is of course aware of this historic function, which is why her arguments are so invested in exposing the lack of allegiance of 'militant' critique to the corporate flattening of the humanities as (post)humanities. The affirmative denial of the class basis of critique can be seen in Felski's text, which in this way directly echoes Latour, as I explain in Chapter 12, in its anxiety that the 'exceptionalism' of critique as 'outside' the ideological has become 'normative' and permeated the culture. It does not occur to Felski or Latour to ask why the affective critique of outside critique as 'exceptional' is needed if it is so obviously un-exceptional because outside critique has become normative. Furthermore, how can the 'exclusiveness' of critique, which Felski claims perpetuates an out-of-touch academic jargon, be taken as a sign of the 'legitimation crisis' of the humanities when its popularity shows

---

73   Fredric Jameson, 'Future City', *New Left Review* 21 (2003), pp. 65–79; Slavoj Žižek, 'The Spectre of Ideology', in *Mapping Ideology*, ed. by Slavoj Žižek (New York: Verso Books, 2012), pp. 1–33; Mark Fisher, *Capitalist Realism: Is There No Alternative?* (London: Zero Books, 2022).

74   As Engels explains, 'Negation in dialectics does not mean simply saying no, or declaring that something does not exist, or destroying it in any way one likes', but is 'determined [ ] by the general and [ ] particular nature of the process' in the social totality ('Anti-Dühring', *Karl Marx/Frederick Engels: Collected Works*, 50 vols [Moscow: Progress Publishers, 1987], 25, pp. 5–312 [p. 131]).

it to be in tune with the times?[75] The reason for the incoherence here becomes clearer when Felski indicates the political interests behind her argument for 'limiting' critique when she represents her views as part of a 'groundswell of voices, including scholars in feminist and queer studies as well as actor-network theory, object-oriented ontology, and influential strands of political theory' who all, she says, consider Marxist scholars, who alone advance outside critique, 'risible' for our condemnation of immanent critique 'for not being critical or oppositional enough' because of their 'failure to live up to its radical promise'.[76] It seems that what has put the (post)humanities is crisis is not the 'normativity' of radical outside critique after all, but the 'exclusivity' of the reformist cultural criticism in what are feared to be 'militant' times. To grasp the class interests at work here, one needs only ask why the 'new materialist' scholars such as Felski are given grants in the millions of dollars to 'research' ways in which to 'limit' critique to 'redescribing' the literary surfaces of texts in agential language and turn critique away from its militant task of changing the world outside the text, while those who do the bulk of the teaching in the humanities are adjuncts who lack basic health care and cannot even pay their rent from teaching alone.[77]

Thinking Blue/Writing Red proposes to work through the class pessimism of the dominant post-class cultural theory (thinking blue) as a necessary mediation for an-other kind of thinking that foregrounds class as the basis for transformation of the totality (writing red). The essays collected here offer an alphabetpedia of how critique-al theory has been voided of class in the textwares of the North Atlantic bourgeois left, which has normalized the supremacy of capital and justified its bankrupt politics. In this anti-theory climate, the classical Marxism being advanced here, especially the chapter which opens the book on Orthodox Marxism, has been placed under a discursive ban and rejected for publication in the left public sphere (by such journals and fora as *Monthly Review, Jacobin, Sublation Magazine,* and Zer0 Books, e.g.), because it violates the rule of pragmatic accommodation and

---

75 Felski, *Limits of Critique*, p. 5.
76 Ibid., p. 8.
77 Lorenzo Perez, 'UVA English Professor Lands Large Danish Grant to Explore Literature's Social Use', *UVA Today*, 25 March, 2016, news.virginia.edu/content/uva-english-professor-lands-large-danish-grant-explore-literatures-social-use [accessed 8 June 2024].

endless negotiations on the terrain of capital and wage-labor relations that constitutes the 'politics' of the cultural left.[78] Its publication now is therefore an act of re-new-ing classical Marxism in the contemporary by putting it in active contestation with the dominant today.

---

78 By contrast, the essay on orthodox Marxism has also been the most widely translated and published outside the North Atlantic left.

THEORY

1.
Marxism

What is Orthodox Marxism?

Any effective political theory will have to do at least two things: it will have to offer an integrated understanding of social practices and, based on such an interrelated knowledge, offer a guideline for praxis. My main argument here is that among all contesting social theories now, only Orthodox Marxism has been able to produce an integrated knowledge of the existing social totality and provide lines of praxis that will lead to building a society free from necessity.

But first I must clarify what I mean by Orthodox Marxism. Like all other modes and forms of political theory, the very theoretical identity of Orthodox Marxism is itself contested — not just from non- and anti-Marxists who question the very 'real' (by which they mean the 'practical' as under free-market criteria) existence of any kind of Marxism now but, perhaps more tellingly, from within the Marxist tradition itself. I will, therefore, first say what I regard to be the distinguishing marks of Orthodox Marxism and then outline a short polemical map of contestation over Orthodox Marxism within the Marxist theories now. I will end by arguing for its effectivity in bringing about a new society based not on human rights but on freedom from necessity.

I will argue that to know contemporary society — and to be able to act on such knowledge — one has to first of all know what makes the existing social totality. I will argue that the dominant social totality is based on inequality — not just inequality of power but inequality of economic access (which then determines access to health care, education, housing, diet, transportation,...). This systematic inequality cannot be explained by gender, race, sexuality, disability, ethnicity, or nationality. These are all secondary contradictions and are all determined by the fundamental contradiction of capitalism which is inscribed in the relation of capital and labor. All modes of Marxism today explain social inequalities primarily on the basis of these secondary contradictions and in doing so — and this is my main

https://doi.org/10.11647/OBP.0324.01

argument — legitimate capitalism. Why? Because such arguments authorize capitalism without gender, race,... discrimination and thus accept economic inequality as an integral part of human societies. They accept a sunny capitalism — a capitalism beyond capitalism. Such a society, based on cultural equality but economic inequality, has always been the not-so-hidden agenda of the bourgeois left — whether it has been called 'new left', 'postmarxism', 'radical democracy', or 'democratic socialism'. This is, by the way, the main reason for its popularity in the culture industry — from the academy (Frederic Jameson, David Harvey, Donna Haraway, Jodie Dean,...) to daily politics (Michael Harrington, Ralph Nader, Jesse Jackson, Bernie Sanders,...) to.... For all, capitalism is here to stay and the best that can be done is to make its cruelties more tolerable, more humane. This humanization (not eradication) of capitalism is the sole goal of *all* contemporary lefts (marxism, feminism, anti-racism, queeries,...).

Such an understanding of social inequality is based on the fundamental understanding that the source of wealth is human knowledge and not human labor. That is, wealth is produced by the human mind and is thus free from the actual objective conditions which shape the historical relations of labor and capital. Only Orthodox Marxism recognizes the historicity of labor and its primacy as the source of all human wealth. In this text I argue that any emancipatory theory has to be founded on recognition of the priority of Marx's labor theory of value and not repeat the technological determinism of corporate theory ('knowledge work') that masquerades as social theory.

Finally, it is only Orthodox Marxism that recognizes the inevitability and also the necessity of communism — the necessity, that is, of a society in which 'from each according to his abilities, to each according to his needs' is the rule.[1]

---

1   Karl Marx, 'Critique of the Gotha Programme', *Karl Marx/Frederick Engels: Collected Works*, 50 vols (Moscow: Progress Publishers, 1984), 24, p. 87.

Why Everyone has Suddenly Become an Orthodox Marxist

A parody of politics has taken over left politics in the US and Europe. A parody in which — after the dead-end of the designer socialisms of postmarxisms — suddenly everyone is an 'orthodox' Marxist: from Žižek who in the introduction to a selection of his work writes of the need to 'return to the centrality of the Marxist critique of political economy'; to Michael Sprinker who referred to himself as a 'neo-conservative marxist'.[2] In calling himself a 'neoconservative', Sprinker was embracing with pride Butler's definition of the term in her 'Merely Cultural' in which she equates it with 'leftist orthodoxy'.[3] Then there is Paul Smith who now, after mocking Orthodox Marxism in *Discerning the Subject* and *Universal Abandon*, says he has a 'fairly orthodox understanding of what Marx and the Marxist tradition has had to say about capitalism'.[4]

Parody is always the effect of a slippage, and the slippage here is that in spite of the sudden popularity of 'orthodox' Marxism, the actual theories and practices of the newly orthodox are more than ever before *flexodox*. It seems as if once more Lenin's notion that when the class antagonism emerges more sharply 'the liberals [...] dare not deny the class struggle, but attempt to narrow down [and] to curtail [...] the concept' has been proven by history.[5] 'Orthodox' Marxism has become the latest cover by which the bourgeois left authenticates its credentials and proceeds to legitimate the economics of the ruling class and its anti-proletarian politics.

Take Paul Smith, for example. In Orthodox Marxism, class is the central issue. (I put aside here that in his writings on subjectivity, for example, Smith has already gotten rid of the 'central' by a deconstructive logic.) What Smith does with class is a rather interesting test of how

---

2   Michael Sprinker, 'Forum on Teaching Marxism', *Mediations*, Spring (1998), pp. 68–73 (p. 68); Slavoj Žižek, 'Preface: Burning The Bridges', *The Žižek Reader*, ed. by Elizabeth Wright and Edmond Wright (Oxford: Blackwell Publishing Ltd., 1999), pp. vii-x (p. ix).

3   Judith Butler, 'Merely Cultural', *Social Text*, 52/53, 15.3/4, Fall/Winter (1997), pp. 265–77 (p. 268).

4   Paul Smith, *Millennial Dreams* (New York: Verso Books, 1997), p. 3.

5   V. I. Lenin, 'Liberal and Marxist Conceptions of the Class Struggle', *V. I. Lenin Collected Works*, 45 vols (Moscow: Progress Publishers, 1977), 19, pp. 119–24 (p. 122).

Orthodox Marxism is being used to legitimate the class interests of the owners. Smith reworks class and turns it into a useless Habermasian communicative act. He writes that 'classes are what are formed in struggle, not something that exists prior to struggle'.[6] To say it again: the old ideological textualization of the 'new left' is not working any more (just look at the resistance against globalization), so the ruling class is now reworking the 'old left' to defend itself. Against the Orthodox Marxist theory of class, Smith evacuates class of an objective basis in the extraction of surplus-labor in production and makes it the effect of local conflicts. In short, Smith reverses the Orthodox Marxist position that, 'It is not the consciousness of men that determines their existence, but their social existence that determines their consciousness', and turns it into a neomarxian view that what matters is their consciousness.[7] In this he in fact shares a great deal with conservative theories that make 'values' (the subjective) as what matters in social life and not economic access.

Žižek provides another example of the flexodox parody of Marxism today. Capitalism in Orthodox Marxism is explained as an historical mode of production based on the privatization of the means of subsistence in the hands of a few, i.e., the systemic exploitation of labor by capital. Capitalism is the world-historic regime of unpaid surplus-labor. In Žižek's writings, capitalism is not based on exploitation in production (surplus-labor), but on struggles over consumption ('surplus-enjoyment'). The Orthodox Marxist concepts which lay bare the exploitative production relations in order to change them are thus replaced with a 'psycho-marxist' pastiche of consumption in his writings, a revisionist move that has proven immensely successful in the bourgeois cultural criticism. Žižek, however, has taken to representing this displacement of labor (production) with desire (consumption) as 'strictly correlative' to the concept of 'revolutionary praxis' found in the texts of Orthodox Marxism. Revolutionary practice is always informed by class-consciousness and transformative cultural critique has always aimed at producing class-consciousness by laying bare the false consciousness that ruling ideology institutes in the everyday.

---

6   *Millennial Dreams*, p. 60.
7   Karl Marx, 'A Contribution to the Critique of Political Economy', *Karl Marx/Frederick Engels: Collected Works*, 50 vols (Moscow: Progress Publishers, 1987), 29, pp. 257–417 (p. 263).

Transformative cultural critique, in other words, is always a linking of consciousness to production practices from which a knowledge of social totality emerges. Žižek, however, long ago abandoned Orthodox Marxist ideology critique as an epistemologically naïve theory of ideology because it could not account for the persistence of 'desire' beyond critique (the 'enlightened false-consciousness' of *The Sublime Object of Ideology, Mapping Ideology,...*). His more recent 'return to the centrality of the Marxist critique' is as a result a purely tropic voluntarism of the kind he endlessly celebrates in his diffusionist readings of culture as desire-al moments when social norms are violated and personal emotions spontaneously experienced as absolutely compulsory (as 'drive'). His concept of revolutionary Marxist praxis consists of re-describing it as an 'excessive' lifestyle choice (which for Žižek are analogous to pedophilia and other culturally marginalized practices).[8] On this reading, Marxism is the only metaphorical displacement of 'desire' into 'surplus-pleasure' that makes imperative the 'direct socialization of the productive process' which causes the subjects committed to it to experience a Symbolic death at the hands of the neoliberal culture industry.[9] It is this 'affirmative' reversal of the right-wing anti-Marxist narrative that makes Žižek's writings so highly praised in the bourgeois 'high-theory' market — where it is read as 'subtle' and an example of 'deep thinking' because it confirms a transcendent position considered to be above politics by making all politics ideological. If everything is ideology, then there can be no fundamental social change, only formal repetition and reversal of values (Nietzsche). Žižek's pastiche of psycho-marxism thus consists in presenting what is only theoretically possible for the capitalist — those few who have already met, in excess, their material needs through the exploitation of the labor of the other and who can, therefore, afford to elaborate fantasies of desire — as a universal form of agency freely available to everyone.

Psycho-marxism does what bourgeois ideology has always done: maintain the bourgeois hegemony over social production by commodifying, through an aesthetic relay, the contradictions of the wages system. What bourgeois ideology does above all is deny that the

---

8   Slavoj Žižek, *The Ticklish Subject: The Absent Centre of Political Ontology* (New York: Verso Books, 1999), pp. 381–88.

9   Ibid., p. 350.

mode of social production has an historic agency of its own independent of the subject. Žižek's 'return' to 'orthodox' Marxism erases its materialist theory of desire: '[o]ur desires and pleasures spring from society' and do not stand in 'excess' of it.[10] In fact, he says exactly the opposite and turns the need for Orthodox Marxist theory now into a phantom desire of individuals: he makes 'class struggle' an effect of a 'totalitarian' desire to polarize the social between 'us' and 'them' (using the 'friend/enemy' binary found in the writings of the Nazi jurist Carl Schmitt).[11]

What is basic only to Orthodox Marxist theory, however, which is what enables it to produce class-consciousness through a critique of ideology, is its materialist prioritization of 'need' over 'desire'. It is only Orthodox Marxism which recognizes that although capitalism is compelled to continually expand the needs of workers because of the drive for profit, it at the same time cannot satisfy these needs because of the logic of profit. 'Desire' is always an effect of class relations, of the gap between the material level and historical potential of the forces of production and the social actuality of un-met needs.

In spite of their formal 'criticality', the writings of Žižek, Spivak, Smith, Hennessy and other theorists of designer socialisms produce concepts that legitimize the existing social relations. The notion of class in their work, for example, is the one that now is commonly deployed in bourgeois media. In their reporting on what has become known as the 'Battle of Seattle', and in the coverage of the rising tide of protest against the financial institutions of US monopoly capital that are pillaging the nations of the global South, the corporate media represents the emergent class struggles as a matter of an alternative 'lifestyle choice'.[12] On this diffusional narrative, 'class' is nothing more than an opportunity for surplus-pleasure 'outside' the market for those who have voluntarily 'discarded' the normal pleasures of US culture. It is the same 'lifestyle' politics that in the flexodox marxism of Michael Hardt and Antonio Negri is made an autonomous zone of 'immaterial labor' which they locate as the 'real communism' that makes existing society

---

10   Karl Marx, 'Wage Labour and Capital', *Karl Marx/Frederick Engels: Collected Works*, 50 vols (Moscow: Progress Publishers, 1977), 9, pp. 197–228 (p. 216).

11   Žižek, *Ticklish Subject*, p. 226.

12   Nicholas Riccardi, 'Hey Hey, Ho Ho, Catch Our Anti-Corporate Puppet Show!', *The Los Angeles Times*, 13 August 2000, https://www.latimes.com/archives/la-xpm-2000-aug-13-tm-3457-story.html

post-capitalist already so that revolution is not necessary.[13] What is at the core of both the flexodox marxism and the popular culture of class as 'lifestyle' is a de-politicization of the concepts of Orthodox Marxism which neutralizes them as indexes of social inequality and reduces them to merely descriptive categories which take what is for what ought to be. Take the writings of Pierre Bourdieu for example. Bourdieu turns Marx's dialectical concepts of 'class' and 'capital' which lay bare the social totality into floating 'categories' and reflexive 'classifications' that can be formally applied to any social practice because they have been cut off from their connection to the objective global relations of production. Bourdieu, in short, legitimates the pattern of class as 'lifestyle' in the bourgeois media by his view that 'class' is an outcome of struggles over 'symbolic capital' in any 'field'. I leave aside here that his diffusion of the logic of capital into 'cultural capital', 'educational capital', and the like is itself part of a depoliticization of the relation between capital and labor and thus a blurring of class antagonism as I explain this in more detail in a later chapter ('Capital').

Without totalizing knowledge of exploitation — which is why such dialectical concepts as 'capital' form the basis of Orthodox Marxist class theory — exploitation cannot be abolished. The cultural idealism of the de-politicized voiding of Marxist concepts fits right in with the 'volunteer-ism' of the neoliberals and 'compassionate' conservatives which they use to justify their massive privatization programs. Considering class struggle politics as a matter of cultural struggles over symbolic status is identical to the strategy of considering the dismantling of social welfare as an opportunity for 'local' agency freed from coercive state power, i.e., the bedrock of the 'non-governmental' activism and 'community' building of the bourgeois reformists. When George W. Bush claimed to mobilize what he called the 'armies of compassion' against the 'Washington insiders' and return 'power' to the 'people', it is the old cultural studies logic that all politics is 'people vs. power bloc', a warmed over populism that makes politics a matter of building de-politicized cross-class coalitions for bourgeois right, utopic models of a post-political social order without class struggle possessing equality

---

13 *Empire* (Cambridge: Harvard University Press, 2000); *Multitude: War and Democracy in the Age of Empire* (London: Penguin Books, 2004); *Commonwealth* (Cambridge: Belknap Press, 2009).

of representation that excludes the revolutionary vanguard. As Marx and Engels said of the 'bourgeois socialists' of their day, such utopian measures at 'best, lessen the cost, and simplify the administrative work, of bourgeois government'.[14] Žižek's 'affirmation' of revolutionary Marxism as a 'totalitarian' desire that polarizes the cultural 'lifeworld' between 'friends' and 'enemies' is another relay of 'class-as-an-after-effect of struggle' of the networked left. What the parody does is make class struggle a rhetorical 'invention' of Marx(ists) analogous to the bourgeois 'rights' politics of the transnational coalitional regime of exploitation ruling today, and erases the need for a global theory of social change. Orthodox Marxism cuts through the closed atmosphere of the 'friends' of the networked left and their embrace of a voluntarist 'compassionate' millenarianism with a critique from outside so to expose the global collective need for a revolutionary social theory and red cultural studies to end exploitation for all.

The Left Partys

The goal of the left *bal masqué* is perhaps most clearly represented in the image for the 'Marxism 2000' conference on millennial marxism — the poster for *Rethinking Marxism* which is the organ of the contemporary neoliberalism masquerading as 'Marxism'. The poster, which opportunistically appropriates Diego Rivera's 'Dance in Tehuantepec' (1935), completes the ironic slippage the bourgeois left has taken as the purpose of post-al theory: the troping of concepts as puncepts. The image on the poster is of peasants performing a (folk) dance and the caption reads, 'The Party's Not Over'. The transcoding of the Party of the proletariat to the party of folk-dancers is the transcoding of revolution to reform that Žižek's 'Orthodox Marxism' performs.

The idea is that social inequality is an effect of the persistence of cultural rituals that need to be addressed separately from class exploitation and revaluated from within as cultures of resistance. The 'folk'-sy theme accommodates the populist romanticization of people on the neomarxian Thompsonite left (Smith, Sprinker) as well, where class

---

14   Karl Marx and Frederick Engels, 'The Manifesto of the Communist Party', *Karl Marx/Frederick Engels: Collected Works*, 50 vols (Moscow: Progress Publishers, 1976), 6, pp. 477–519 (p. 514).

is reduced to the 'lived experience' of traditions of 'resistance' which say good-bye to the urban working class as a revolutionary agency that critiques all conventions. The flexodox left wants a party-ing proletariat (Hennessy) rather than a Party of the proletariat to put a smile-y face on exploitation.

The hollowing out of Marxism in the name of (Orthodox) Marxism by such theorists as Smith, Sprinker, and Žižek is based on the ideological un-said of the bourgeois right of property and its underpinning logic of the market which are represented as natural ('inalienable') 'human rights', or, more commonly in daily practices, as individual rights. Revolutionary struggles against these 'rights' (of property) are assumed to be signs of dogmatism, ruthless impersonality, vanguardism and totalitarianism — all 'obvious' markers of Orthodox Marxism. The remedy put forward by these theorists is to resist the revolutionary vanguard in the name of 'democracy from below', which is itself a code phrase for 'spontaneity'. Spontaneity — the kind of supposed 'freedom' which is the fabric of bourgeois daily life — is itself a layered notion that, in its folds, hides a sentimentalism that in reality constitutes 'democracy from below' and its allied notion of the 'individual', and the 'human subject'. Žižek and other 'high theorists' manage to conceal this naïve emotionalism (of which soap operas are made) in the rather abstract language of 'theory'. What is subtly implicit in the discourses of 'high theory', however, becomes explicit in the annotations of middle theory — that is, in bourgeois cultural commentary and criticism. Rosemary Hennessy's *Profit and Pleasure* is the most recent and perhaps most popular attack on Orthodox Marxism in the name of Marxism itself. Instead of looking at the cultural commentary in Hennessy's book (the book is actually a reprinting of older essays, and is thus even more historically significant as a documentary record of the continual emptying of Marxism in the 1980's and 1990's), I will look at its 'Acknowledgments'. This text is not something 'personal' and 'separate' from the cultural commentary and criticism of the essays in the body of her book. The 'Acknowledgments' text represents in fact a summing up — and a mutual confirmation between Hennessy and those she 'acknowledges' — of the core assumptions and ideas that inform the practices of the bourgeois left now.

As the 'Acknowledgments' text makes clear, the cultural commentary of Hennessy's *Profit and Pleasure* is rooted in the notion that politics is

basically a community activity. In bourgeois cultural criticism, the idea
of 'community activity' is a code term that signals the substitution of
shared 'ideas', 'assumptions', and 'emotions', for 'class' solidarity.[15]
What, therefore, lies at the core of 'community' is not a structure (class)
but a 'feeling' (emotional intensity). Hennessy, who is not as subtle as
Žižek or even Smith, is quite open about the valorization of 'feeling'
('opened her heart', 'feisty politics', 'precious friendship', 'a path with
heart', 'warmth and love').[16] The mark of membership in her post-al
community is 'heartache': in this evaluative social scheme, she who has
felt the most 'heartache' (emotional intensity), is the most authentic
member of the community. This appeal to a 'comradeship' based on
the intensity of 'feeling' clearly indicates that no matter what Marxist
or quasi-Marxist language Hennessy uses elsewhere in her book, she
basically believes that people's lives are changed not by revolutionary
praxis but by encountering other 'feeling' people: 'During the last year
of writing this book, I met [...] and my life has not been the same since
[...]'.[17] The lesson of this encounter, Hennessy indicates, was not the
classic lessons of Marxism that social change is a product of structural
change, but that social change comes about by means of something
called 'revolutionary love' (*'amor revolutionario'*) which — according to
her — has taken her 'time and time again to the other side' (*'llevarme una
y otra vez al otro lado'*).[18] The other lesson is the danger of vanguardism:
'revolutionary love' has also reminded her that 'power is finally and
always in the hands of the people' (*'el poder es finalmente y siempre en los
manos de la gente'*).[19] People as spontaneous actors.

On this view, Orthodox Marxism is dogmatic and totalitarian. So
to 'correct' its 'faults', Hennessy empties its revolutionary vanguard
of its commitment and puts feeling (manifested by 'heartache') in
its place. What is, of course, so significant is that Hennessy installs
such sentimentality as the ultimate layer of her Marxism in the name
of Marxism itself. This is what makes the work of bourgeois writers

---

15 Richard Rorty, 'Solidarity or Objectivity?', *Objectivity, Relativism, and Truth*
    (Cambridge University Press, 1991), pp. 21–34.
16 Rosemary Hennessy, *Profit and Pleasure: Sexual Identities in Late Capitalism* (London
    and New York: Routledge, 2000), pp. xii-xiii.
17 Ibid., p. xiii.
18 Ibid.
19 Ibid.

like Žižek, Smith, Sprinker, and Hennessy effective and welcome in the academy and the culture industry: they do not (unlike regular right-wingers) attack Marxism, but they reduce its explanatory power and its revolutionary force by substituting spontaneity for revolutionary praxis. For these writers, social transformation is the effect not of revolutionary praxis but of a spontaneous and emotionally intense exchange between two kindred 'spirits'. It is the spirit that moves the world. What in Hennessy is presented as Marxism or feminism turns out to be a souped-up version of the old bourgeois cultural feminism which, running away from revolution, retreats once again into community, spontaneity, affectivity, and above all the autonomous subject who gives and receives love above and beyond all social and economic processes.

One of the ways such writers hollow out Marxism of its Marxism and produce a Marxism beyond Marxism is by their overt acknowledgement of the way Marxism is treated in the bourgeois culture industry. Hennessy, for example, writes that Marxism in English Departments (the trope of the culture industry) is both 'courted and tamed'.[20] In other words, by announcing her awareness of the way that Marxism is tamed, she hopes to inoculate herself from the charge that she is doing so. The message the reader is supposed to get is this: because she knows Marxism is always being 'tamed', she herself would never do that. Under cover of this ideological self-inoculation, Hennessy then goes on to produce her 'tamed' version of Marxism which is only metaphorically 'marxist' because it is void of all the concepts and practices that make Marxism *Marxism*.

My larger point is of course that the most effective writings for the ruling class are located in the middle register, in that register of writing usually praised as lucid, clear, jargon-free, and above all, 'readable'. Žižek is abstract; Hennessy is concrete. This is another way of saying that the work of Hennessy and other such 'tamers' of Marxism is always a work of synthesis and consolidation — they make concrete the work of high theory; it is for this reason that their work forms the very center of the culture industry. Finally, to be clear, the question here is not to play a game of determining the 'good' from the 'bad' Marxism. What is good Marxism — what is effective in overcoming inequality — is

---

20   Ibid., p. 2.

determined by history itself. The question is whether what is being done actualizes the historical potential made possible by the development of the forces of production and thus brings about change in the existing social relations of production (overcomes class inequality) or whether it plays within the existing actuality and thus turns the limits of the actually existing into the very limits of reality as such. And in doing so, it reifies the present social relations of production. Flexodox Marxists like Hennessy accept the proposition that capitalism is here to stay and thus reject as 'impractical' any pressure put on the external supports of capitalism (capital and labor relations) and then work within capitalism — on the basis of community and emotional intensity — to make its ongoing process of the exploitation of the labor of the world's workers more 'humane' and tolerable.

Capitalism is, according to Hennessy's soap-operatic leftism, something that one should always keep in mind but not seriously consider overthrowing. She is too cynical to take even her own views seriously:

> This means that eliminating the social structures of exploitation that capitalism absolutely requires and so violently enacts at the expense of human needs must be on the political agenda, at the very least as the horizon that sets the terms for imagining change.[21]

Capitalist exploitation is a heuristic consideration not a revolutionary imperative. Beyond the theatrical moves of the bourgeois left, however, Orthodox Marxism is emerging as the only understanding of the new global formations that lead to transformative praxis.

Orthodox Marxism has become impossible to ignore because the objective possibility of transforming the regime of wage-labor into a system in which the priority is not profit but meeting the needs of all is confronted as a daily actuality. The flexodox left turns the emergent class struggles into self-enclosed struggles for symbolic power so to represent class hegemony in the relations of production as capable of being changed through cross-class 'coalitions', when in fact exploitation is everywhere in the world maintained by such coalitions which are losing their legitimacy and breaking apart under the weight of their own contradictions precisely because the class divide is growing under their

---

21   Ibid., p. 232.

rule and beyond their borders. Orthodox Marxism demonstrates that the productive forces of capitalism have reached tremendous levels and have the ability to feed, clothe, and house the world many times over but are fettered by capitalism's existing social relations: its fundamental drive to privately consume the social resources of collective labor. That the left today has, in dramatic fashion, been forced to return (if only rhetorically) to Orthodox Marxism marks the fact that the struggle to transform capitalism has reached a stage of development that necessitates a systemic theoretical basis for revolutionary praxis. The hegemonic left now wants to incorporate Orthodox Marxism into its dogmatic coalitional logic as a discourse which depends for its identity on 'class' as 'real': which is a code for the 'lived experience' or the transcendental ineffable politics (Lacan) of class as an outside inferred from the inside (the side of subjective 'values') and as such held to be unavailable for positive knowing. Which is another way of saying that class is a matter of 'persuasion' and 'seduction' rather than production.

What the resulting flexodox marxism cannot explain therefore is that class

> is not a matter of what this or that proletarian, or even the whole proletariat, at the moment *regards* as its aim. It is a question of *what the proletariat is*, and what, in accordance with this *being*, it will historically be compelled to do.[22]

Orthodox Marxism does not consist of raising 'class' as a dogmatic banner of the 'real', but in the critique of false consciousness which divides the workers by occulting their collective interest by shifting the focus from their position in social production, their material antagonism with the capitalist class. 'Class as real' (a spectral agency) cannot explain, and therefore cannot engage in, the material process through which capitalism, by its very own laws of motion, produces its own 'gravedigger' in the global proletariat. What the flexodox return to, and hollowing out of the concepts of Orthodox Marxism proves, among other things, is that 'the ideas of the ruling class are in every epoch the ruling ideas' and history progresses despite this ideological hegemony

---

22　Karl Marx and Frederick Engels, 'The Holy Family, or Critique of Critical Criticism', *Karl Marx/Frederick Engels: Collected Works*, 50 vols (Moscow: Progress Publishers, 1975), 4, pp. 5–211 (p. 37).

through the agency of labor. In short: 'The history of all hitherto existing society is the history of class struggles'.[23]

Orthodox Marxism has become a test-case of the 'radical' today. Yet, what passes for orthodoxy on the left — whether like Smith and Žižek they claim to support it or like Butler and Rorty they want to 'achieve our country' by excluding it from 'U.S. Intellectual life' — is a parody of orthodoxy which hybridizes its central concepts and renders them flexodox simulations.[24] Yet, even in its very textuality, the orthodox is a resistance to the flexodox. Contrary to the common-sensical view of 'orthodox' as 'traditional' or 'conformist' 'opinions', is its other meaning: ortho-doxy not as flexodox 'hybridity', but as 'original' 'ideas'. 'Original', not in the sense of epistemic 'event', 'authorial' originality and so forth, but, as in chemistry, in its opposition to 'para', 'meta', 'post', and other ludic hybridities: thus 'ortho' as resistance to the annotations that mystify the original ideas of Marxism and hybridize it for the 'special interests' of various groups.

The 'original' ideas of Marxism are inseparable from their effect as demystification of ideology — for example the deployment of 'class' that allows a demystification of daily life from the haze of consumption. Class is thus an 'original idea' of Marxism in the sense that it cuts through the hype of cultural agency under capitalism and reveals how culture and consumption are tied to labor, the everyday determined by the workday: how the amount of time workers spend engaging in surplus-labor determines the amount of time they get for reproducing and cultivating their needs. Without changing this division of labor, social change is impossible. Orthodoxy is a rejection of the ideological annotations: hence, on the one hand, the resistance to orthodoxy as 'rigid' and 'dogmatic' 'determinism', and, on the other, its hybridization by the flexodox as the result of which it has become almost impossible today to read the original ideas of Marxism, such as 'exploitation', 'surplus-value', 'class', 'class antagonism', 'class struggle', 'revolution', 'science' (i.e., objective knowledge), 'ideology' (as false consciousness). Yet, it is

---

23   Karl Marx and Frederick Engels, 'The German Ideology', *Karl Marx/Frederick Engels: Collected Works*, 50 vols (Moscow: Progress Publishers, 1976), 5, p. 59; 'Manifesto', p. 482.

24   Richard Rorty, *Achieving Our Country: Leftist Thought in Twentieth-Century America* (Cambridge: Harvard University Press, 1998); Judith Butler, 'Left Conservatism II', *Theory & Event*, 2:2 (1998).

only these ideas that clarify the 'elemental' truths through which theory ceases to be a gray activism of tropes, desire and affect, and becomes, instead, a red, revolutionary guide to praxis for a new society freed from exploitation and injustice.

Marx's original scientific discovery was his labor theory of value. Marx's labor theory of value is an elemental truth of Orthodox Marxism that is rejected by the flexodox left as the central dogmatism of a 'totalitarian' Marxism. It is only Marx's labor theory of value, however, that exposes the mystification of the wages system that disguises exploitation as a 'fair exchange' between capital and labor and reveals the truth about this relation as one of exploitation. Only Orthodox Marxism explains how what the workers sell to the capitalist is not labor, a commodity like any other whose price is determined by fluctuations in supply and demand, but their labor-power — their ability to labor in a system which has systematically 'freed' them from the means of production so they are forced to work or starve — whose value is determined by the amount of time socially necessary to reproduce it daily. The value of labor-power is equivalent to the value of wages workers consume daily in the form of commodities that keep them alive to be exploited tomorrow. Given the technical composition of production today, this amount of time is a slight fraction of the workday, the majority of which workers spend producing surplus-value over and above their needs. The surplus-value is what is pocketed by the capitalists in the form of profit when the commodities are sold. Class is the antagonistic division between the exploited and their exploiters. Without Marx's labor theory of value, one could only contest the after effects of this outright theft of social labor-power rather than its cause which lies in the private ownership of production. The flexodox rejection of the labor theory of value as the 'dogmatic' core of a totalitarian Marxism is, therefore, a not-so-subtle rejection of the principled defense of the (scientific) knowledge workers need for their emancipation from exploitation because only the labor theory of value exposes the opportunism of knowledges (ideology) which occult this exploitation. Without the labor theory of value, socialism would only be a moral dogma that appeals to the sentiments of 'fairness' and 'equality' for a 'just' distribution of the social wealth that does the work of capital by naturalizing the exploitation of labor under capitalism giving it an acceptable 'human face'.

It is only Orthodox Marxism that explains socialism as an historical inevitability that is tied to the development of social production itself and its requirements. Orthodox Marxism makes socialism scientific because it explains how, in the capitalist system, based on the private consumption of labor-power (competition), the objective tendency is to reduce the amount of time labor spends in reproducing itself (necessary labor) while expanding the amount of time labor is engaged in producing surplus-value (surplus labor) for the capitalist. This is mainly done through the introduction of machinery into the production process by the capitalists themselves to lower their own labor costs. Because of the competitive drive for profits under capitalism, it is historically inevitable that a point is reached when the technical mastery — the amount of time socially necessary on average to meet the needs of society through the processing of natural resources — is such that the conditions of the workers worsen relative to the owners and becomes an unbearable global social contradiction in the midst of the ever-greater masses of wealth produced. It is therefore just as inevitable that at such a moment it makes more sense to socialize production and meet the needs of all to avoid the explosive social conflicts perpetually generated by private property than to maintain the system at the risk of total social collapse on a world scale. 'Socialism or barbarism' (Luxemburg) is the inevitable choice faced by humanity because of capitalism. Either maintain private property and the exploitation of labor in production, in which case more and more social resources will go into policing the growingly desperate surplus-population generated by the technical efficiency of social production, or socialize production and inaugurate a society whose founding principle is 'from each according to his abilities, to each according to his needs' and 'in which the free development of each is the condition for the free development of all'.[25]

The time has come to state it clearly so that even the flexodox opportunists may grasp it: Orthodox Marxism is not a free-floating 'language-game' or 'meta-narrative' for arbitrarily constructing local utopian communities or spectral activist inversions of ideology meant to seduce 'desire' and 'mobilize' (glorify) subjectivity — it is an absolute

---

25   Marx and Engels, 'Manifesto', p. 506; Karl Marx, 'Critique of the Gotha Programme', *Karl Marx/Frederick Engels: Collected Works*, 50 vols (Moscow: Progress Publishers, 1984), 24, pp. 75–99 (p. 87).

prerequisite for our emancipation from exploitation and a new society freed from necessity! Orthodox Marxism is the only global theory of social change. Only Orthodox Marxism has explained why under the system of wage-labor and capital, communism is not 'an ideal to which reality will have to adjust itself' but 'the *real* movement which abolishes the present state of things' because of its objective explanation of and ceaseless commitment to 'the self-conscious, independent movement of the immense majority, in the interest of the immense majority' to end social inequality forever.[26]

---

26 Marx and Engels, 'German Ideology', p. 49; 'Manifesto', p. 495.

2.
(Post)humanity

Animal Matters and Sublime Pets

Increasing unevenness in capitalist relations, which have led to the global financial crisis of 2007–08, have normalized an ethical turn in the humanities and led to 'new' theories that could account for the rising inequalities in cultural terms.[1] Poststructuralism and the decentered theory of the social it authorized lost its explanatory power with the waning of the neoliberal consensus of deregulation and monetarist economics in the 1990s, which continue to be challenged around the world by various anti-globalization, anti-austerity, and people's and worker's movements for imposing measures that have produced greater global inequality. Hardt and Negri's theory of the 'multitude' that accounts for inequality as exclusion from the circuits of 'immaterial labor', Agamben's juridical account of inequality as a 'state of exception' to democratic norms, and Rancière's writings on democracy as the hegemonic co-optation of the proletariat as 'the part of no-part', are prominent among the 'new' theories to have emerged since the crash of 2007–08. What these theories highlight is the way that the 'knowledge economy' — the high-tech sector of production that manufactures the cultural products that shape people's consciousness — increases the alienation of labor and therefore the alienation of humans from humans. Insofar as these theories account for inequality immanently from within culture they heighten the awareness of differences within the taken for granted notions about what it means to be human and the way such common-sensical ideas naturalize inequality by the denial of the humanity of 'others' (as what Agamben calls 'bare life', e.g.). In more middle register writings, the discourses of (post)humanist cultural theory produce an uncomfortable sense of alienation that embraces the animal as a way to overcome it and, so, one finds Derrida and Haraway writing about

---

1   Gary Hall, *New Cultural Studies: Adventures in Theory*, ed. by Clare Birchall (Athens: Georgia University Press, 2007).

    https://doi.org/10.11647/OBP.0324.02

how they commune with their pets. 'Pettism' is put forward in their writings as a therapeutic response that covers over a causal theory of the increasing inequality of cybercapitalism. It is within and between these various discourses that the 'posthumanities' — as the University of Minnesota Press series devoted to the field is called — finds its tutor-texts for thinking about the cultural disruptions of global capitalism. The 'post' of the (post)humanities signals awareness of not only the exclusionary basis of the concept of Man, as did (post)structuralist post-humanist philosophy, but also represents a new sentimental embrace of non-human otherness and a Heideggerian ethics of care as 'being-with' the animal(s) to respond to the growing social alienation of global capitalism. As in all 'posts' (postfordist, postindustrial, poststructuralism, postmodern,...), a cultural zone 'beyond' the conflict between capital and labor is announced that naturalizes class inequality as the basis of human societies.[2]

The 'post' of (post)structuralist post-humanism and the 'post' of the new-er (post)humanism are, despite their historical differences, ideologically the same: they attempt to 'solve' in the theoretical imaginary contradictions that have arisen from the conflict between capital and labor. The founding texts of (post)structuralism were of course post-humanist in their focus on textuality and discourse, but the opposition to humanism today has changed since Derrida and Foucault's critiques of humanism in the '60s and '70s and it is less concerned with deconstructing logocentrism and the languages of Man than it is with the cultural inscription of bodies around the human/animal distinction. These discursive changes are not driven by knowledge but instead reflect changes in the mode of production. Poststructuralism — the theories premised on linguistic play and the indeterminacy of meaning — was invested in demonstrating that the human is not the autonomous being cognitively self-identical to itself as represented by Humanist and Enlightenment philosophy because such humanist notions of identity and essence are always subject to mediation by language. It thus criticized as logocentric humanism any conception of thought that placed thought above discursive mediation because

---

2   Mas'ud Zavarzadeh, 'Post-Ality: The (Dis)Simulations of Cybercapitalism', in *Transformation 1: Marxist Boundary Work in Theory, Economics, Politics and Culture* (Montreal: Maisonneuve Press, 1995), pp. 1–75 (p. 1).

the unsaid assumption of such an essentialist notion of the subject is that language is merely a medium of communication between abstract intelligences, as if language were simply a token or tool that delivers the pre-determined content of thought.[3] This earlier post-humanism represented the philosophical position that cultural media are material and as such constitutive of the human rather than the opposite: the traditional Aristotelian humanist idea that media represent a passive and neutral medium through which is 'expressed' the spiritual essence of Man. However, the (post)structuralist critique of humanism has to be situated within the social relations in order to understand its hidden class politics.

The post-humanism of (post)structuralist theory was considered useful and 'made sense' under conditions in which the ruling class sought to deregulate the social-democratic welfare-state on a global scale as these regimes depended on the discourse of humanism to ideologically justify their particular distribution of social resources as serving the universal good. The humanism of welfare-state philosophy that was dominant at that time — which Cold Warriors and Western Marxist critics alike considered 'totalitarian' — was opposed for imposing a hegemonic unity that was exclusionary of cultural differences and that thereby deprived the margins of a voice, or, in more common language, individual rights. The post-humanism of difference theory thus served to legitimate in philosophy the re-distribution and privatization of the social resources of the state beginning in the late 1970s that has overwhelmingly strengthened the market forces. On the left, the neoliberal counter-revolution that was serving to commodify the globe was represented in terms of the politics of the sign as heralding 'new times' and laying the groundwork for a 'radical democracy' that was 'liberating' the 'popular' forces from 'totalitarian' power. Poststructuralism was the philosophical thug that was used to smash the welfare-state and to portray the privatization of social wealth during the 1980s as the basis for a new-found freedom, in much the same way that the CIA used abstract expressionism to undermine socialist ideology after World War II.[4]

---

3   Jacques Derrida, 'The Ends of Man', in *Margins of Philosophy*, trans. by Alan Bass (Chicago: Chicago University Press, 1972), pp. 111–36.

4   Frances Stoner Saunders, *The Cultural Cold War: The CIA and the World of Arts*

(Post)humanism today, by contrast, is an attempt to reconstruct a social identity in common after the deconstruction of the human and the crisis of inequality promoted by the policies of neoliberalism and its post-al philosophy that announces the end of man, ideology, and class. Theory cannot go back to humanism, which has been delegitimated as an outdated 'state philosophy' by the market forces, but it cannot continue to defend radical difference either because of the association of difference theory with the hegemony of neoliberal power that helped to bring about the current global crisis of inequality and with the more general costs associated with global capitalism, such as the destruction to the environment, the escalation of imperialism and war, and the general degradation of the quality of life that come in their wake. What has emerged to contain the contradictions of capitalism today is the (post)humanism of Derrida, Haraway, Wolfe et. al. showcased by the Minnesota Press series, which critiques capitalism as an oppressive 'biopower' that subjugates life only to announce a new non-oppressive and co-operative being in common — what Donna Haraway calls the 'transspecies', Derrida calls *l'animot*, and Žižek, the 'biogenetic commons'. In this theory of a new post-exploitative present made of biopower and biopolitical cultural resistance, the concept of the human is still considered ideologically incoherent only it is not because of social mediations that defer and delay its self-presence through spacing which deny its purported autonomy. Rather, (post)humanism now announces the end of the human species as a distinct entity in nature because of the emergent knowledge that the human is biogenetically hybridized with non-human others (animals, microbes, etc.) — a condition taken to be enabled by biopower, especially the knowledge practices of biogenetics. Haraway bases her understanding of transspecies, for example, on the fact that biogenetics has discovered that 'human genomes can be found in only about 10 percent of all the cells that occupy the mundane space I call my body; the other 90 [...] are filled with the genomes of bacteria, fungi, protists, and such'.[5] What contemporary (post)humanism thus

---

and Letters (New York: The New Press, 2001); Gabriel Rockhill, 'The CIA Reads French Theory: On the Intellectual Labor of Dismantling the Cultural Left', *The Philosophical Salon: A Los Angeles Review of Books Channel*, 28 February 2017, https://thephilosophicalsalon.com/the-cia-reads-french-theory-on-the-intellectual-labor-of-dismantling-the-cultural-left.

5   Donna Haraway, *When Species Meet* (Minneapolis: Minnesota University Press,

rejects is not only the discourse of Man as a universalist cultural construct that marginalizes cultural differences but also, and more importantly, Marx's concept of human 'species being', on the claim that species-being suppresses the biological difference inscribed within nature (in the genetic code) and thereby perpetuates the regime of what Derrida has called 'carnophallogocentrism': 'the interventionist violence that is practiced [...] in the service of or for the protection of the animal, but most often the human animal'.[6]

And yet, the (post)humanism which 'makes sense' now in terms of legitimating class inequality is, as in the past, the one that serves the dominant sector of capital that, among other things, through its command of the resources of the state makes the most profits. The (post)humanism of transspeciesism and the biogenetic commons reflects changes in property. Specifically, it reflects the shift from forms of public wealth invested in social welfare programs to privatized wealth and speculative capital that are more and more invested in the biotech and 'green' industries and that, therefore, stand to make the biggest profits in the new millennium, as these industries represent the main avenues of capital valorization and accumulation through which capitalism is currently commodifying the environmental crisis. (Post) humanism, in short, is a social theory after the massive privatization of the social; the transspecies a 'commons' founded on the continuation of extracting surplus-value from labor and the suppression of the class-consciousness needed to end exploitation.

Species-Being and *L'Animot*

In his introduction to the Posthumanities series published by the University of Minnesota Press, Cary Wolfe gives a map of the (post) humanities that promises to go beyond what he considers the deadlock of contemporary cultural theory, specifically, because of its residual humanism. Central to Wolfe's story of the (post)humanities is Derrida's 'thinking concerning the animal' as if it marked a new moment in cultural theory beyond the regional conflicts of the past that opens

---

2008), p. 3.

6   Jacques Derrida, *The Animal That Therefore I Am* (Bronx: Fordham University Press, 2008), p. 25.

theory to more global horizons.[7] Derrida is made to support Wolfe's view of (post)humanism as that which 'opposes the fantasies of disembodiment and autonomy inherited from humanism itself'.[8] What Wolfe's (post)humanities series canonizes are the texts of Derrida's later 'ethical turn', such as *The Animal That Therefore I Am*, in which are found annotations of experience and the quotidian which are represented as sublime ('secret') moments of sensual embodiment that produce a 'pathetic' version of history as existential 'suffering'.[9] This is in contrast to Derrida's earlier more analytically rigorous writings, such as his reading of Lacan, in which, for example, is found his critique of 'embodiment' as a support of logocentric thought. I will briefly rehearse Derrida's critique of Lacan in order to explain why Derrida's later ethical turn to embodiment is not, as Wolfe imagines, a 'new' cutting-edge discourse but represents the dumbing-down of theory in the service of capital.

In his response to Lacan, Derrida argued that the primacy of the signifier that developed within psycho-analytic thought after Saussure, posits a 'speaking-subject' that sustains the 'ontotheology' of 'Western metaphysics'. In other words, he argued that the 'materiality' of the signifier ('voice') is used as a subordinate and idealized ground for the telos (ends) of presence as 'speech', hence, as the condition of possibility for the traditional idealist autonomy of the subject in Western humanism, even if finally as a 'split-subject' in Lacan.[10] What Wolfe turns to in Derrida is not his earlier critique of the 'body' as central to humanist idealism, but his later more sentimental texts in which, as Derrida puts it, 'animal words' proliferate 'in proportion as my texts [...] become more autobiographical'.[11] In short, Wolfe privileges writings in which, rather than self-reflexively accounting for the conditions of theory, Derrida instead offers mere annotations of experience. If 'humanism' is premised on maintaining a split between the material ('voice') and the conceptual ('speech') in which the former is taken to be subordinate to the latter, as Derrida had previously argued against Lacan, then the later Derrida, whom Wolfe invokes and who turns to 'embodiment' as a basis for the

---

7   Ibid., p. 7.
8   Cary Wolfe, *What Is Posthumanism?* (Minneapolis: Minnesota University Press, 2010), p. xv.
9   Derrida, *Animal*, p. 26.
10   Jacques Derrida, *Positions* (Chicago: Chicago University Press, 1981), pp. 108–9.
11   Derrida, *Animal*, p. 35.

ethical, is not (post)humanist but humanist with a vengeance; hence the easy sentimentality of his later texts and their quick canonization in religion departments. In other words, Derrida has engaged in a simple reversal of the mind/body binary, a binary which is central to Western humanist philosophy, that not only maintains its terms but, more importantly, advances a cultural politics that defines the good within the epistemic coordinates of the dominant ideology in which nature is sentimentalized (as the affective) and theory depoliticized (as ethics).

It is because of this accommodation of the dominant ideology that today the 'question of the animal' in Derrida's later writings is made a matter of embracing the 'passion of the animal'.[12] Rather than situate affective experience within the historical series, Derrida reifies experience by fetishizing the 'feelings' that overtake him when his pet cat looks at him naked in the bathroom, especially the feeling of 'shame' at 'seeing oneself seen naked under a gaze behind which there remains a bottomlessness [...] uninterpretable, unreadable, undecidable, abyssal and secret'.[13] 'In these moments of nakedness' standing before his pet cat Derrida locates 'an "experience" of language about which one could say, even if it is not in itself "animal," that it is not something that the "animal" could be deprived of', which he puts forward as an ethical model of what he claims is 'the most radical means of thinking the finitude that we share with animals'.[14] Leaving aside that what Derrida is here calling an experience of finitude is really not an experience but a trope for his commitment to Saussure's synchronic theory of language which understands language ahistorically rather than as 'an arena of class struggle', such an experience of bodily finitude is necessary, according to Derrida, so as to understand how the 'industrial, mechanical, chemical, hormonal, and genetic violence to which man has been submitting animal life for the past two centuries' shapes the cultural 'inequality [...] between, on the one hand, those who violate not only animal life but even and also this sentiment of compassion, and, on the other hand, those who appeal to an irrefutable testimony to this pity'.[15] In other

---

12   Ibid., p. 12.
13   Ibid., pp. 4, 12.
14   Ibid., pp. 166, 28.
15   V. N. Vološinov, *Marxism and the Philosophy of Language*, trans. by Ladislav Matejka and I. R. Titunik (Cambridge: Harvard University Press, 1993), p. 23; Derrida, pp. 26, 28–29.

words, it is only by embracing our animal mortality as embodied beings with singular experiences that inequality becomes intelligible, not as a material antagonism, but as a cultural 'war [...] waged over the matter of pity'.[16] On these pathetic terms, what is to be opposed most of all is speciesism because it establishes a hierarchical binary that puts 'the whole animal kingdom with the exception of the human' into a 'vast encampment' for the purpose of industrial 'genocide' and thus foments the culture wars over values.[17] In nakedly communing with his pet cat, Derrida thus experiences a moment of animal liberation from humanist thought in which he apparently believes 'everything can happen' and indulges in a kind of thinking without thinking ('the passion of the animal') that, following Heidegger's 'need to strike out "being"', dismisses thinking in materialist terms about inequalities of power, which are at root class conflicts over the resources of labor inscribed in what Marx calls human 'species-being'.[18]

Derrida understands the 'question of the animal' in strictly immaterial (emotional and ethical) terms, occulting the actual relation of humans to nature. He does this work of occulting the material labor relations that make up the human species by inventing a hybrid 'animal-word' (*l'animot*) through which to interpret the social conflicts over inequality, which he considers to be primarily cultural as they are the result of unethical practices: 'the interventionist violence that is practiced [...] in the service of or for the protection of the animal, but most often the human animal'.[19] *L'animot* is a portmanteau combining the French terms for 'animal' and 'words' which sounds the same as the plural of 'animal'. What this term does in Derrida's writing is to represent recent 'developments of zoological, ethological, biological, and genetic forms of knowledge' — knowledges which are, in other words, productive of the hi-tech commodification of hybrid forms of life that for Haraway defy species classification and lay the basis for a 'transspecies' consciousness — as the basis for a new ethical awareness he calls the 'passion of the animal', or, 'embodied knowledge' (that is made 'naked, vulnerable, and

---

16   Derrida, *Animal*, p. 29.
17   Ibid., pp. 41, 34, 26.
18   Ibid., pp. 12, 39; Karl Marx, 'Economic and Philosophical Manuscripts of 1844', *Karl Marx/Frederick Engels: Collected Works*, 50 vols (Moscow: Progress Publishers, 1975), 3, pp. 229–346.
19   Derrida, *Animal*, p. 25.

unfathomable').[20] *L'animot*, in other words, marks a 'double session' that, to begin with, inverts the material (species-being) with the immaterial (biogenetics) by showing how they include rather than oppose each other so as to reveal their dependence on a disavowed third term — the 'passion of the animal', which is represented as a type of '"experience" of language about which one could say, even if it is not in itself "animal," that it is not something that the "animal" could be deprived of'.[21] This 'experience of language', although marked in emotional terms and inscribed within the affective, is of course not a spontaneous feeling brought about by humans tampering with nature, nor is it simply an insight that came to Derrida as he nakedly communed with his pet cat in the bathroom. In fact, the concept that the experience of language here that is not in itself, but is also not something we can be sure animals do not posses, is Derrida's (post)humanist ethical gloss on the differential concept of language that he takes from Saussure but presents in less alienating language: language as a structure without a subject because, '[i]n language there are only differences without positive terms'.[22] Derrida, in other words, is defining animal life as inherently decentered because it is subject to cultural processes of meaning production, in which case any differences between humans and animals is a language effect (e.g., as in the difference between philosophical and poetic discourses about animals that Derrida discusses).

Nevertheless, although Derrida is not so crudely biologically literal as Haraway in his notion of human-animal hybridity that in the (post) humanities signals the arrival of a post-exploitative being in common, he still puts forward a notion of the animal that functions as an ethical limit-text within the discourse of theory in which the 'passion of the animal' marks a liberated zone of affective experience as if it existed outside the history of class struggle. By 'striking out being' in the 'abyssal rupture' of communing with his pet cat and experiencing the passion of the animal, Derrida reinscribes a notion of history as the determination of the material by the immaterial, as if 'spirit' moves the world rather

---

20 Ibid., p. 25.
21 On 'double session' see, Jacques Derrida, *Dissemination* (Chicago: Chicago University Press, 1983), pp. 191–207; Derrida, *Animal*, p. 166.
22 Ferdinand de Saussure, *Course in General Linguistics*, ed. by Charles Balley and Albert Sechehaye, trans. by Wade Baskin (McGraw Hill, 1966), p. 120.

than labor.[23] Accordingly, what he calls 'thought', 'logocentrism', or the 'dominant form of consensus' (because it puts 'the whole animal kingdom with the exception of the human' into a 'vast encampment'), is made responsible for industrial 'genocide'.[24] And yet, the 'experience of language' that Derrida's 'animal words' embody is itself a form of 'thinking the animal' more ethically as finitude, passion, shame, vulnerability, rather than instrumentally and genocidally in the culture 'war [...] waged over the matter of pity'.[25] In other words, Derrida reinscribes the human/animal binary as an ethical difference within knowledge and, therefore, in the terms of his text, maintains the same domination of the animal by the human that perpetuates the 'veritable war of the species' he laments.[26] As always, deconstruction reinscribes what it opens to question by failing to go outside the epistemological and implicating knowledge within the historical series of class practices.

Insofar as *l'animot* marks the animal as essentially unknowable (the sublime 'secret' of the pet), it privatizes animal life, fixing it, for ethical reasons, as a singularity unconnected to labor relations, and this despite the fact that animal life is historical and evolves along with changes in the human life which dominates the earth. As Marx explains, '[t]he whole character of a species, its species-character, is contained in the character of its life activity [...]. Admittedly animals also produce [...] [b]ut an animal only produces what it immediately needs [...], whilst man produces universally'.[27] On Marx's dialectical materialist logic, *l'animot* therefore indexes a change in the social relations of production rather than simply marking a singular experience humans have come to share with animals as a result of the technological intervention into nature. How we interact with and conceive of animal life, including our own species-being, always reflects our practical interaction with nature within necessary social relations at a certain level of development. Derrida's opposition of 'thinking' as the liberation of (animal) passion from the 'dominant thought' of human speciesism reinscribes the human/animal binary as internal to knowledge and occults human

---

23   Derrida, *Animal*, p. 30.
24   Ibid., pp. 26–27, 34, 40–41.
25   Ibid., p. 29.
26   Ibid., p. 31.
27   Marx, 'Economic and Philosophical Manuscripts', p. 276.

species being as the universal production of life, what Marx calls 'life-engendering life'.[28] By 'striking out' Marx's concept of species-being as the universal production of life and reinscribing (non)knowledge as the basis of life, Derrida fixes the animal in the dumb muteness of an 'uninterpretable, unreadable, undecidable, abyssal [...] secret' and mystifies the labor relations upon which all life on earth depends.[29] This is not merely a logical contradiction, however, considering that what is being put forward as a 'new' (posthumanist) ethical thought is actually a reinscription of the body as the biological basis of life and culture as the primary zone of conflicts. More importantly it testifies to ongoing material conflicts in the economic base and takes the side of the ruling class against the workers.

While the dehierachization and reinscription of the human/animal binary in Derrida is represented as a self-enclosed movement within culture (knowledge, ethics, affect), it is actually a mode of side-taking in the class struggles of global capitalism against the workers who need 'outside' knowledge — the positive and reliable knowledge of class inequality that critiques ideology — for their emancipation from capital. Furthermore, without such class-consciousness, humanity will not be able to realize a more sustainable relation to nature. It is not the devaluing 'thought' of animals in humanism that produces their subjugation by humans — although such a 'violent' understanding of thought is necessary for deconstruction to represent the animal as liberated by 'thinking the animal' — but it is instead the exploitation of human species-being by humans for profit that does so. More exactly, it is the estrangement of human species-being through the capitalist exploitation of human labor-power that produces the reified 'thought' of human superiority over nature through the exercise of pure reason on the one hand, as well as the ethical 'thinking' of the embodied 'passion' of the animal as its corrective on the other. The closed circuit of knowledge (species thought/embodied thinking of the animal) in Derrida's text is itself a reification of human labor activity which considers human species-being in a one-sided way, as 'knowledge' of the body (animal life). Making animal life into an unfathomable abyssal secret of embodiment may seem like a challenge to the interventionist

---

28   Ibid., p. 276.
29   Derrida, *Animal*, p. 12.

violence of 'carnophallogocentrism' (Derrida), but in its culturalism it underwrites the idea that inequality is an effect of knowledge rather than the reverse, that all knowledge (even the 'secret' thinking that is taken to be not thinking but feeling the passion of the animal) is rooted in the class inequality of the capitalist mode of production and reflects it at the level of theory — either for or against capital or labor. By inscribing 'thought' as dominant and 'embodiment' as subjected (but secretly free 'thinking') Derrida normalizes the class relations which in actuality reify knowledge of species-being as a whole, not by humanity intellectually imposing on animals, but by imposing animality on humans, that is, by reducing the life activity of humans to animal life, which is the 'dominion of immediate physical need' imposed on humanity by capitalism.[30]

And yet, the one-sided production of estranged labor undertaken for wages which reduces the worker to immediate physical need so as to increase surplus-value for the capitalist is what is today everywhere in crisis. Behind the succession of financial bubbles and crashes at the millennial turn (which go under the names of 'Savings & Loan', 'dot com', 'Enron', 'the housing bubble', and now, the 'pandemic crash') is the overproduction endemic to capitalism as it 'rationalizes' production so as to increase profits: the technical innovations introduced in production to increase the surplus-value of labor have the overall effect of decreasing the abstract socially necessary labor-time overall, which is the source of value, and this is what encourages speculation in the financial markets because of the low rate of return on industrial capital investment. What the crisis shows is that the private consumption of social wealth that regulates production for profit is coming into contradiction with the global mass of labor which has transformed the planet, the very process of accumulation that has 'simplified the class antagonisms' and confronts humanity with the necessity for socialism, as even the likes of Federal Reserve Chairman Alan Greenspan was finally forced to recognize after the crash of 2007–08.[31] Marx's concept of 'species-being'

---

30 Marx, 'Economic and Philosophical Manuscripts', p. 276.
31 Marx and Engels, 'Manifesto', p. 485; According to Greenspan: 'Clearly the increased concentrations of income that have emerged under technological advance and global competition, have rekindled the battle between the cultures of socialism and of capitalism — a battle some thought had ended once and for all with the disgrace of central planning. But over the past year, some of the critical pillars underlying

as the 'life activity' of humans is crucial for understanding and changing the world and it therefore necessarily comes into conflict with the dissimulations of capitalism such as the 'abyssal difference' of the (post) humanist transspeciesism that reifies life as embodied knowledge found in Derrida. In short, what the world is confronted with is not a cultural 'war [...] waged over the matter of pity' due to the normalization of 'genetic violence' against animal life, which is a secondary cultural effect of the exploitation of labor.[32] Rather, the question is will the human species be ruled by the law of profit so as to enrich a few or realize a world free from need by producing in accordance with the needs of life as a whole?

As Engels explains in *Dialectics of Nature*, it is the exploitation of human labor — which is what is at the center of capitalism and not 'genetic violence' (Derrida) — that produces 'the idealist world outlook', which defines the human in a one-sided way as 'outside' or 'above' nature, such that human nature is understood as 'arising out of thought instead of [human] needs'.[33] Engels' observation that the spiritual humanism of the bourgeoisie 'dominates men's mind' to such an extent that even the 'materialistic natural scientists' are 'unable to form any clear idea of the origin of man' in labor has proven prescient for understanding the cyber ideology of today in which knowledge is made the source of value.[34] Engels' account of the dominance of ideology is embedded in a materialist understanding of the contradictions of capitalism. He explains that while the mastery of nature by the human species 'consists in the fact that we have the advantage over all other creatures of being able to learn its laws and apply them correctly' in material production, this economic 'mastery', however, by no means is meant to suggest that men 'rule over nature like a conqueror over a foreign people, like someone standing outside nature'.[35] Rather, to the contrary, as he goes on to clarify, the more social labor takes control of natural processes the more 'men not only feel but also know their oneness with nature',

---

market competition arguably have failed' ('Markets and the Judiciary', *Patently-O Blog*, 2 October 2008, https://patentlyo.com/media/docs/2009/03/Greenspan.pdf).

32   Derrida, *Animal*, p. 29.

33   Frederick Engels, 'Dialectics of Nature', *Karl Marx/Frederick Engels: Collected Works*, 50 vols (Moscow: Progress Publishers, 1987), 25, pp. 452–65 (p. 459).

34   Ibid., p. 459.

35   Ibid., p. 461.

and, furthermore, 'the more impossible will become the senseless and unnatural idea of a contrast between mind and matter, man and nature, soul and body'.[36] Capitalism, however, despite its compelling humans to realize their relation to the social world and nature and thus making them potentially free to 'produce in accordance with the standard of every species', represents a material obstacle to such universal development.[37] While on the one hand capitalism 'advances [...] the natural sciences' and puts us in 'a position to realize, and hence to control, also the more remote natural consequences of at least our day-to-day production activities', on the other it 'is predominantly concerned only about the immediate, the most tangible result' of production so that 'the more remote effects of actions directed to this end turn out to be quite different, are mostly quite the opposite in character'.[38]

Derrida, in opposition to Engels, places species-being under erasure and mystifies the relation between human and non-human life, instead inscribing the contradictions as internal to knowledge practices. In an initial move, he locates the question of the animal as part of an ongoing culture war between anthropocentric discourses on the one side that define animals in general against an unquestioned human norm and the discourses of 'thinking' on the other, which 'strike out being' (following Heidegger) and destabilize the traditional binary between human/animal by posing the question of animal 'suffering'.[39] He frames the cultural debate as a 'war waged over the matter of pity' emergent in the wake of the biotech revolution of the last two centuries because it confronts humanity with the ethical dilemma of the mass production of living organisms for the sole purpose of being consumed (for food, fashion, experiments, etc.).[40] Having been made aware by the biogenetic intervention into animal life that thinking is always embodied, the ensuing cultural war necessarily 'concerns what we call "thinking"' as the West has understood 'reason' to be the essence of what it means to be human. The sides in this culture war are thus not 'for' or 'against' animal rights on Derrida's framing, but for or against

---

36   Ibid., p. 461.
37   Marx, 'Economic and Philosophical Manuscripts', p. 277.
38   Engels, 'Dialectics of Nature', pp. 461, 463–64.
39   Derrida, *Animal*, pp. 25–28.
40   Ibid., p. 29.

thinking what Derrida calls the 'abyssal difference' that structures the surface 'inequality [...] between, on the one hand, those who violate not only animal life but even and also this sentiment of compassion, and, on the other hand, those who appeal to an irrefutable testimony to this pity'.[41] The difference that matters, 'the most radical means of thinking' on these terms, is purely a linguistic matter: how to formulate 'an "experience" of language about which one could say, even if it is not in itself "animal", that it is not something that the "animal" could be deprived of' and thereby bear witness to 'the passion of the animal' as resistant to thought.[42]

L'animot is Derrida's neologism to describe how bioengineered life deconstructs the binary of human/animal from within and produces a 'thinking' (that is not a thinking but a feeling) of 'the abyssal limits of the human', a 'passion' (without thinking) to be found in 'those moments of nakedness' in the 'eyes' (body) of the animal.[43] The new forms of life produced by biogenetic capitalism (*l'animot*) are thus held to 'necessitate' new forms of thinking animal life that go beyond the surface difference of inequality to uncover 'abyssal difference', a thinking without thinking, the 'passion of the animal', or 'embodied thinking', 'naked', 'open', 'vulnerable', the 'nonpower at the heart of power', 'the most radical means of thinking the finitude that we share with animals', and 'all the living things that man does not recognize as his fellows, his neighbors, or his brothers'.[44] *L'animot* marks a zone of thinking without thinking (the affective) as the ethical basis of whatever life beyond inequality that Derrida represents as coming from communing with one's pet at a time of global genocidal genetic violence.[45] However, what this 'pathetic' framing of the question silently assumes is that 'knowledge' work, the production of hybrid transspecies life-forms produced by biogenetic industries, has displaced human species-being (labor) as the base of the social. In actuality, the production of *l'animot*, whether discursively by deconstruction or concretely in biogenetics, is itself an effect of the social relations of production as a whole, the

41   Ibid., pp. 28–29.
42   Ibid., pp. 28, 166.
43   Ibid., p. 12.
44   Ibid., pp. 28–29, 34.
45   Ibid., p. 26.

labor arrangements which determine our place in nature as a collective species-being. Without the knowledge of labor as species-being ('life-engendering life': Marx) there can be no fundamental transformation of capitalism but only cultural reforms of its more obviously outdated practices (what Derrida calls 'violence').

For all his opposition to 'historicism', Derrida ascribes the agency of history to the history of ideas (biogenetics, philosophy, thought, thinking, passion, Heidegger, Saussure,...) and assumes a bottom-line technological 'necessity' of coming to an ethical accommodation with inequality, rather than producing a critique-al knowledge of the social totality as estranged labor, for social change.[46] Critique, unlike ethics, entails a knowledge of the totality of the social relations of production as a whole and how they shape signs, meanings, values, subjectivity, etc. For instance, biogenetic technology is not an autonomous activity driven by human egoism (whether conceived in terms of thought, knowledge, passion, or domination), but a part of capitalist production driven by profit which is realized from the extraction of surplus-labor from wage-labor. Speculating on 'the question of the animal' — thinking about thought about animals but from their mysterious embodied perspective — is not a 'radical' thinking that gets at the 'root' of inequality. 'The root', as Marx says, is 'man himself': humans, that is, not as 'setting out from what men say, imagine, conceive, nor from men as narrated, thought of, imagined, conceived' but as 'real, active men [...], on the basis of their real life-process', in short, as social animals whose life activity (labor) is universal in scope.[47] In fact, Derrida's 'animal-words' (*l'animot*) themselves display the profit to be had in the production of ideological hybrids and how this alienated intellectual production that puts individual profit making before meeting people's needs naturalizes the estranged species life of capitalism that produces the inequality and environmental destruction in the first place, making it seem unchangeable (because of unfathomable 'abyssal differences' in Derrida's discourse).

---

46   Ibid., p. 29. On 'critque-al' in opposition to 'critical' see, Teresa L. Ebert, *The Task of Cultural Critique* (Urbana: University of Illinois Press, 2009).
47   Karl Marx, 'Contribution to the Critique of Hegel's *Philosophy of Law'*, *Karl Marx/ Frederick Engels: Collected Works*, 50 vols (Moscow: Progress Publishers, 1976), 3, pp. 3–129 (p. 182); Marx and Engels, 'German Ideology', p. 36.

What Wolfe is unable to account for in his mapping of the (post) humanities with Derrida at its center is how ideas of the material and materiality have changed in cultural theory under the impact of changes in the structure of property. Contemporary discourses on (post)humanism represent a further fold in the canonical post-humanist discourses found in the earlier writings of Derrida ('The Ends of Man'), Foucault ('the end of Man' announced in *The Order of Things*), and Barthes ('Death of the Author').[48] While the texts of poststructuralist theory placed Man under erasure as a discursive construct and found Western humanism to be a coerced consensus that undermined its purported project of universal enlightenment, the contemporary discourses of (post)humanism affirm the body as a post-ideological zone of opacity and subversive singularity (bare life, passion of the animal, transspecies) that escapes all norms and testifies to a 'coming community' (Agamben), or, a 'democracy to come' (Derrida).[49] The turn to the body is justified in 'ethical' terms as addressing contemporary biopower, the cultural impact of biotech engineering and cybertech industries, on the argument that in the wake of a new 'knowledge economy' the material has changed: textuality has hybridized with corporeality (biogenetic life) and, as a result, the dogmas of (post)structuralist theory are made to circulate as the self-evidencies of 'experience'.[50] The 'materiality of the signifier' (de Man) or the 'materiality of the letter' (Lacan) has been displaced by 'incorporeal materiality' (Foucault) or the 'materiality of ideology' (Žižek) in which knowledge is held to be a singularly sublime and excessive drive that both constitutes and disrupts the phenomenal in a mysterious contingent way.[51] This is the 'materialism without substance

---

48   Michel Foucault, *The Order of Things: An Archaeology of the Human Sciences* (New York: Vintage, 1973); Jacques Derrida, 'The Ends of Man', in *Margins of Philosophy*, trans. by Alan Bass (Chicago: Chicago University Press, 1972), pp. 111–36; Roland Barthes, 'The Death of the Author', in *Image, Music, Text*, trans. by Stephen Heath (New York: Hill and Wang, 1977), pp. 142–48.

49   Giorgio Agamben, *The Coming Community*, trans. by Michael Hardt (Minneapolis: Minnesota University Press, 1993); Jacques Derrida, 'Force of Law: The "Mystical Foundation of Authority"', in *Acts of Religion*, trans. and intro. by Gil Anidjar (London and New York: Routledge, 2002), pp. 228–98.

50   Sherry Turkel, *Life on the Screen: Identity in the Age of the Internet* (New York: Simon & Schuster, 1997).

51   Jacques Lacan, *Écrits: A Selection*, trans. by Alan Sheridan (New York: W. W. Norton & Co., 1977); Michel Foucault, 'Theatrum Philosophicum', in *Language, Counter-Memory, Practice*, ed. with an intro. by Donald F. Bouchard, trans. by Donald F.

[or] the concept of social class' (Derrida) of an 'event'-al historiography centered around the 'Messianic cessation of happening' (Benjamin) in the everyday in which power intervenes in the daily in the form of what Agamben calls the 'state of exception' and reduces the human to 'bare life' (Agamben).[52] What actually has changed, however, is not the rise of knowledge as a constitutive power over the social but the way the State — which as Marx and Engels say is nothing but 'a committee for managing the common affairs of the whole bourgeoisie' in their struggle against the workers — is being used to normalize the process of capital accumulation on a world scale.[53]

Deconstruction was useful under neoliberalism when the question for the ruling class was how to privatize the state and increase surplus-value from within the territory of the nation because of its opposition to the welfare-state as a 'totalitarian' imposition upon cultural differences. But now that the state has become relatively 'deterritorialized' by being subordinated to multinational corporations whose interests are no longer limited to exploiting the territory of a nation but to amassing surplus-value around the world, deconstruction has proven to be irrelevant in containing the contradictions of transnational capitalism and new-er more 'ethical' theories have emerged to do so. What changed in theory is the concept of the material.[54] Previously primarily understood as a purely textual matter (the 'materiality of the signifier': de Man), the material is now 'immaterial', a power over life that is held to exceed positive and reliable knowledge and that can thus only be experienced bodily as a sensual affect: whether as what Agamben calls 'bare life', or as the 'biogenetic life' of Haraway's 'transspecies', or, the 'multitude' of

---

Bouchard and Sherry Simon (Ithaca: Cornell University Press, 1977), pp. 165–98 (p. 169); Paul de Man, *The Resistance to Theory* (Minneapolis: Minnesota University Press, 1986); Slavoj Žižek, 'The Spectre of Ideology', in *Mapping Ideology*, ed. by Slavoj Žižek (New York: Verso Books, 2012).

52   Jacques Derrida, *Specters of Marx: The State of the Debt, The Work of Mourning & the New International* (London and New York: Routledge, 1994), pp. 69, 212; Walter Benjamin, 'Theses on the Philosophy of History', in *Illuminations* (New York: Schocken, 1977), p. 263; Giorgio Agamben, *Homo Sacer: Sovereign Power and Bare Life*, trans. by Daniel Heller-Roazen (Stanford: Stanford University Press, 1998).

53   Karl Marx and Frederick Engels, 'The Manifesto of the Communist Party', *Karl Marx/Frederick Engels: Collected Works*, 50 vols (Moscow: Progress Publishers, 1976), 6, p. 486.

54   This shift was officially formalized at the 'The Idea of Communism' conference in London on March 2009 at which Žižek, Badiou, and Negri participated.

affective labor (Hardt and Negri), or in terms of personal (in)fidelity to an unrepresentable 'truth-event' (Badiou), or, as in Žižek's notion of the Real as sublime 'social substance' whose unequal coverage constitutes class as a pathological death drive in his texts. In these terms, what (post)humanism investigates, unlike the theoretical post-humanism dominant under early neoliberalism, is 'biopower', which, as Foucault argued, demands thick description of the technological conditions that call into question the human mastery of nature and that often times seems to place humanity's 'existence as a living being in question'.[55] Žižek has taken to calling such an approach 'dialectical materialism' because of its focus on 'the 'inhuman' core of the human' as 'the gap between humanity and its own inhuman excess', which he calls the 'materiality of ideology' coincident with the 'desubstantialization' of the 'commons' by the market.[56] The result in terms of Žižek's understanding

---

55   Michel Foucault, *The History of Sexuality: An Introduction* (New York: Vintage, 1990), p. 143.

56   Slavoj Žižek, *The Parallax View* (MIT Press, 2006), p. 5; Slavoj Žižek, 'Ecology — A New Opium for the Masses', *Next Nature*, 16 February 2009, https://nextnature.net/story/2009/ecology-a-new-opium-for-the-masses. Žižek's 'dialectical materialism' is the opposite of the dialectical materialism of Engels. Dialectical materialism in Engels' writings is the philosophical basis of Marxism because it represents the only consistent understanding of materialism which explains how change enters being not from a spiritual 'beyond', as Hegel imagined, but from the motion of matter itself, which is thought to be static and inert in 'mechanical materialism' (empiricism). It represents the principle that 'the concept of a thing and its reality, run side by side like two asymptotes, always approaching each other yet never meeting' ('Letter to Conrad Schmidt'), or, in other words, that our concepts are abstractions of material reality with which they do not 'coincide' but nevertheless 'correspond' in a 'circuitous' way ('asymptotically'). As Engels explains, such an approach is necessary so as not to fall into the false consciousness that our concepts are merely pragmatic 'fictions'. As Lenin put it: dialectical materialism is a 'guard against mistakes and rigidity' ('Once Again on the Trade Unions', pp. 70–107), such as the dogma that the relation of concepts to reality is arbitrary (i.e., eclecticism), because dialectical materialism maintains the principle that although truth 'is something we cannot ever hope to achieve completely' the continual approximations made toward it are an 'indicator of its connection with human wants', its 'use and connection with the surrounding world'. In other words, it demonstrates how the 'thing-in-itself' is always a 'thing-for-us'. Žižek's 'dialectical materialism' should more accurately be called an 'eclectical immaterialism' because behind all the examples, jokes, films, biographies, philosophers, etc. he rehearses to illustrate the (gray-on-gray) theme of the traumatic Real, is the principle that 'a reduction of the higher intellectual content to its lower economic [...] cause' (*Parallax*, p. ix) is 'bad' epistemology because it covers over the 'absent cause' of ontology (the Lacanian 'lack' that drives desire) which 'eludes' representation, or, put differently, 'the materiality of ideology'. Such an interpretation makes 'dialectical materialism' a

of history is devastating as he makes a fetish of alienation, of how, in Marx's words, 'an inhuman power rules over everything' in capitalism, whereby, as Engels adds, 'the more remote effects of actions [...] turn out to be [...] quite the opposite in character' of what was intended by the producers.[57] In doing so, Žižek redefines humanity as the unconscious rather than conscious species-being, driven by desire rather than need, and re-conceives history in Benjamin's messianic terms as an inevitable path to global catastrophe from which the only escape is a religious leap of faith — what Žižek calls 'pure voluntarism'.[58] And yet, what is strangely missing from these discussions, hence the continuation of the 'post', is a materialist understanding of the material as what Marx calls 'species-being' (or 'life activity, productive life').[59]

As Marx and Engels explain: 'Men can be distinguished from animals by consciousness, by religion or anything else you like. They themselves begin to distinguish themselves from animals as soon as they begin to *produce* their means of subsistence'.[60] This needs to be read literally. What they are saying is not, as is so often claimed, that labor, tools, production, or economics distinguishes humans from animals instead of consciousness, religion, or anything else you like, but rather that humans can be discursively distinguished from animals by anything (including labor, tools, production, economics,...) and yet whatever that 'thing' is thought to be, it necessarily is a product of human life activity, or, human species-being, rather than merely a fixed idea. As Marx acknowledges elsewhere: 'animals also produce' and 'the life of the species, both in man and in animals, consists physically in the fact that man (like the animal) lives on organic nature', so it is not simply production as such which distinguishes humans from non-human animals for Marx.[61] Nevertheless, despite Marx's recognition of the commonality, he yet maintains that human life activity is different than animal life activity because the life activity of humans is not

---

trope of desire that occults need in his writing that, as in all ideology, mystifies the social.

57   Marx, 'Economic and Philosophical Manuscripts', p. 314; Engels, *Dialectics*, pp. 463–64.
58   Slavoj Žižek, *First as Tragedy, Then as Farce* (New York: Verso Books, 2009), p. 154.
59   Marx, 'Economic and Philosophical Manuscripts', p. 275.
60   'German Ideology', p. 31.
61   'Economic and Philosophical Manuscripts', pp. 275–76.

completely determined for them as it is for animals by purely biological and environmental conditions:

> The animal is immediately one with its life activity. It does not distinguish itself from it. It is its life activity. Man makes his life activity itself the object of his will and of his consciousness. He has conscious life activity. It is not a determination with which he directly merges. Conscious life activity distinguishes man immediately from animal life activity.[62]

It is important to note that it is not the natural possession of 'consciousness' that distinguishes human beings from the rest of animal life for Marx here. Rather, it is the social mode of activity through which human beings produce their life under diverse and changing conditions that they have learned not only to consciously adapt to, but also to transform, that does so. Human beings confront their life activity — the 'metabolism' of their own labor mixed with natural resources — in practice as well as an object of thought, as something they are necessarily made aware of themselves having produced through their own labor practices over time. Human beings in their life activity, therefore, confront nature not as something given that subsists in-itself but always as a material basis for the realization of their own purposes:

> [W]hat distinguishes the worst architect from the best of bees is this, that the architect raises his structure in imagination before he erects it in reality. At the end of every labour process, we get a result that already existed in the imagination of the labourer at its commencement.[63]

This objectification of human life is of course a result of the fact that human life activity (i.e., labor) transforms nature, including human nature (e.g., language as an adaptation of natural sounds for the purpose of communication), whereas animal life activity does not. In other words, humans socially produce a transformation within the material conditions they inhabit in the very process of producing what is immediately necessary to sustain themselves, whereas the other animals do not. Consequently humans also produce and transform *themselves* in order to adapt to the ever changing conditions. The difference between the human and the animal to which Marx draws attention throughout

---

62 Ibid., p. 276.
63 Karl Marx, *Capital. A Critique of Political Economy*, vol. I, *Karl Marx/Frederick Engels: Collected Works*, 50 vols (Moscow: Progress Publishers, 1983), 35, p. 188.

his writings is concretely demonstrable in the fact that 'an animal forms only in accordance with the standard and the need of the species to which it belongs, whilst man knows how to produce in accordance with the standard of every species'.[64] More importantly, however, this is also a critique-al distinction to make between humans and animals in order to produce awareness of the way in which human labor, which is imposed by material necessity and productive of the 'know how' to produce all life, is 'estranged' under capitalism; the mode of production in which 'all things are other than themselves' because 'an inhuman power rules over everything' due to the law of value that emerges from out of the commodification of labor.[65] The objectification and transformation of our species-being may be the basis of human life, but the commodification of labor is the objectification of human life itself that reduces the subject of labor herself into an object on the market that is consumed by another who owns the means of production, for the purpose of accumulating capital. Capitalism thus 'makes man's species-life a means to his physical existence' so that humanity 'produces only under the dominion of immediate physical need' rather than 'produce in freedom' from necessity.[66] In other words, capitalism systematically expropriates abstract social labor and privatizes it in the hands of a few, and thus turns labor, the life activity of the species, into physical work undertaken for mere subsistence (wage-labor). The result is that capitalism 'humanizes' nature, turning it into material wealth, and in the process 'dehumanizes' humanity by reducing labor to a means of capital accumulation by the capitalist and a task undertaken by the worker for wages merely to maintain their physical existence.

It is important to clarify Marx's theory of species-being because today — as Engels said of the 'materialistic natural scientists' of his day who were 'unable to form any clear idea of the origin of man' owing to the fact that 'under ideological influence' they did 'not recognize the part played by labor therein' — even the marxists fail to grasp it.[67] Terry Eagleton, for instance, has defended Marx's concept of species-being but, echoing Weber's understanding of capitalism as 'spiritual'

---

64   Marx, 'Economic and Philosophical Manuscripts', p. 277.
65   Ibid., p. 110.
66   Ibid., pp. 68–69.
67   Engels, *Dialectics*, p. 178.

in essence, he turns it into the useless romantic idea that human nature inherently 'resists' the ethos of capitalism.[68] According to Eagleton, capitalism depends on a 'ruthlessly instrumental logic' that demands 'everything [...] must have its point and purpose', so as to build up the expectation of a 'reward' for 'acting well' and, moreover, it reserves punishments for acting in ways that do 'not have a goal'.[69] In response to his culturalist theory of capitalism, he posits an equally culturalist understanding of what is to be done to transform capitalism. When he argues that defending the idea of 'the material "species being" of humanity' is a radical act of transgression, he actually puts forward a pseudo-materialist understanding of 'species-being' by representing humanity as having a cultural root and, in turn, representing culture as purposeless activity for its own sake.[70]

Leaving aside for the moment the 'spiritual' way Eagleton discusses capitalism, is 'the idea of fulfilling your nature' that he finds exemplified in culture really 'inimical to the capitalist success ethic'?[71] Capitalism after all depends on constant technical innovation because individual capitals realize relative surplus value by cutting the amount of time workers engage in necessary labor to reproduce the value equivalent of their wages and increasing the amount of time spent in unpaid surplus labor which forms the basis of the capitalist's profit.[72] To argue that 'it is in our nature to go beyond ourselves' and 'give birth to culture, which is always changeable, diverse and open ended' and thus 'resistant' to instrumentality, is to naturalize the law of value that drives capitalism by embedding the drive for innovation in human nature.[73] Making culture the root of humanity also homogenizes culture as reflecting a universal 'sense of belonging' that 'humanizes' both oppressor and oppressed rather than a site of class antagonism over the material resources that determine whose needs are being met and whose are not, who is 'humanized' by capital and feels at home in the world as it is, and who is 'dehumanized' by it and has nothing to lose.[74]

---

68 Terry Eagleton, *After Theory* (New York: Basic Books, 2003), p. 120.
69 Ibid., pp. 115–19.
70 Ibid., pp. 119–20.
71 Ibid., p. 110.
72 Marx, *Capital*, I, Chapt. 10, 'The Working Day', pp. 239–43.
73 Eagleton, *After Theory*, p. 119.
74 Ibid., p. 21.

But what about Eagleton's argument that culture is not only essentially anti-capitalist, but is also the material root of human nature and as such an incontestable 'absolute truth'?[75] On this argument, he claims that in the same way that 'you cannot ask why a giraffe should do the things it does', one cannot ask why humanity produces culture, or, in other words, ask 'what is the purpose of culture?'.[76] In both cases, however, nature is taken to be a static and unchanging thing, as if giraffes ever existed outside an ever changing and evolving material environment which, actually, always does explain why they should do what they do and not something else, which is, of course, what Darwin's theory of natural selection is all about. Not only does Eagleton assume that what makes a giraffe is immanent to the giraffe outside the material environment in which it must find food, shelter and other giraffes, thus effectively giving the giraffe in place of its actual nature a normative cultural identity (a kind of Aristotelian soul inscribed in its genes, supposedly), but he also naturalizes culture by treating it as a kind of secretion that is spontaneously produced by human beings naturally. Eagleton, following an aesthetic tradition within Western (Hegelian) Marxism since Adorno, defends 'the concept of culture' as 'the cultivation of human powers as ends in themselves' on the argument that not only is an immanent understanding of culture 'resistant' to the law of value, but, furthermore, that it is embedded in human nature.[77] And yet, such a self-reflexive concept of culture is not coincident with humanity as a species: a long period of natural evolution from bipedalism and the opposable thumb to economic (i.e., conscious) organization and tool-making precedes language and 'art', the first cultural practices which take on the formation of the subject specifically as their purpose. It is only by suppressing knowledge of human evolution and the origins of culture in labor that culture can be made to seem 'purposeless' (i.e., something naturally subjective rather than socially objective). But, not only is culture always purposeful ('language *is* practical, real consciousness', as Marx and Engels say) because it is economic in essence — it produces a consciousness of the material process necessary to sustain life and helps wrest control over the material world so that humans are not the

---

75   Ibid., p. 103.
76   Ibid., p. 116.
77   Ibid., p. 24.

slaves of chance and necessity — it also has cross-purposes that arise, for instance, when short and long term purposes come into conflict, such as when the needs of immediate survival conflict with long term sustainability, or, as when culture serves to 'contain' conflicting class interests (ideology).[78]

What is radical about the theory of humanism that Marx advances in his early writings is how it foresees the need of overcoming alienation, the negative activity of humanity that consists of endless 're-appropriation' of our estranged 'essence', if we are ever to become truly human. He argues, 'Only through the supersession of this mediation — which is itself, however, a necessary premise — does positively self-deriving humanism, *positive* humanism, come into being'.[79] For Marx, human nature is not as Eagleton imagines: a given, static, and inert thing that 'resists' the outside world. Instead, humanity is a part of nature that, even if no longer quite an animal like any other, nevertheless remains something less than fully human, an 'instrument of labor' like any other used as a means to an end, until such time that it acquires 'control and conscious mastery of these powers, which, born of the action of men on one another, have till now overawed and ruled men as powers completely alien to them'.[80]

Without an understanding of what makes the human and why (the mode of production), it is impossible to make a fundamental critique of the capitalist exploitation of human labor-power — the estranged labor that produces and 'humanizes' wealth for the capitalist and impoverishes and 'dehumanizes' the worker — and instead things appear topsy-turvy so that inequality appears to be the result of a 'bad' consciousness — 'instrumental reason' (Adorno); 'ready-to-hand thought' (Heidegger); 'the spirit of capitalism' (Weber); 'carnophallogocentrism' (Derrida); 'privatization of the commons' (Badiou, Negri, Žižek) — to be re-formed through more ethical discourses, or, in other words, through spiritual idealization ('learning to live well'). But this inversion of the material relations into ideology is itself an act of estranged labor inserted into the division of labor and represents the product of professional ideologists. In short, it is another instance of how labor power is exchanged for

---

78   Marx and Engels, 'German Ideology', p. 44.
79   Marx, 'Economic and Philosophical Manuscripts', pp. 341–42.
80   Marx and Engels, 'German Ideology', pp. 51–52.

wages (means of consumption) rather than to meet human needs as a whole. Ethical discourses and 'spiritual' fixes are commodified ways of individually learning to come to terms with the exploitation of labor by capital, rather than a way to socially change the world for the good of all.

It is the domination of capital that subjects labor to meeting physical needs (wages) and that makes culture into ideology, a reified activity to rationalize production and normalize the worker to her own subjection, rather than a material force for social emancipation from inequality. This is why although Marx argues that 'the *initial stage* of the movement [the re-appropriation of estranged human life] [...] depends on whether the true *recognized* life of the people manifests itself more in consciousness or in the external world — is more ideal or real', he nevertheless maintains that the abolition of 'real' estrangement (private property), as distinct from the negation of estranged 'ideas' (reified thought), 'embraces both aspects' while the contrary is not the case.[81] In other words, the Hegelian inversion of 'substance' as 'subject' which negates the estrangement of ideas from their material basis when they are considered self-caused (as forms of 'thought') is itself an ideological false consciousness, what Marx calls an 'occult' or 'mystifing critique', precisely in the sense that it does not 'embrace' the universal estrangement of labor under capitalism, but only concerns itself with the alienated 'labor of thought' (Hegel).[82] In the same way, the deconstruction of the human/animal binary inscribed within what Derrida calls 'carnophallogecentric thought' that is effected by 'thinking (the passion) of the animal' as it surfaces bodily in all inscriptions of knowledge does not 'embrace' the material as the estrangement of human species-being as a whole but only contests the 'ideal' subjection of 'thinking' and necessarily reifies the material as ahistorical 'matter' (the body as a certain 'experience of language'). In other words, Derrida simply rehearses how 'thought' too is 'other than itself' but does not surface the social forces that explain why 'an inhuman power rules over everything'.[83] Without a materialist explanation, thinking remains alienated and blissfully at home with social inequality. The critique of 'ideal' estrangement (ideological

---

81   'Economic and Philosophical Manuscripts', p. 297, 332.
82   Ibid., p. 345; G. W. F. Hegel, *The Phenomenology of Mind* (Harper & Row Publishers, 1967), pp. 90–91, 128.
83   Marx, 'Economic and Philosophical Manuscripts', p. 314.

'thought') necessarily leaves intact the estrangement of human powers as alien powers embodied in capital which does not change due to changes in discourse and which 'always exceed the fate of signs'.[84]

Other (Post)human Stories

(Post)humanism is a regime of knowing that represents the material, which is at root class inequality, as an effect of the immaterial (knowledge) and advocates for change as a spiritual movement of ideas (ethics). It for instance argues that at the root of injustice and inequality is biogenetic 'violence' that renders species undecidable from within and liberates thinking the 'passion of the animal' as the experience of language ('language about which one could say, even if it is not in itself "animal," that it is not something that the "animal" could be deprived of'), or what Derrida calls 'animal writing'.[85] Humanism on this view is 'speciesism', a mode of policing the 'ontological divide' between the human and non-human (animal) others in 'thought'. It seems that in (post)humanist discourses, the more science advances the understanding of nature and the more life on earth depends on understanding human species-being as the universal production of the whole earth ('life-engendering life': Marx), the more impossible it becomes to know with any certainty what is human, and yet, such developments actually prove Marx's materialist theory that 'productive life is the life of the species'.[86] It follows that if, during their productive lives, human beings are reduced to the mere maintenance of physical life while the value of labor is transferred to the commodity, then humanity, and along with it everything else, will appear 'other than itself' and 'inhuman'. In place of a materialist theory of species as productive life, the social is represented in (post)humanist cultural theory in an alienated way, as an inhuman 'hauntology' of ghostly traces, a hybrid creation of 'immaterial labor' embodied in transspecies form.[87] In actuality the immaterial (knowledge) is determined by the material (class) and the ethical turn of the (post)humanities is nothing

---

84 Mas'ud Zavarzadeh and Donald Morton, *Theory, (Post)Modernity, Opposition* (Montreal: Maisonneuve Press, 1991).
85 Derrida, *Animal*, pp. 25–26.
86 'Economic and Philosophical Manuscripts', p. 276.
87 On 'hauntology' see, Derrida, *Specters*.

more than a justification of the new more profitable forms of global capital today.[88]

The 'question of the animal' (Derrida) is part of a broader 'ethical' turn in the humanities that frames issues of injustice and inequality, which are rooted in class, in cultural terms (knowledge) that accommodate capitalism as the normal basis of human societies. On the one hand it shows a concern to extend to animals the awareness of difference that social movements have brought to questions of gender, race, and sexuality, and on the other it represents sensuality and sentimental attachments as an emergent animal perspective that will transvalue all values, and so one finds Derrida nakedly communing with his cat and Haraway writing about making love with her dog through 'oral intercourse' as if such sentimental attachments could remake 'reality'.[89] In (post)humanist writings, the agency of change is 'animal writing'; what Derrida does when he writes '*l'animot*' is to 'liberate [...] animal words' and is an example of what Haraway calls 'dog-writing', a kind of writing that

> brings together the human and non-human, the organic and technological, carbon and silicon, freedom and structure, history and myth, the rich and the poor, the state and the subject, diversity and depletion, modernity and postmodernity, and nature and culture in unexpected ways.[90]

(Post)humanist writing consists of telling stories of 'co-habitation, co-evolution, and embodied crossspecies sociality' on the assumption that such 'stories are bigger than ideologies' and determine 'the world we might yet live in' because 'reality is an active verb'.[91] Central to the (post)humanities is the kind of 'animal writing' performed by Derrida and Haraway as the limit of the radical now, which has consolidated itself into an academic discipline known as 'animal studies'. Animal studies is committed to raising awareness of how humanity has conceived of and related to animals and, as well, prioritizes the question of how animals

---

88   *e2: The Economies of Being Environmentally Conscious* (PBS, 2006).
89   See, e.g., Ralph R. Acampora, *Corporal Compassion: Animal Ethics and Philosophy of Body* (Pittsburgh: University of Pittsburgh Press, 2006); Donna Haraway, *The Companion Species Manifesto: Dogs, People, and Significant Otherness*, (Chicago: Prickly Paradigm Press, 2003), pp. 2–3, 6.
90   Derrida, *Animal*, p. 37; Haraway, *Companion Species*, pp. 3–4.
91   Ibid., pp. 3, 4, 6, 17.

experience the world in non-human ways that are held to provide an 'other' awareness (embodied knowledge) through which to change the ways humans relate to animals, the world, and each other so as to be more respectful of differences ('love'). The question of the question of the animal, however, is not exhausted by such ethical concerns, nor is it produced immanently within cultural discourses. The ethical turn to the consideration of the animal is a question because capitalism is now transforming the biosphere and developing newer forms of property and class conflict in ways that put the exploitation of human species-being itself in question and raise awareness of the necessity of the class struggle for socialism. The 'question of the animal' is the reformist answer to the class inequalities of capitalism that serves the ruling class which wants a 'sustainable' capitalism with less overt injustice but with class inequality as the root of the system in exploited labor still intact.

The 'question of the animal' is not a questioning of capitalism. Rather, it is a questioning of the humanist legitimation of an outdated ('modern', 'industrial', 'nationalist') capitalism and on the side of a newer (post)humanist global capitalism.[92] This is why one finds that the new (post)humanist capitalists speak the same (post)humanist animal language of a Derrida or Haraway, as when Joel Salatin, a farm owner/activist, remarks:

> A culture that views a pig as a pile of protoplasmic inanimate structure to be manipulated by whatever creative design the human can foist on that critter will probably view individuals within its community and other cultures in the community of nations with the same kind of disdain, disrespect and controlling-type mentality.[93]

Humanist capitalism is a 'controlling-type mentality' (carnophallogocentrism; speciesism); (post)humanist capitalism is more 'in touch' with the 'commons' (critter life, transspecies, pettism). In other words, humanist capitalism is 'violently' industrial, nationalist, and monocultural: it penetrates local cultures and causes them to destroy their forests for export or to hunt species to extinction for trade, for example. In contrast, (post)humanist capitalism is more 'ethical',

---

92 See, e.g., Harriet Ritvo, *The Animal Estate: The English and Other Creatures in the Victorian Age* (Cambridge: Harvard University Press, 1987).

93 *Food, Inc.*, dir. Robert Kenner (Magnolia Pictures, 2008).

postindustrial, transnational and multicultural: it cooperates with local growers to preserve their ecospheres and invents sustainable forms of agriculture and urbanism and protects wildlife for the knowledges they may give to future generations. Humanist capitalism is gray. (Post) humanist capitalism is green. But green capitalism, like gray capitalism, is still a rejection of the red — the emancipatory theory of labor in which 'from each according to his abilities, to each according to his needs' is the rule, and 'men not only feel but also know their oneness with nature' because they 'produce in accordance with the standard of every species' universally.[94]

The (post)humanities advocates the standpoint of the animal as 'resistant' in its opacity to the systematic use of animals for profit (speciesism) because it values the singularity and difference of the animal, but global capitalism itself necessitates such an ethical awareness because of the new forms of property, such as the genetic engineering of food or the protection of ecospheres for pharmaceuticals research and development. On the left these new forms of capital are made into 'immaterial' forms of 'biopower' (Foucault, Agamben), or, ironically, in more (neo)marxist terms, as the privatization of the commons of 'general intellect' (Negri, Wark, Žižek), as if knowledge were the source of wealth. Biopower represents the commodification of labor by capital as the result of a compulsive acquisitive drive for material resources, a will-to-power to control the 'commons' and regulate 'life', and not the class practice of the capitalist to accumulate more surplus-labor from human labor-power. The displacement of the material by the immaterial as the underlying logic of the system in (post)humanist theory is an argument for an ethical capitalism that focuses on the effects of capitalism (social domination) rather than its cause (labor exploitation) and in this way makes individuals seem responsible for its inequalities and justifies a volunteerism to reform it in localities (pettism) rather than critique the logic of class relations.

But capitalism today realizes the most surplus-value precisely through such ethical practices, through, for instance, the exercise of 'soft power' in 'humanitarian aid' missions by US military forces in response

---

94   Karl Marx, 'Critique of the Gotha Programme', *Karl Marx/Frederick Engels: Collected Works*, 50 vols (Moscow: Progress Publishers, 1984), 24, p. 87; Engels, *Dialectics*, p. 461; Marx, *Manuscripts*, p. 277.

to so-called 'natural disasters' as in Haiti in 2010, and the development of 'green alternatives' for industry:

> A new poetry of buildings [...] born of a deeper beauty — not merely sleek design but rather part of its DNA, ingrained in the materials, its source, its inner workings, possessing an unseen soul [...] a building can do more than stand [...] it can live and contribute.[95]

These newer forms of property, unlike the old forms, are represented as the outcome of immaterial processes (knowledge-work) that are inherently 'clean' (i.e., more efficient, less-wasteful and therefore ethical or 'smart') and therefore 'green' (more just). And yet these forms of property do not lessen but actually deepen class exploitation by, for example, using the material resources of the state to first subsidize their development and then to protect their monopoly on the new products (as Monsanto does with the patents on its genetically modified seeds for example or as Pfizer does with the patents on its medicine). They commodify the environmental crisis into marketable products and polarize the social even more between the 'haves' and 'have nots'. These new forms of exploitation are ideologically enabled by the new '(post) humanist' theories of the material which I will now turn to consider more closely.

Materialist (Post)humanism

The canonical figuration of the (post)humanities with Derrida at the center marginalizes theories of (post)humanism that regard it as the dominant ideology of global capitalism, such as Žižek's for instance. Turning to Žižek's writings, one finds a very different way of making sense of (post)humanism according to its 'outside'. On Žižek's framing, the (post)humanities is really the terrain in which 'we should locate today's struggle between idealism and materialism' as 'class struggle' over the Real.[96] The 'idealists' are the contemporary 'immaterialists' who reduce phenomena to an absolute plane of immanence without an outside

---

95 'The Green Apple', nar. by Brad Pitt, *e2: The Economies of Being Environmentally Conscious* (PBS, 2006).

96 Žižek, *The Parallax View*, p. 166; Slavoj Žižek and V. I. Lenin, 'Afterword: Lenin's Choice', *Revolution at the Gates: The 1917 Writings* (New York: Verso Books, 2014), p. 190.

cause, such as Heidegger (Being), Derrida (Text), Deleuze (Flows) and Negri (Multitude). Without accounting for an outside cause, such views produce an 'unconditional voluntarism' that is at home in the world as it is, following the dictates of compulsory consumption heedless of the social costs.[97] The 'materialists', conversely, are those who 'embed' the 'immaterial' phenomena of culture within its underlying preconditions — capitalism. Leaving aside for the moment the question of Žižek's understanding of the outside, class, capitalism, and materialism, how does his theory lead us to understand the 'question of the animal' that is central to Derrida's formulation of the (post)humanities?

Žižek has stated his agreement with Fukuyama's assessment of the possibility of the imminent demise of capitalism by allowing markets deregulated access to the 'lifeworld': 'We are in danger of losing everything: the threat is that we will be reduced to abstract subjects devoid of all substantial content, dispossessed of our symbolic substance, our genetic base heavily manipulated, vegetating in an unlivable environment'.[98] Despite this agreement, Žižek does not share Fukuyama's idea of human freedom as cultural competition for status or his global regulatory fantasies. Žižek is opposed to the essentialist account of human nature that underlies Fukuyama's writings which figure as properly human the 'struggle for recognition' (culture) as an extension of the animal struggle for existence (need). According to Žižek, all struggles are 'surplus' struggles at the root of which is the class struggle over surplus-value, which gives form to the cultural struggles beyond the economic struggle and makes it impossible to ideologically close the gap between 'what is' (inequality) and what 'should be' (democracy).[99] Class struggle, in short, is the 'absent cause' (Althusser) at the center of existence that generates ideological 'solutions' but that itself 'eludes symbolization' and explanation. The question for Žižek is how to figure this gap between the 'symbolic' surface conflicts and the underlying structural contradiction of capitalism in such a way as to resist its recuperative suturing in the Symbolic edifice of the culture, a strategy

---

97 Žižek, *Parallax*, p. 165.
98 Francis Fukuyama, *Our Posthuman Future: Consequences of the Biotechnology Revolution* (London: Picador, 2003); Žižek, *Tragedy*, p. 97.
99 Slavoj Žižek, *Less Than Nothing: Hegel and the Shadow of Dialectical Materialism* (New York: Verso Books, 2012), p. 246.

he calls 'Bartleby politics' (i.e., as in 'I prefer not to' repeat the ideology). In other words, his project is how to 'resist' attachment to a 'big Other' or 'grand narrative' of history that would seem to 'guarantee' a progressive outcome and thereby promote the usual politics that support the system rather than provoke a 'leap of faith' outside the logic of history.[100] Žižek thus opposes 'traditional history' with 'effective history' as in Foucault's reading of Nietzsche, which dissolves the ongoing historicity of labor in the 'event'-fulness of ideology (reversal of values).[101] What this does to the concept of class in Žižek's writings is crucial for understanding their ideological function. Žižek turns class into a marker of cultural status. His 'class' is not a matter of 'oppressor and oppressed' but of symbolic 'inclusion and exclusion' from the dominant culture: 'slum dwellers [...] are "free" in the double meaning of the word even more than the classic proletariat ("freed" from all substantial ties; dwelling in a free space, outside the police regulations of the state)'.[102] His writings have become so popular in the left theory market and on the Internet because of the way they turn class from an economic structure of inequality to an empty political trope, citing Rancière's ideological gloss on the proletariat as 'the part of no-part' that whitewashes exploitation and alibis capitalism.[103] His answer to social injustice and inequality is, as in market criteria, how to construct an 'effective' (which always means popular in terms of marketing) understanding of class by representing class as disavowed desire and perverse pleasure rather than alienated

---

100 Such a voluntarist leap 'outside' history is of course already 'inside' the discourse of anarchism, which can be traced through the writings of the Young Hegelians, to Stirner, Nietzsche, and Sorel, through the Surrealists, the College of Sociology (Bataille, Benjamin), and the Situationists, as a text that, moreover, has always put itself forward as dissenting from the 'orthodoxies' of dissent and as offering a 'third way' between capitalism and socialism and whose libertarian discourse has itself become the official ideology of the neoliberal state (deregulation). Žižek, however, has taken to cloaking it as revolutionary Marxism ('Repeating Lenin' n. pag.). But for Marxism, 'the history of all hitherto existing society is the history of class struggles' between 'oppressor and oppressed' ('Manifesto', p. 482). Hence it follows that 'there is no middle way (for mankind has not developed any 'third' ideology), and generally speaking, in a society torn by class opposition there could never be a non-class or an above-class ideology' (Lenin, 'What Is To Be Done?: Burning Questions of Our Movement', *V. I. Lenin Collected Works*, 45 vols [Moscow: Progress Publishers, 1977], 5, pp. 347–529 [p. 384]).
101 Foucault, 'Nietzsche, Genealogy, History', in *Language, Counter-Memory, Practice*.
102 Marx and Engels, 'Manifesto', p. 482; Žižek, 'Ecology', n. pag.
103 Žižek, *Tragedy*, p. 99.

labor and unmet need. In other words, class is posited as a site of 'surplus-enjoyment' in the culture in which the term is either invested with negative or affirmative pleasure rather than class as a matter of who is clothed, fed, housed, educated, healthy, and *why*. In this way he makes class into a market identity as in bourgeois sociology. So, on the one hand, class is a negative Real that eludes symbolization at the level of culture ('the part of no-part') and, on the other, it is a positive call to action to struggle against the privatization of the 'commons' (what he calls communism) on the part of 'egalitarian collectives' united by the categorical imperative that 'truth is partial' rather than 'objective'.[104] In terms of ideology, what this situating of class in relation to culture rather than production entails is the insistence that behind the symbolic humanization and naturalization of capitalism as the horizon of struggle is an 'inhuman' excess ('the materiality of ideology'), a death-drive implanted in human beings by the market that produces a 'surplus-pleasure' to be found both in the sacrifice of one's normal identity as a consumer and symbolic rebirth as an ethical subject. For Žižek, the contemporary represents the moment when the inhuman drive of capitalism that enslaves the individual to the loop of desire and prioritizes it before the social good is extended into the Symbolic (the cultural sphere), which puts it up for contestation and resignification in ways that may challenge the consumerism and technocratic reason of the dominant ideology such as to make possible a truly authentic ethical act to commit oneself to the overthrow of capitalism.

Clearly, in Žižek's terms, Haraway's 'transspecies' and Derrida's '*l'animot*' are as equally problematic as Fukuyama's defense of the human because they all ideologically obscure a real contradiction between the inside (capitalism) and the outside (communism). They all reduce the class struggle, which structures culture, to the terms of the cultural as a plane of immanence in which (class) antagonism is normalized as the self-difference within class, and disappear the struggle between classes over the 'inhuman' social Real (the 'commons').[105] And yet Žižek's understanding of the outside is also not outside but inside, what he calls

---

104 Žižek, 'Repeating Lenin', n. pag.
105 *Class and Its Others*, J. K. Gibson-Graham, Stephen A. Resnick, and Richard D. Wolff (eds), foreword by Amitava Kumar (Minneapolis: Minnesota University Press, 2000).

the ethical Act, or, following Badiou, 'fidelity to the event' or the 'idea of communism' (i.e., defense of the commons), that makes class into a marker of different lifestyles: the 'working class' is thus a plurality of market identities that consists of 'intellectual laborers, the old manual working class, and the outcasts' each with their own 'identity politics' ('multiculturalism'/'populist fundamentalism'/'gangs') formed in response to state 'privatization' that 'desubstantializes' the 'commons' (the 'general intellect') and thus makes them 'free [...] to invent some mode of being-together'.[106]

Žižek's opposition to the humanism of 'state philosophy', which he locates both in the Fukuyamian attempt to delimit a properly human sphere of ethics from an encroaching 'inhuman' otherness and in the postmodern left who fetishize a sublime otherness (pettism), is finally not so radical because he represents capitalism as an 'inhuman' drive that nullifies the revolutionary agency of the proletariat, which is the material, not symbolic, critique of everything existing, and 'the *real* movement which abolishes the present state of things' because of its centrality to capitalism.[107] Žižek rejects what he calls the 'old' and 'naïve' theory of surplus-value of Marx and in place of Marx's class theory of culture, he puts his own cultural theory of class as a matter of who is included/excluded from the hegemonic form of 'enjoyment'.[108] He claims that the proletariat no longer exists as the mass of workers exploited at the point of production and that Marx's theory of value as the exploitation of labor is out of date because there is no more exploitation now that knowledge is the source of value ('general intellect') and profit is not made from surplus-labor but 'rent' (of copyrighted software for example).[109] Leaving aside that what he

---

106 Žižek, *Tragedy* 147; 'Ecology', n. pag.

107 Marx and Engels, 'German Ideology', p. 49.

108 Slavoj Žižek, 'The Monstrosity of Christ: Paradox or Dialectic?', YouTube, 21 September 2009 https://youtu.be/RqVAiBbSjbI?t=4202 [accessed 8 June 2024].

109 *Tragedy*, p. 145; The result of Žižek's rejection of Marx's labor theory of value is bourgeois ideology: 'I don't believe Bill Gates is exploiting his workers because he pays them relatively well' ('Monstrosity of Christ', n. pag.). In short, exploitation is not a matter of production but market exchange that disappears when the terms of exchange are 'fair'. I leave aside how Žižek has already undermined the logic of 'fair' that allows him to conclude there is no exploitation when he says that the logic of profit is 'arbitrary' because it is determined through the use of juridical force (copyright). What is behind Žižek's (il)logic is the (ideo)logic of capital that mystifies the source of value in human labor.

describes is actually double profit — not only does the capitalist own the labor embodied in the commodity but also the wages to access it through monopoly control of the market — in place of the proletariat as 'the *real* movement which abolishes the present state of things', Žižek instead substitutes those he calls 'toxic subjects', 'outcasts', or 'slum dwellers' basing this on their exclusion from authentic recognition by the culture for what is in effect, on his reading, their cynical non-affirmative consumption, which he romanticizes as 'Bartleby politics'.[110] Žižek rewrites 'class' in cultural terms as those who are not 'included' in the 'symbolic social substance' (i.e. 'commons', 'general intellect') and whose exclusion becomes its own source of pleasure: '"freed" from all substantial ties [...] they have to invent some mode of being-together'.[111] In Žižek's psycho-marxist theory, in contrast to classical Marxist theory, 'toxic subjects' are not understood as subjects of history whose agency is material and the effect of the structure of capitalism that exploits them. Instead, they are subjects understood as 'free agents', conscientious objectors to the class war between exploiters and exploited, who act spontaneously in the market as counter-hegemonic ethical agents and who never question the exploitation of labor by capital at the root of capitalism but simply question its ideological supremacy because they feel alienated from it. In short, they are good petty-bourgeois subjects who see themselves as free individuals, as in bourgeois ideology. Capital of course depends on these 'free subjects' to normalize the exchange of labor for wages as a relation that is freely entered into and to mystify the exploitation of labor by capital. For all his denouncing of the 'resistance' politics (Laclau, Butler, Critchley, et al.) which fundamentally accepts capitalism as the silent and unquestioned 'background', Žižek's notion of politics is finally no different. It amounts to resisting the privatization of the 'commons', which in his writings means resisting the 'private' (instrumental) use of reason by the State (citing Kant), so that the 'immediate universal' substance ('general intellect') may display itself unhindered, without representation and regulation, as a screen on which to project more 'authentic' images of surplus-enjoyment. In short, he wants a de-regulated symbolic economy, or, more commonly,

---

110 Marx and Engels, 'German Ideology', p. 49; Slavoj Žižek, 'Learn to Live Without Masters', *Naked Punch*, 3 October 2009, http://www.nakedpunch.com/articles/34.

111 Žižek, 'Ecology', n. pag.

freedom of speech. His insistence on the 'materiality of ideology' as the limit of the possible is done so as to figure movement to the outside in libertarian terms, as simply opting out ('I prefer not to') or 'demanding the impossible' (as in the old May '68 slogan). It is the lack of a materialist theory of value that leads Žižek, like Negri, into spiritualism and voluntarism as a political strategy and to the embrace of bourgeois ideology; as when he claims that Paul of Tarsus is a true Leninist for such moral platitudes as that radical change begins as 'a change in you'.[112] Žižek fetishizes the 'encounter with the Real' as identification with that which is not yet culturally 'schematized' and thereby holds out the hope of an alternative schematization; 'When the normal run of things is traumatically interrupted the field is opened up for discursive ideological competition'.[113] What is ruled out by such an adventurist cultural politics of the spectacle (which led Žižek to support the fascist populism of the Trump campaign in 2016) is the advancement of revolutionary politics based on the class struggle over material resources and meeting people's needs.[114]

Žižek 'surpasses' Negri on the transpatriotic left by saying that it is those who are excluded from the commons of 'general intellect' that are

---

112 Slavoj Žižek, *The Puppet and the Dwarf: The Perverse Core of Christianity* (Cambridge: MIT Press, 2003), p. 9; Slavoj Žižek, 'An Interview with Slavoj Žižek: "On Divine Self-Limitation and Revolutionary Love"', with Joshua Delpech-Ramey, *Journal of Philosophy and Scripture*, 1:2, Spring (2004), pp. 32–38 (p. 36).

113 Žižek, *Tragedy*, p. 17.

114 This is perhaps most obvious in Žižek's justification of the 2008 bank bailouts, which, he argued, was necessary given that the 'real economy' depends on the 'virtual economy' in the sense that everything has first to be financed in order to be produced (*Tragedy*, p. 14): an ideological inversion characteristic of the capitalist system that in fact makes exchange-value a priority over use-value and thereby gives finance capital executive power in determining the social distribution of resources. Leaving aside the fact that the bailout did not stimulate the 'real economy' and unemployment continued to grow at an unprecedented rate, financial capital is not productive capital that is invested in labor and machinery to realize surplus-value but is instead speculative capital that simply shifts money around and re-distributes already produced surplus-value. Žižek's inversion of the 'real' into the 'virtual' economy dissolves labor as the source of value into speculative financial transactions as if capital were the source of value. What is Real is thus the 'bottom line' incontestable Truth of the market ('virtual economy') over meeting people's needs for health care, education, housing, communications, and economic stability ('real economy'). The reality remains, however, that the 'virtual economy' of financial speculation emerges out of the 'real economy' due to the falling rate of profit relative to investment in the production process, which is why the bailout did not stimulate investment and produce jobs as advertised.

revolutionary, not those who participate in it by producing new ideas of sociality.[115] These 'outcasts' are the ones whose consumption does not add value — because they do not affirm the political ideology of ethical capitalism through which products are marketed today — and therefore does not support the 'new' cultural capitalism which unlike the 'old' capitalism is based not on surplus-labor but surplus-pleasure. By withholding their affirmation, they practice a cynical consumption that then marks them symbolically for exclusion (as 'toxic subjects', 'outcasts', 'terrorists', etc.). This is of course a meta-cynical theory which finds spontaneously in the market a disaffected lifestyle that offers a ready-made model of revolution without the need for theory ('I prefer not to') and the hard task of building a revolutionary party. But, as Lenin argues in his critique of spontaneity, 'without revolutionary theory there can be no revolutionary movement'.[116]

Žižek is meta-cynically playing with the concrete surfaces of meaning in culture which on his own terms is a way to 'privatize the commons' and justify an ethical capitalism. The value Žižek adds to the 'general intellect' is the idea that cynical (non-affirmative) consumption spontaneously undermines capitalism, an idea which simply makes its peace with the ongoing exploitation of labor embodied in the commodity. The 'idea of communism' he defends (following Badiou) is a romantic sublime indebted to Heidegger's ethos of 'letting being be' which, like the 'refusal of work' doctrine of the autonomist marxists, is a theology of crisis in which the 'weak' are represented as 'strong in spirit' and in which we see the intellectuals abandon their social duty to educate the laboring masses (the exploited) in their struggle against the exploiter (capital) by becoming cheerleaders for whatever is popular at the time. On this logic 'the poor are actually extraordinarily wealthy' because 'despite the myriad mechanisms of hierarchy and subordination' they are 'creative' and 'express an enormous power of life', or, in Žižek's terms, '"freed" from all substantial ties' they are '"free" [...] to invent some mode of being-together'.[117] Unlike Hardt, Negri, and Starbucks, however, Žižek does not insist that spiritual values necessarily lead to a good society

---

115 Žižek, *Tragedy*, pp. 39–41.
116 V. I. Lenin, 'What Is To Be Done?', p 369.
117 Antonio Negri and Michael Hardt, *Multitude: War and Democracy in the Age of Empire* (London: Penguin Books, 2004), p. 131, 129; Žižek, 'Ecology', n. pag.

because there are no guarantees that it will (now that history has been 'desubstantialized'), and it may just as well strengthen the State. When one considers the role of the state in the 'authoritarian capitalism' he locates in The People's Republic of China, the normalization of which he sees as inevitable, his passionate embrace of 'the Cross of the postrevolutionary present' as an example of how the 'lowest' is the 'highest' (Hegel's 'infinite judgment') is particularly cynical.[118] Žižek's messianic embrace of the oppressed is, in other words, conditional upon their remaining oppressed. Hence all the awkward and oft-repeated Gulag jokes at the expense of his 'enemies' to lighten things up, as if to say, 'I am not really serious, I would not take power and incarcerate and indoctrinate you — like them'. But the jokes have a serious message; they signal the cynical belief in an eternal capitalism and are a mark of class belonging among those who are engrossed in inventing pleasures above and beyond the struggle over material need, which they are allowed to enjoy because as bourgeois apologists they justify consuming the labor of the other.

Žižek finds, in the indirect style of deconstruction in which materiality is reduced to textual mediations, a hidden belief in substantial 'reality' that indicates its silent complicity with the dominant ideology, what he calls 'objective belief'.[119] Objective belief functions by taking the subject out of the picture as if the Real simply exists without the active participation of subjects who normalize it precisely by disavowing the complicity of their attempts to ameliorate things through such mechanisms as activism, charity, and ethical consumption, which support the status quo. Žižek embraces the 'monstrosity of Christ' and 'Bartleby politics' as marginalized figures of non-participation in the dominant ideology who embody the self-sacrificing ideals of egalitarian collectivity by 'doing nothing' but 'thinking' during moments of social crisis. But how effective is this counter-strategy? Žižek reverses Marx's eleventh thesis when he argues that 'the first task today is precisely not to succumb to the temptation to act [...] but to question the hegemonic'.[120] In doing so, he leaves intact the ideological notion that the eleventh thesis is the formula for an ethical calling (i.e., Badiou's 'fidelity to the Event'). By contrast, Marx's argument about philosophers interpreting the world

---

118 *Parallax*, p. 5
119 Slavoj Žižek, *On Belief* (London and New York: Routledge, 2001).
120 'Repeating Lenin', n. pag.

rather than changing it is not an ethical call to spontaneous activism, but a materialist guide for praxis based on the recognition that 'it is not the consciousness of men that determines their existence, but their social existence that determines their consciousness'.[121] In other words, Marx is not posing the question of whether one should choose to think or act, as Žižek imagines, but revealing the complicity of thought in social praxis. Žižek's view is exactly the opposite: it invites one to imagine that theory and practice are separate self-enclosed activities which allow for the possibility of the choice of one of them, and that by choosing 'thinking' and rejecting ideology ('I prefer not to') silently assumes that consciousness determines social existence. In other words, he apparently believes that by 'combating solely the phrases of this world' he is changing it, or as he puts it, 'When the normal run of things is traumatically interrupted the field is opened up for discursive ideological competition'.[122] Žižek's 'dialectical materialism' is really a version of Hegel's objective idealism in which ideas determine the material, which is why he rejects ideology critique as 'a reduction of the higher intellectual content to its lower economic [...] cause' for immanent critique which aims at 'the inherent decentering of the interpreted text' by surfacing 'its 'unthought' [...] disavowed presuppositions and consequences'.[123] Thinking the unthought and disavowed (i.e., encountering the traumatic Real that contradicts ideology in daily life) is represented by Žižek as more important than surfacing the determination of thought by the social totality (class). In short, Žižek substitutes ideological inversion for a materialist critique that uncovers the economic forces that structure the totality as a guide to praxis. His understanding of 'class' as inclusion/ exclusion in the 'social substance of ideology' is itself a dissimulation of class privilege in that it assumes the world is shaped by ideas, the material by the immaterial, as in all bourgeois ideology.

What people think and believe, however, whether the dominant ideology or revolutionary ideas, are always a reflection of the class relations that determine the limits of the possible. If the world appears

---

121 Karl Marx, 'Preface' to *A Contribution to the Critique of Political Economy, Karl Marx/ Frederick Engels: Collected Works*, 50 vols (Moscow: Progress Publishers, 1987), 29, pp. 261–65 (p. 263).
122 Marx and Engels, 'German Ideology', p. 30; Žižek, *Tragedy*, pp. 39–41.
123 *Parallax*, p. ix.

determined by ideology, this is simply a result of the fact that in practice labor is itself 'estranged' at the point of production, and what appears to be an equal and fair exchange of labor for wages is in actuality the exploitative extraction of surplus-labor from the worker by the capitalist, which subordinates labor to capital. The objective appearance of the exchange of labor for wages in the market is itself already ideological and disguises the class inequality between capital and labor without the need of any extra cultural reinforcement (i.e., surplus-pleasure). Moreover, this objective ideology, which is daily reproduced in material practice, can only be penetrated by Marx's labor theory of value, which explains that what the worker sells to the capitalist is not her labor (a commodity like any other) but her labor-power — a 'special commodity whose use value possesses the peculiar property of being a source of value'.[124] Žižek's 'surplus' theory of ideology in which ideology is made into a phantom value, a surplus-pleasure beyond normal pleasure, which he places as the object (a) of all struggles, does what bourgeois ideology has always done which is to disguise the outright theft of labor-power by the capitalist, not in the everyday surfaces of consumption but daily at the point of production, in the 'working day'.[125]

For Žižek, species-being (i.e., Marx's explanation of 'life activity', 'productive life', 'life-engendering life'), which explains labor as the source of value, is a piece of New Age-y mysticism ('cosmic awareness' or 'holistic immersion') that must be dismissed because 'nature doesn't exist', 'there is no Evolution', and 'one should thus learn to accept the utter groundlessness of our existence'.[126] In this he is echoing Badiou who rejects any 'figure which makes man into a species' on the grounds that to do so reduces politics to the mere maintenance of animal life as in the biopolitics of 'state philosophy'.[127] Species-being is thus posited as a 'new opium of the masses' through which late capitalism manages its contradictions by adopting a 'co-operative' ontology (humanist speciesism). On this view, species-being (labor) is a socialist ideology that has been incorporated into the maintenance of capitalism and what is really radical is commitment to the 'idea of communism', not

---

124 Marx, *Capital*, I, p. 177.
125 Marx, *Capital*, I, pp. 239–43.
126 *Tragedy*, p. 94; 'Ecology', n. pag.
127 Alain Badiou, *The Century* (Boston and New York: Polity Press, 2007), p. 174.

as the movement of history, but as a categorical imperative that 'truth is partial' and cannot be grounded in any 'big Other' because now that the 'commons' has been privatized 'substance is subject', as Hegel thought, and we are 'free [...] to invent some mode of being-together'.[128] On Žižek's view, class is thus a 'sublime object' of ideology, with all of its religious aroma, rather than the material basis of what exists. Desire and not need is at the center of the social. Desire, however, not as human but as inhuman. It is not, in other words, desire as it arises out of the social relations through which men and women meet their needs, but desire as a trope to mark the fact that his analytics remains immanent to the dominant ideology of compulsory consumption (the law of enjoyment). Desire is 'inhuman' because Žižek considers it a 'compulsive' force that negates the autonomy of the ego (will, reason, etc.), pace Freud ('death drive'). Yet in this way 'desire' is de-humanized — it is not understood as emerging from the social relations — and becomes in fact an ideology or 'false consciousness': a way to 'imagine [...] false or seeming motive forces' in place of 'the real motive forces' that compel individuals.[129] In short, Žižek's notion of death drive as the inhuman compulsion of desire is simply a mystification of what Marx calls 'the silent compulsion of economic relations'.[130] It is libidinal economy masquerading as political economy in the attempt to imagine a (post)humanist reversal of values in which the human being embodies the 'passion of the animal' (Derrida), which is a trope that mystifies the actual reduction of humans by capital to bare animal existence.

Because capitalism has clearly become destructive in its effects and cannot meet the needs of the masses (the primary producers of wealth), the dominant ideology of bourgeois society has become (post) humanist and inscribes the notions that, (1) the human is not a unique and singular being but a shifting construct made from out of spectral values, affects, desires, etc. that emerges from the 'ontological divide' in Western discourse erected between the 'human' and 'non-human' in culture and (2) culture as a realm of values cannot be considered distinct from nature as 'not culture' and 'value-less' because such distinctions

---

128 'Ecology', n. pag.
129 Frederick Engels, 'Letters on Historical Materialism', *The Marx-Engels Reader*, ed. by Robert C. Tucker (New York: Norton, 1978), pp. 760–68 (p. 766).
130 *Capital*, I, p. 726.

are always 'embodied': value hierarchies mark subjects by inhabiting the 'matter' of bodies and are always 'lived' by (human, non-human, posthuman) individuals.

What the first premise denies is that labor (human species-being) is the unique and singular source of value because it is only due to social labor that humans have the special capacity to know and transform nature as a whole, not only in accordance with human needs but also the needs of nature. This quality of human laboring activity being 'life-engendering life' (Marx) and not merely a life-maintaining activity is what makes humans not simply a species like any other but also one whose form of activity takes historically specific forms ('modes of production'). It also explains why labor in its current form, as the commodity whose consumption in the production process increases value beyond its immediate use, is a transitional and historical form of species-life. Making the human a spectral category whose internal displacements reveal the impossibility of positive and reliable knowledge of the real is to disappear the surplus-value extracted from human labor that comprises all value in commodity culture (even the value of so-called 'natural resources' which cannot be utilized without the application of labor).

The second premise erases the distinction between culture and nature through the category of 'embodiment' — as in Foucault's 'materialism of the incorporeal' in which knowledge is always an effect of how power inscribes bodies. In doing so, this premise further assumes that 'matter' is a 'thing' (body). But while what is material is always bound up with a conception of value, such a conception is itself always valued relative to the development of the forces of production. If today, for instance, it is 'bodies that matter' (Butler, Grosz) rather than 'textuality' (Barthes, Derrida, de Man), it is not simply the result of an ethical turn but the result of textual materialism appearing outdated in the transnational cyber-economy of smartphones, social media, the Internet of things, deep learning, artificial intelligence, and Web 4.0. The international language of the televisual economy, what one cultural critic calls the 'iconomy', is visual literacy (just look at international airport signage or IKEA instructions), and, as any global blockbuster film will show (e.g., *Avatar*), visual literacy must be discursively formulaic and appeal to the immediacy of the senses (embodiment) in order to realize a profit.[131] Embodiment, the matter of the body as the limit-text of thinking materiality in (post)humanist cultural theory, is valued now because it reflects in ideology the new global property forms developed to commodify the environmental crisis by re-tooling industry through what is being called 'sustainable design' on the grounds that with existing technologies it is possible to reduce the human footprint by 90%.[132] On this market logic, 'All of life is actually a design project today' and what matters most is thus the sensual 'interface' between the consumer and the new products.[133] In short, the notion of matter changes not simply because of a cultural change in values but because of changes in the mode of production and the forms of property.[134]

The material is a social relation not a 'thing'. In other words, what is material is the structure of need, which is inscribed in the relation between wage-labor and capital; labor at a certain level of historical development is embodied in private property (capital) to which there corresponds an ideological form of consciousness. In this sense, the material is not simply 'matter' — whether conceived as 'sensuous' 'thingness', or, as in the (post)humanist logic, the embodiment of knowledge, codes, affects, and so forth. Making the limit of the material the matter of bodies is really just a way to make reliable knowledge of these material relations — and their limits — conceptually unattainable by defining the material in terms of its opacity to consciousness (the unfathomable secret core of matter that Kant called the 'thing-in-itself' and Graham Harman the 'withdrawn object') and thereby authorizing lived experience (the phenomenal) as the limit-text of knowing.[135] However, '"lived" experience is not a given [...] but the spontaneous "lived experience" of ideology in its peculiar relationship to the real'.[136] More specifically,

---

131 On 'iconomy' see, Terry Smith, *The Architecture of Aftermath* (Chicago: Chicago University Press, 2006).

132 *The 11th Hour*, dir. by Nadia Conners and Leila Conners Petersen (Warner Bros., 2007).

133 Bruce Mau, *The 11th Hour*.

134 Kimberly DeFazio, 'Designing Class: Ikea and Democracy as Furniture', *The Red Critique*, No. 7, November/December 2002, http://redcritique.org/NovDec02/designingclass.htm.

135 Graham Harman, *Object-Oriented Ontology: A New Theory of Everything* (New Orleans: Pelican, 2018).

136 Louis Althusser, *Lenin and Philosophy* (New York: Monthly Review Press, 1971),

lived experience is the logic of consumption that serves big business by encouraging 'alternative' consumption in the time of overproduction.

Today materialism is being discussed in terms of its effects at the level of consciousness — that is, as 'materialism of the incorporeal' (Foucault) or the 'materiality of ideology' (Žižek) — on the assumption that the material is the 'matter' perceived by the senses, behind which lies the 'immaterial' ideas that determine its form. However, what is being called 'immaterial' and 'emotional labor' and made into the form-giving agency that Hardt and Negri call the 'multitude' and Žižek calls the 'commons' is simply a trope for that moment of production in which the object of labor is the subject herself that has always been a part of the labor process now as ever. This is, by the way, why Hardt and Negri can attribute this reflexive idea to Marx by citing his phrase, '*l'homme produit l'homme*'.[137] This simply means that labor is a dialectical activity. Labor, in other words, is not a 'one-sided' working upon things but an 'all-sided' activity that produces the subject as well as the object. Furthermore, it is a social process of production that is undertaken in accordance with material necessity:

> Production not only supplies a material for the need, but it also supplies a need for the material [...] [it] not only creates an object for the subject, but also a subject for the object [...] Production thus creates the consumer.[138]

Obviously, calling the production of subjectivity 'immaterial' simply maintains an ideological distinction between mental and manual labor, one that presupposes an empiricist understanding of the material as matter. In this matterist view, labor is defined by the type of 'thing' it produces and hence 'immaterial' when the 'thing' produced is subjectivity or affective attachments ('emotional labor' or services). When Hardt and Negri say that they agree with Marx that 'humans produce and humans are produced' but follow Foucault in rejecting Marx's 'humanism' and, moreover, when they reject Marx's dialectical

---

p. 223.

137 Antonio Negri and Michael Hardt, *Commonwealth* (Cambridge: Belknap Press, 2009), p. 136.

138 Karl Marx, *Grundrisse: Foundations of the Critique of Political Economy (Rough Draft)* (London: Penguin Books, 1993) p. 92; 'Economic Manuscripts of 1857–8', *Karl Marx/ Frederick Engels: Collected Works*, 50 vols (Moscow: Progress Publishers, 1986), 28, pp. 17–537 (pp. 29–30).

critique for Kant's transcendental critique, this is their way of denying that labor is more than a 'thing' — it is what Marx calls species-being ('life activity, productive life').[139]

Labor (species-being, life activity, productive life) is the structure of necessity that explains the seemingly disparate and apparently concrete as an effect of the social transformation of nature. Labor is the determinate relation behind any explanation of the world we see and it can only be ignored in the imaginary: What is 'imagined' however is also explained by labor. In short, labor is dialectical — what is usually 'ascribed to the mind', or, 'to the development and activity of the brain', is in actuality a product of the 'idealistic world outlook' which has emerged and is maintained due to advances in labor from simple and straightforward practices to more complex and opaque combinations.[140] Marx's concept of species being is root knowledge for uncovering the 'part played by labor' (Engels) in the so-called 'posthumanist' culture because 'labor is the unique and singular source of value' that is being 'resignified' in 'imaginative' ways to reform capitalism in localities but that yet explains contemporary culture in all its forms as alienated and exploited labor demanding transformation of the totality.

Badiou's 'formalized in-humanism' for instance, takes the 'inhuman' effects of social praxis under the existing capitalist relations of production as the basis upon which to adopt Foucault's anti-humanism against the 'anthropology' of Marx: 'the man of inhuman beginning, who installs his thought in what happens and abides in the discontinuity of this arrival'.[141] What is regarded as human on these terms is always the projection of agency onto the past, a retroactive application of identity into the contingent events, forces, and wills that make up history, following Nietzsche's reversal of causality from an objective determination into an affective one.[142] Yet, what is being marked as 'inhuman' here, the 'event'-fulness of history, is in actuality a testimony to the materiality of labor, and not of discontinuity. The 'lag' between 'what happens' and how it is 'thought' is explained not by 'discontinuity' but by the process of the

---

139 *Commonwealth*, pp. 6, 136.
140 Engels, *Dialectics*, p. 459.
141 Badiou, *The Century*, pp. 174, 178.
142 Friedrich Wilhelm Nietzsche, *The Will to Power*, trans. by Walter Arnold Kaufmann and R. J. Hollingdale (New York: Random House, 1967), pp. 293–300.

material causation of thought as humanity

> inevitably sets itself only such tasks as it is able to solve, since closer
> examination will always show that the problem itself arises only when
> the material conditions for its solution are already present or at least in
> the course of formation.[143]

What is being called 'in-human' is in actuality the product of human
labor at a certain point of historical development in which the 'needs of
nature' (Marx) are currently being ignored because of the immediate
imperative to profit a few from the exploitation of human labor-power.
In other words, thinking humanity as an 'in-human' projection is simply
to re-turn the human to a figure of free thinking (the messianic) and to
disappear the labor relations that always shape thinking. What is taking
place in (post)humanist cultural theory are more stories that perform in
their folds a willful ignorance about labor, the universal species-being
that is alone the agent of history.

Popular (Post)humanism: *Wendy and Lucy*

The 'question of the animal' in the (post)humanities is a sign of a deep
cynicism toward global explanations and a compulsive naïveté, a making
do with less so as to feel at home in the world as part of the 'vulnerable'
'pathos' of the commons — 'the nonpower at the heart of power', 'the
passion of the animal'. It codifies in theory the species-friendly consumer
practices of the upper middle class that justifies capital investments in
environmental solutions for industry as heralding a green capitalism.
Behind it there is rehearsed a series of assumptions that suggest the
world is a harsh, dehumanized place from which springs the need for
human contact but, as no one can be trusted without consensus as to
the social good, one must connect with the animal(s) as a way back
to 'commonality' with nature as well as with human others.[144] With

---

143 Marx, 'Preface', p. 263.
144 'Pettism' is an example of how bourgeois ideology 'affects the nerves', as Lenin
is reported to have said regarding music, and portrays animal life in such a way
that 'makes you want to say kind, silly things, to stroke the heads of the people'
under conditions in which 'you mustn't stroke anyone's head, you'd get your hand
bitten off', so instead you (buy and) pet a companion animal (Maxim Gorky, *Lenin*
[Oxford: Oxford University Press, 1967], pp. 44–45).

one's pet — which, arguably, all animals are today in the sense that their existence depends on human species-being (labor) — one comes to a subtle communion with whatever nature and the world looks new. Its alienated appearance is transformed from a digital wasteland bereft of life into a cooperative organism in a constant flux of becoming. What has been wasted, such is the messianic promise, will be recycled and made anew. Exploitation is past and has been replaced by caring, service, and cooperation. This series of ideological assumptions is found across the cultural spectrum from the discourses of 'high theory' (Derrida) to 'popular culture' (e.g., films such as *Okja, Rise of the Planet of the Apes,* and *Etienne*!). The result is an 'eco-fiction' whose stories 'take[] place in a world where cooperation and mutual aid have replaced the ruthless self-interest of capitalism, and where the decisive binary, and hierarchy, between humans and the nonhuman world has dissolved'.[145]

Take the 'indie' film *Wendy and Lucy*, for instance. The 'meaning' of the film cannot be separated from its 'poetics'.[146] The minimal dialogue, the low-fi sound (the humming on the soundtrack) and image production values, the trendy androgyny of its main character, her DIY lifestyle as she crosses the northwest looking for work, hipster superstar Will Oldham's cameo appearance as a crusty anarcho-punk (Icky),... are all strategically designed to signal to the audience the 'alternative' credentials of the film in relation to mainstream commercial film-making — it is not an 'industry' film but a postindustrial film with a 'heart'. The story as well is also concerned to show how alternative forms of culture (lifestyles) emerge from out of impoverished conditions, not only across cultural lines (as with Wendy's friendship with the security guard), but across species as well.

Wendy and her dog Lucy are driving from Indiana, where she had been living with her sister Deb and Deb's boyfriend Dan, to Alaska because she's heard 'they need people' to work. The story picks up with Wendy and Lucy as they are crossing Oregon and mainly centers around their separation when Wendy is arrested for shoplifting dog food. The fact that Wendy has money to purchase the dog food is an ironic emphasis of the point made by the store employee who aggressively detains her and

---

145 Lynne Feeley, 'How Eco-Fiction Became Realer Than Realism', *The Nation*, 18 August 2022, https://www.thenation.com/article/culture/elvia-wilk-death-landscape
146 *Wendy and Lucy*, dir. by Kelly Reichardt (Warner Bros., 2008).

insists she be made an 'example' of by having her arrested: 'if a person can't afford dog food, they shouldn't have a dog'. On this market logic Wendy's attachment to Lucy must submit to a coldly dispassionate cost-benefit analysis so as to avoid transgressing the law of profit. Wendy's evident anxiety throughout the film to be reunited with Lucy is partially to be explained no doubt by her own guilty complicity with this common sense morality: If she valued Lucy so much why did she not just pay for the dog food? The film deploys a series of binary oppositions that underline the same point that, on the one hand, the logic of the market and authentic feelings are antithetical but, on the other, the authenticity of feelings can only be expressed through market transactions. Icky, the crust punk who tells the story of how he recklessly destroyed an expensive piece of machinery working in the Alaskan fisheries, represents the inhuman other who has rejected the market while other (equally unattractive) characters in the film are meant to represent those whom the market has failed (e.g., the cyborgian figure in the wheelchair who is briefly glimpsed while the Walgreens guard muses in voiceover about how people 'waste' their days since the mill closed).

Not only is Wendy alienated from Deb and Dan — who, despite the fact that she has not asked for anything and only wants some expression of kindness and sympathy, can only repeat that they cannot help her when in emotional desperation she calls them long distance — but Wendy is also shown to be alienated from her peers, both the cluelessly lawless crust punks she encounters on her travels, as well as the zealously lawful store employee who busts her. The social alienation that is depicted — where the logic of the market disrupts a shared sense of common humanity and empathy with others — has the effect of an inversion that humanizes Lucy the dog while making pet ownership seem like a radically transgressive act. Wendy's ownership of Lucy, the logic of the film suggests, represents 'caring' for the other at a time when it has become socially impossible for people to care for each other. Significantly, the only people Wendy is able to talk to in non-instrumental terms are those who show feelings for Lucy — the crust punk girl and the Walgreens security guard — suggesting that more important than socio-political divisions, such as between Law (protection of property) and Anarchy (disregard for property), is the moral divide between those who feel a connection with animals and those who do not. It is perhaps to the same point that work in a fishery in Alaska seems to be the only industrial work left in America. In other words, 'they need people' in Alaska... to kill animals. In short, the problem with capitalism is alienation from others and the natural world, a problem that the film suggests can be fixed by bonding with (by personally owning) animals at a time when capital is indifferent to the social costs it inflicts and people are made redundant and no longer able to care for themselves. The fact that Wendy leaves Lucy with a foster home also suggests, however, that caring for the other and private ownership are synonymous and can yet provide a way to compensate for the brutal violation of shared feelings, which is due after all to Wendy's personal lack of resources. Even though Wendy and Lucy both cry when separating, viewers are reassured it is what is best for Lucy and that Wendy is acting like a mature and responsible person by sacrificing her only friendship to the logic of the market. The viewer is then ideologically reconciled to submitting to exploitation by being reassured that in future Wendy will assume greater personal responsibly so as to avoid such heart-wrenching separations from her loved ones.

Wendy and Lucy is a '(post)humanist' text for two reasons: firstly, it represents society as 'dehumanized' and the dehumanization as the outcome of industrial production, and, secondly, it proposes as a solution to the spiritual deadening of humanity forming emotional attachments with non-human creatures (pettism). Pettism, in actuality, is the ideology of a green capitalism in which the biggest profits stand to be made from retro-fitting industry to be more environmentally sustainable. Furthermore, it reinforces the division of labor, between 'hi-' and 'lo-tech' workers for example, through the inculcation of more up-to-date cultural values — treating animals humanely as life companions becomes a sign of ethical distinction. What is elided by such a lifestyle politics of course is how class inequality underlies values.

Wendy and Lucy is also a 'post-apocalyptic' tale in which human beings have lost all semblance of 'humanity' and can no longer form connections with others and is in this way similar to the other post-apocalyptic tales currently on the market.[147] In *The Road* the ultimate

---

147 *Wendy and Lucy* is part of a new genre of writings/films like *The Road* (Cormac McCarthy/dir. John Hillcoat), *Never Let Me Go* (Kazuo Ishiguro/dir. Mark Romanek), *Time of the Wolf* (dir. Michael Haneke), and *Children of Men* (P.D. James/dir. Alfonso Cuarón), that deal with traditional science fiction themes (post-

expression of inhumanity is to be treated like so much meat by those who have reverted to cannibalism.[148] Significantly, in the film based on the book the last scene in which The Boy is united with The Family on the beach assures the audience of the humanity of these characters by a series of close-ups that move from the parents to the children and, lastly, their dog. What this image of the dog represents of course is that these post-human characters are truly human (they 'carry the fire' in the parlance of The Boy) because not only do they not treat people like animals (for food) but they treat animals humanely as equals despite being reduced to absolute poverty themselves. Similarly, Wendy's abandonment of Lucy to a foster home that can provide for her because

---

apocalyptic world, cloning, etc.) but in the codes of realism, which have as their primary effectivity the defamiliarization of the present and the immediate in terms of an overdetermining but 'absent cause'. Like much of contemporary art, the new hybrid-genre of 'sci-lit' throws the audience *in medias res* and compels the viewer to make sense of a fundamentally ambiguous narrative in a ruined world full of the ghosts of narratives past all of which have lost their substantive power to compel belief. It is as if the sci-lit text puts the viewer in the place of a child who, while pressured to make sense of their surroundings, is not in a position to have the means to do so and is thus compelled to invent their own framework of understanding. Such an intelligibility can also be seen to be at work in the 'twee' aesthetic that has become so iconic in contemporary pop art (Mark Ryden, Marcel Dzama, Anthony Goicolea,...) — traceable to the 'outsider' art of Henry Darger — that depicts adult themes in a naïve way, as if all previous frames of reference of those 'supposed to know' have ossified and yet because events still demand to be made sense of by being given a narrative form it must at the least be modest and humble. The insistence on narrative having a 'meaning' in the wake of the impossibility of substantive consensus in a media saturated environment is what makes contemporary art, at least at a formal level, post-postmodern, or, 'metamodern' (Van den Akker). It is not massive 'incredulity' toward 'grand narratives' that makes it impossible for them to secure belief, as Lyotard defined the postmodern condition. Rather, it is the opacity that ideology must of necessity assume as it is forced to manage the unmet needs of the many which is compelling them to believe that another world is needed that militates against any substantive, decided, consensual, meaning. And yet, the left's insistence on the invention of an 'imagined' narrative of community in the context of its estranged forms in its willful ignorance of labor reflects the ideology of contemporary cyber-capitalism as a regime of 'immateriality' in which knowledge rather than labor is considered productive of value. The 'immaterial' ideology is itself, however, a reflection of the increasing ratio of 'constant' (dead objectified labor) to 'variable' (living productive labor) capital in the production process (Marx, *Capital*, I, pp. 307–316). In other words, it is the estrangement and appropriation of labor that explains the alienation of human agency in social consciousness which imagines agency as being 'immaterial' and change as merely a change in ideology. In the immaterial ideology the material is an effect of knowledge (*techne*) — it is 'spirit' that moves the world, not labor.

148 *The Road*, dir. by John Hilcoat (Dimension Films, 2009).

she is too poor to do so herself is also meant to signal her humanity in a de-humanized world (the 'strength of the weak', 'the passion of the animal'). Unlike *The Road*, however, in which the source of the (post) humanist 'apocalypse' is not directly represented or explained, *Wendy and Lucy* does, in a way, give a 'crisis diagnosis' of the dehumanization of the social in its depiction of human beings as having lost control of technology.[149]

The point of Icky's story about wrecking an expensive piece of machinery at work while on drugs is that he was unable to stop the machine; the drawn out details and seemingly pointless repetition of Wendy's arrest are clearly shown to be due to the police not having mastered their technology; the de-industrialization of the town is shown to be producing 'monsters' (e.g., the 'creepy' man in the woods, the 'mutant' wheelchair figure); and the playful way the film doubles the lo-fi music of the soundtrack (which seems to represent Wendy humming a tune in her head) in the digitized muzak of the grocery store in which she is arrested suggests that the most intimate and authentic part of a person is really a scripted reflex of mass consumer culture. In these ways the film argues that the dehumanization of the social is due to the negation of the human by technology, and it represents humans as having lost control of the machine which now controls them.

However, in its crisis diagnosis that technological dehumanization is at the root of the social crisis *Wendy and Lucy* also makes a material explanation impossible and proposes instead a spiritual solution to the crisis ('pettism') that goes along with an 'alternative' consumerist ideology.[150] But, as Engels makes clear in *Dialectics of Nature* the destructiveness of capitalism on the environment is not primarily a problem with technology or a technological problem. Primarily it is a problem with the use of technology by capital for the short-term realization of profit in the context of market competition which does not concern itself with the long-term results to the biosphere (the 'social

---

149 Seyla Benhabib, *Critique, Norm and Utopia. A Study in the Foundations of Critical Theory* (New York: Columbia University Press, 1986), p. 109.

150 *The Road* also alibis capitalism in the way it, through its many product placement ads, represents the products of consumer culture (Coca-Cola, Cheetos, Vitaminwater, etc.) as 'life saving' and fails to show the connection of commodity production with the causes of the apocalyptic event in the wake of which the story takes place (Sarah Berman, 'The Year in Film', *Adbusters*, January/February [2010], p. 87).

metabolism' between labor and nature in Marx's terms). By ascribing the social crisis to a loss of humanity caused by technology, *Wendy and Lucy* blocks awareness of the social basis (the class arrangements) that explains why technology under capitalism is not an emancipatory but an enslaving and destructive force in the long run and, thus, why the working class alone is the agent of history in a material position and with a material interest to abolish capitalism.

Wendy and Lucy reifies the effects of the exploitation of labor by capital by representing technology as the material base instead and in this way produces a spiritual interpretation of technology (it is 'dehumanizing') for which there is a false spiritual solution (pettism) that stimulates further consumption (ownership of 'companion' animals). The film's occulting of labor, however, is the primary means for immunizing capitalism from social critique and thus blocks changing it. The (post) humanist critique of dehumanization is itself dehumanizing because it understands the social as 'immaterial' at root rather than material — it is the disappearance of jobs and the end of meaningful work in the post-industrial economy rather than the commodification of labor in the production process that explains the existing social relations. In actuality, the 'loss of control' over technology that is supposed to explain the (post)humanist world as a world of immaterial production is really a local effect of exploited and estranged labor in general. Even the idea that emotionally connecting with pets represents the basis of an alternative immaterial economy forgets that dogs are embodied labor.[151] It is because labor has been socialized and the world is 'more and more splitting up into two great hostile camps, into two great classes directly facing each other: Bourgeoisie and Proletariat', while control of the production process is privatized in the hands of a few to make profit from unpaid surplus-labor, that industry is enslaving humanity on a self-destructive course.[152] The solution begins with producing awareness

---

151 'The dog and the horse, by association with man, have developed such a good ear for articulate speech that they easily learn to understand any language within their range of concept. Moreover they have acquired the capacity for feelings such as affection for man, gratitude, etc., which were previously foreign to them. Anyone who has had much to do with such animals will hardly be able to escape the conviction that in many cases they now feel their inability to speak as a defect, although, unfortunately, it is one that can no longer be remedied because their vocal organs are too specialized in a definite direction' (Engels, *Dialectics*, p. 173).

152 Marx and Engels, 'Manifesto', p. 485.

of the social power of labor to transform the existing in accordance with human needs, which includes understanding the needs of the biosphere as a whole, and engaging in a critique of the 'immaterial' (post)humanist ideology that negates labor in the cultural imaginary. Pettism, rather than representing a realistic solution for immaterial times, actually reflects a bourgeois relation with animals that negates in the imaginary the labor relations that shape the human interaction with non-human nature. It is the distortion of needs by private property that reduces animals to food for the 'all too human' masses on the one side and 'companions' for the privileged '(post)humanists' on the other who because their needs have already been met through the labor of the other are free to 'feel' the 'passion of the animal'.

The 'question of the animal' is a desire-al and affective form of knowing (embodied knowledge) that immunizes global capitalism from critique by representing its alternative as a new transspecies commons (pettism). But, the 'passion of the animal' always leads to one conclusion: 'The real difference between cat-lovers and dog-lovers has nothing to do with income, education or habits of work. It is [...] a matter of morals'.[153] It presents class inequality as affective cultural differences and considers it is thereby respecting animal difference, but it actually thus insures the continued production/use of animals for profit which will only end when production is carried out in accordance with meeting human needs, which includes the needs of nature as Engels says, rather than the exchange of labor for wages.

The most radical means of thinking the existence that we share with animals is not some 'abyssal' knowing beyond knowing ('passion') ourselves as sublimely (post)humanist animal-others, but knowing the root of our species-being which 'both in man and in animals, consists physically in the fact that man (like the animal) lives on organic nature'.[154] As Marx argues, a 'species-character is contained in the character of its life activity' — which for humans is not only a matter of how physical existence demands labor in the transformation of inorganic nature 'in the form of food, heating, clothes, a dwelling, etc'., but also, as well, requires

---

153 Felipe Fernández-Armesto, 'A dog's dinner of an idea', *Times Higher Education*, 18 February 2010, https://www.timeshighereducation.com/comment/columnists/a-dogs-dinner-of-an-idea/410391.article.

154 Marx, 'Economic and Philosophical Manuscripts', p. 275.

'spiritual nourishment' that must be realized through the processing of 'plants, animals, stones, air, light, etc'. by 'human consciousness' into 'objects of natural science [and] objects of art'.[155] It is only in knowing species-being in these terms that we become aware of our relation with the natural world and thus are in a position to live in a non-destructive relation to the environment as well as other species. As Engels explains, the more 'men not only feel but also know their oneness with nature [...]' the more impossible will become the senseless and unnatural idea of a contrast between mind and matter, man and nature, soul and body' and humanity will be in 'a position to realize, and hence to control, also the more remote natural consequences of at least our day-to-day production activities'.[156]

As Marx explained, it is the activity of labor that distinguishes the human species from all others and 'makes all nature his *inorganic* body' because the 'life activity' of the human species is 'universal' ('life-engendering life')

> The life of the species, both in man and in animals, consists physically in the fact that man (like the animal) lives on organic nature; and the more universal man (or the animal) is, the more universal is the sphere of inorganic nature on which he lives.[157]

According to the (post)humanist left, to produce a critique-al knowledge of production as species-being can only be 'speciesism' that perpetuates violence on the other ('carnophallogocentrism'). Yet, without such a concept what cannot be explained is the material basis that underlies and connects humanity with the rest of nature nor, therefore, 'how to produce in accordance with the standard of every species' given that humans produce universally by transforming all of nature into their 'inorganic body' and a means to reproduce their own life.[158] When Marx and Engels write that men are distinguished from animals, not by some abstract principle ('consciousness, religion, anything else you like'), but by their mode of production, it is because the human species is maintained in its existence by and through the production of animal life,

---

155   Ibid., p. 275.
156   Engels, *Dialectics*, p. 461.
157   Marx, 'Economic and Philosophical Manuscripts', pp. 275–76.
158   Ibid., pp. 275, 277.

including our own material life ruled by objective necessity. The human species is the underlying mode of production that in capitalism produces the appearance of a division between man and animal as well as undoes this opposition by producing new forms of life and organization beyond mere animal life that can only be fully emancipated under communist production (conscious life activity).

3.
Globality

Sudamerica

The social uprisings in Argentina, Venezuela and Peru in 2001 against the neoliberal state — behind which stands the multinational coalition of financiers, businessmen and trade union bureaucracies that are forcibly imposing free market policies around the world under the banner of democracy — have shown the world that the only alternative to the extreme social inequality and instability of global capitalism is revolutionary class struggle.

The ongoing battle for workers' democracy in Latin America directly contradicts the mantra of neoliberalism that has been endlessly repeated across the political spectrum since the destruction of the Soviet bloc from the left as much as the right, in the academy as much as in the mainstream media; the claim that the world has entered a 'post-class' moment in which class struggle is over because of the new 'knowledge' economy and all that is left is to make do with capitalism.

In this familiar story, cultural changes like the Internet and the new eco-friendly lifestyle politics are supposed to have empowered the people against totalitarian power by decentering and deregulating their lives so that they can find freedom in the local and everyday, the sphere of consumption, rather than, as in the past, through class struggle over the socio-economic conditions of production.

What recent changes in global media and culture did in fact produce was a 'cyber' imaginary that hides from view the class conflict in global capitalism so as to normalize the exploitation of wage-labor by capital that is at the center of capitalism. In other words, it hides from view the fact that capitalism, as Marx and Engels explained over 150 years ago in *Manifesto of the Communist Party*, is at its root based on social inequality — the inequality between the 'bourgeoisie [...], the class of modern Capitalists, owners of the means of social production and employers of wage-labor', and the 'proletariat, the class of modern wage-laborers who, having no means of production of their own, are reduced to selling

    https://doi.org/10.11647/OBP.0324.03

their labor-power in order to live'.[1]

It is this unequal division of labor between owners and workers that makes capitalism exploitative. It does so, as Marx scientifically proved in *Capital*, by forcing workers to engage in 'surplus-labor' (labor beyond that required to meet their needs) so as to realize a profit for the bosses who are themselves free from the need to work for a living because they privately own the social means of production, which requires that the majority to have to work for them.[2]

Capitalism is considered democratic because it is the freedom to make voluntary exchanges in the market without regard to differences of 'rank' or 'merit' but on pure voluntary self-interest. As Marx explained, however, the dream of capitalism that free exchanges between legally equal persons ensures the social good of all, has always to be related to the actuality of capitalism as a social system of production. In actuality, capitalism is not simply a political system that ensures civil rights in a free market, but an economic system of production in which individuals basically stand in a relation of class inequality. They are either members of the working class, and thus free to work or starve because they own nothing but their ability to labor for others, or, capitalists who, owning the means of production as their private property, are free to force the majority to engage in surplus-labor over and above that which is required for meeting the worker's own needs so as to realize a profit for themselves.

Private property in production is what makes the social inequality of class in capitalism: class is the division between those who employ and consume labor (the exploiters) and those who do not but instead produce the social wealth (the exploited). The corporate media uses all its power to hide this class-consciousness from the people to make capitalism appear as the limit of freedom and democracy.

But freedom and democracy under capitalism is only for the few who can afford it because they live off the labor of the many. As capitalism develops on a global scale, the many cannot even meet their basic

---

1   Karl Marx and Frederick Engels, 'The Manifesto of the Communist Party', *Karl Marx/Frederick Engels: Collected Works*, 50 vols (Moscow: Progress Publishers, 1976), 6, pp. 477–519 (p. 482).

2   Karl Marx, 'The Working Day', Chapt. 10, *Capital. A Critique of Political Economy*, vol. I, *Karl Marx/Frederick Engels: Collected Works*, 50 vols (Moscow: Progress Publishers, 1983), 35, pp. 239–43.

needs and are compelled to enter into struggle against the bosses — as Argentina in 2001, after only ten years of neoliberal deregulation, and similarly as Venezuela, whose workers were forced to arm themselves simply to defend the minor redistributions of wealth of the Chavez government, have once again shown.

The reemergent revolutionary struggles in Latin America since 2001 once again prove the basic truth of Marxism: that the global development of capitalism leads to its own downfall by producing a revolutionary working class with nothing left to lose and a world to win by taking power from the owners and running the economy for the social good. This truth, however, is covered up by a thick layer of mystification by the corporate media through a variety of relays and mediations. This mystification serves to naturalize the social inequality at the basis of capitalism and maintain the status quo.

Take the lie that the global North, led by the US, has a moral destiny to bring freedom and democracy to the global South which is crushed by poverty and corruption. The poverty and corruption of course are the result of freedom and democracy — the freedom of the capitalist to exploit human labor power for profit, which is what in actuality 'chases the bourgeoisie over the whole surface of the globe' and 'compels all nations, on pain of extinction, to adopt the bourgeois mode of production; [...] to introduce what it calls civilization into their midst', as *The Manifesto of the Communist Party* says.[3]

The 'moral' story about protecting human rights is told to conceal the material truth about democracy: that it is the freedom to exploit others for profit. The story is needed to alibi the regime of wage-labor and capital as a fact of nature. In other words, it portrays the normal daily exploitation of labor under capitalism as the free expression of human nature in comparison with which its everyday brutality is made to appear 'extreme' and 'irrational' rather than a socially necessary consequence of private property.

The representation of capitalism as natural is of course not natural at all but historical: it is needed now to manufacture consensus that capitalism cannot be changed when it has already become obvious that the material conditions exist to abolish class inequality.

---

3   Marx and Engles, 'Manifesto', p. 488.

As in the case of Venezuela, it has become obvious that what stands in the way of a regime directed toward meeting people's needs, which is what Chavez represents, is not a lack of respect for human rights by immoral and corrupt people in the global South, but the need of big business for a bigger share of the world market. It was the US oil giants represented by the Bush regime, supported by the trade union bureaucracy in the US, that aided the counter-revolutionary coup in Venezuela in 2002 (e.g., by fomenting the oil workers' strike as the core of a 'civil society' movement that tried to abolish the popular social reforms of the Chavez government). It is for profit, not democracy, that the US supported the reactionary coup to overthrow Chavez (not just in words but with financial aid, military weapons and advisors as the British Guardian reported); it is for profit and not for democracy that the US supports Israel, colonized Afghanistan so as to take Iraq, and foments 'color revolutions' around the world, from Yugoslavia to Ukraine.

It is obvious that US foreign policy is guided by profit and not democracy, which is why global public opinion is everywhere outside the US opposed to US 'unilateralism' and 'empire' building. This growing 'obviousness' of democracy as hegemony of the rich threatens the ideology of capitalism by exposing democracy as the bourgeois freedom to exploit the labor and resources of the world. It is also behind the formation of a transnational populist left, however, that goes along with the system of wage labor and capital by marking the obvious hoax of democracy but nevertheless channeling the opposition into a reformist politics to maintain capitalism. By merely contesting its obviously barbaric effects rather than engage in a radical critique of capitalism for a social revolution against wage-slavery that is the cause of the effects, the left supports the ideology of democracy as class rule. It thus goes along with the reactionary backlash ascendant in the wake of the Cold War to make social contradictions into problems of 'governance' of essentially 'unruly' subjects so that the powerless are made to bear responsibility for the contradictions of class society.

What has emerged in the wake of the revolutionary explosions in Latin America in the new millennium is the growing awareness that it is becoming impossible to simply deny the basic truth of Marxism on democracy as class dictatorship. As a result, newer mystifications of capitalism and why it changes have also emerged to stabilize the status quo.

The dominant mode of naturalizing capitalism is to represent the new popular struggles as spontaneous movements of the oppressed, by denying that they are a product of history as class struggle over the conditions of production. Rather than produce awareness of the class interests behind the emerging struggles the populist left portrays them as the outcome of spontaneous rebellions of the people against power. It is thus on the left most of all that one finds the alibi of capitalism as democracy that proposes capitalism may be reformed while the exploitation at its root remains intact. A reformed capitalism is simply a code for a more efficient regime of exploitation and imperialist brutality — it is appeasement of the violent democracy of the owners.

Middling Class

Argentina and Venezuela provide a useful occasion for proving the truth of class against the global post-class ideology because although the class conflict has dramatically exploded into public view in these countries and has since become impossible to deny as an ongoing daily reality, what one finds in the dominant media instead are 'stories' of the 'middling' of class designed to re-describe class as a cultural matter and block the need for class-conscious solutions to the unfolding crisis.

For example, the dominant media focuses on different styles of protest in Argentina like those of the *'cacerolazo'* (pots and pans demonstrations) and *'piqueteros'* (the unemployed and poor workers who protest without pots and pans 'because they have none') instead of explaining why these differences are effects of basically unequal economic relations and not merely cultural. These local differences need to be overcome to realize a new society without class inequality; fixing these differences as cultural matters is a way to divide workers and keep them powerless against their exploiters who are demanding more and more austerity from them.

One effect of the 'middling' of class is to make class appear to be such a complex thing that solutions to the social crisis based on the material conflict of interest in society between capital and labor appear simplistic and unreliable as well as manipulative and suspect. Solutions to the crisis based on class struggle can then easily be dismissed as signs of an out-of-touch nostalgia with a 'dead' ideological past as well as signs of a hopeless 'anti-American' future. One finds routinely in *The New York Times* and *The Washington Post*, for example, such conclusions which reveal more about the basically fascist ideology of a US elite who can only read the political expressions of the needs of the world's people as a pious or perverse death-wish out of touch with 'reality' than they do about the actual impact of global capitalism on working people's lives and what it causes them to do. As the social eruptions in Argentina and Venezuela against neoliberalism were the first to show, however, there is nothing more dead than the 'post' ideology that class is dead. In order to contain this awareness newer class ideologies have become necessary that do not simply deny class struggle but attempt to re-describe it as cultural conflict so as to provide a middle ground for reformist solutions, which maintain the social inequality at the root of capitalism.

Before turning to consider 'left' and even 'marxist' stories of class as culture, which are against class as the structure of necessity, I will briefly read the popular media representations. In this way I will bring out the underlying ideological sameness of the bourgeois order that is usually cloaked behind local idiomatic differences. The 'middling' of class occurs in the mainstream media in a variety of ways that all have in common the erasure of class-consciousness, or, what I am calling the awareness of the material conflict between exploiters and exploited that makes capitalism capitalism, explains why social crisis and poverty exist in the midst of wealth, and why class struggle is necessary.

The different ways of 'middling' class in the media correspond to the local differences in global capitalism which has to manufacture consensus for the status quo from differences that have arisen on the basis of the capitalist division of labor and its need for different kinds of workers; between 'high' and 'low-tech' workers, for example. These local differences, which are the effect of production, are represented as cultural differences of consciousness and behavior in the dominant media so as to contain awareness of the conflicts which arise because of the class division between the 'haves' and 'have nots' that periodically threatens to reveal the basic inequality in capitalism between the interests of capital (a merely formal democracy where economics is directed toward the accumulation of wealth for a few) and those of labor (a social democracy where economics is directed toward meeting the needs of the many).

The most popular way to disguise class with a 'middling' logic is the method of the mainstream news media that appears most non-ideological of all because it uses the codes of 'description' and 'neutrality' to hide the class antagonism at the core of capitalism. For example, in the news coverage of events in Argentina since the 'Argentinazo' uprising December 2001, the difference between the uprisings that took place over food and medicine and the *cacerolazo* demonstrations that formed because of the freezing of bank accounts to meet the balance of payments to the global speculators in Argentine financial markets, is regularly represented as the 'poor rioting' on the one hand, and therefore a matter for the police forces to handle, and 'middle-class rage' on the other, which is given a political significance as legitimate anti-government protest. What this cultural coding of class in the dominant media does is hide the true class basis that is the cause of the conflicts and that goes beyond Argentina.

The profit imperative that guides capitalist competition, as well as the government policies that protect this imperative by continuing to subsidize the wealth of a few and devaluing the small savings of the many, are the reasons there are poor and unemployed workers to begin with. Underlying both the 'poor rioting' and 'middle-class rage' is a single socio-economic system directed toward profit maximization in which the needs of workers are secondary.

It is the profit imperative — which compels the capitalists to invest more and more in technology in order to lower their labor costs so as to more effectively compete with other capitalists — that produces the unemployment. In a system directed toward meeting people's needs, there would be no need for unemployment. The profit motive is also what lies behind the economic bankruptcy of the government, which has seized the small bank deposits of the many in order to pay off the global financial investors. Moreover, these investors are themselves forced to speculate in the international financial markets to realize a profit on their capital because it no longer pays enough of a return to invest in the real economy of plant and equipment that is already highly efficient and overproductive.

In other words, behind the superficial appearance of differences between the problems of the 'poor' and 'middle-class' is the same class logic of capitalism that periodically produces the crisis of overproduction (mass poverty in the midst of social wealth) that acutely affects places in the global South such as Argentina. Such crises occur not because of purely financial mechanisms that exceed any possible political regulation in the new global economy, as the neoliberals claim, but because labor productivity is now so high, due to advanced technological efficiency, that it is no longer profitable to invest capital in production while, at the same time, labor is so cheap, because of the unemployment and cutbacks in social services, that workers cannot afford to buy the commodities they themselves produce.

It is for this reason that even before the financial crash that sparked the 2001 Argentinazo, estimates of Argentine unemployment and underemployment were around 20% and, more importantly, official government estimates of poverty had themselves placed half the population in this category even while Argentina was being celebrated as a model 'democracy'.

The representation of class struggle in Argentina as merely a matter of different problems facing the 'poor' and 'middle' classes and their mode of responding to them does the work of middling class and deflecting class-consciousness. It does so by representing the most needy sections of the working class as an 'irrational' threat to peaceful society whose politics must be met by force and another section of the working class, who have been able to save some money for times of hardship, appear like 'reasonable' people because they do not challenge property relations directly but focus only on the official policies that maintain the status quo. The workers who engage in struggle against the neoliberal policies of the official political institutions are represented as rational 'middle-class' people while those workers whose politics challenge the principle of social inequality directly are the 'rioting poor' who are politically ignorant and only understand force.

In reality, what is being called a 'rational' and 'reasonable' protest because it pressures the government to reform itself is not ultimately in the interests of those called 'middle-class' much less the 'poor'. It is only in the interests of the wealthy who need people to believe that capitalism can be politically reformed and need not be socially transformed, because it is exploitative at root. The actions of those workers who directly challenge existing property relations by expropriating the food and medicine they need to live from those who want to profit from them are called 'rioting poor' and coded as 'irrational' for the same reason: to deflect attention from the primary division in society between exploiters and exploited and the anarchic logic of the economic system based on this division.

Class is made a matter of culture by the dominant media (class as levels of political 'reasonableness') in order to divide and block the unity of the workers. This is done by instilling in them the values of compromise and negotiation with their exploiters so that they consent to their collective exploitation to make profit for a few rather than take power into their own hands and run the economy to meet the needs of the many.

The Left Carnaval

The most effective middling of class — 'effective' in terms of hiding that what is at stake in the wake of the insurgencies of the global South is the truth of class and the future of capitalism — is that which is found on the left because of its overt political questioning of the more oppressive features of capitalism.

Read, for example, the articles on the Argentinazo that appeared in the French monthly *Le Monde Diplomatique*. One such article, for instance, objected to cultural 'commentators' who 'have attempted to play down events, claiming that this was little more than a show of bad temper on the part of the middle classes'.[4] The reason for the objection to the mainstream media's focus on the 'middle classes' here is not to uncover the class conflict at the root of capitalism but to once again pluralize class into cultural differences and blur the basic class division in society. 'The revolt' is thus represented as 'the result of an alliance between the poorest people and the urban middle classes' and not an expression of basic working class collectivity that stands to challenge capitalism at its root.

What is assumed on the left is that class is a political 'alliance' and not an economic structure. The class antagonism between exploiters and

---

4   Diana Quattrocchi-Woisson, 'Ten Days that Shook the World Bank', *Le Monde diplomatique*, February 2002, https://mondediplo.com/2002/02/08tendays.

exploited, it is assumed, has ended and cultural struggles for merely reforming capitalism in its localities have taken its place. Thus, in *Le Monde Diplomatique* the proof of class is not that the 'have nots' must engage in struggle with the 'haves' just to be able to eat (and thereby prove the bankruptcy of capitalism as a regime of democratic equality), rather, it is 'what people were singing on 19 December'. This focus on 'the national anthem and a song that openly poked fun at the state of emergency the authorities had declared' gives capitalism a popular democratic cover.[5] Because the singing included 'the national anthem' and 'poked fun' at the same time, it symbolizes, in this populist left cultural imaginary, an 'alliance' of the ever loyal 'middle class' and desperately cynical 'poor'. This takes the focus off of class as the massive unmet need of the majority and instead celebrates events in Argentina as a carnival of the people. This same writer, predictably, sees in the neighborhood assemblies ('interbarrials') that have emerged across the country — whose program of demands include direct challenges to capitalist rule such as repudiation of the foreign debt, the nationalization of the banks, the renationalization of all privatized utilities, popular election of Supreme Court judges, the taking into state control of pension funds, etc. — not the radical expression of working class needs but a place for more cultural consumption. The interbarrials are reduced to 'talking shops where all manner of daring, innovative ideas circulate', like a Starbucks, only with more interesting and 'colorful' people than usual.[6] The celebration of culture is supposed to signal to the reader the death of class struggle, as can be seen when it is contrasted to the 'rioting' (popular expropriations of food and medicine) as a reflection of 'the despair of people with no political direction or agenda'. Rioting, in other words, is not a class issue of food and the need to change the system but a moral issue of a lack of 'hope'. For *Le Monde Diplomatique*, in short, class is culture (singing, knowledge, feelings) not economic struggle (politics of need).

The shift from economics to culture in considering class is made in order to claim that what was occurring in Argentina was not class struggle that puts workers and owners in conflict over the purpose of democracy — that is, whether 'democracy' is a matter of merely 'equal

---

5   Ibid., n. pag.
6   Ibid., n. pag.

rights' or of economic equality. Instead, it represented the class struggle in Argentina as a matter of 'casting off the most deeply ingrained habits of [...] political culture' on the part of 'a new generation, born under a democracy' in which the goal is for people to have more of 'a say in economic and political decisions [...] with a sort of street veto'.[7] In short, 'democracy' is equated with more bourgeois freedom of speech (which is the freedom to exploit) not economic freedom from need (the power to abolish exploitation).

In another article in the same magazine the same post-class cultural logic is evident with slight variation: 'In the past, demonstrators had always obeyed strike rules, marching in columns behind their union or party banners. This time, they came out simply as citizens' (Gabetta, n. pag.).[8] What this story of generational changes in cultures of protest does is obscure the basic class division in society so as to place class elsewhere as a strictly cultural matter of the 'people' spontaneously acting out against 'power': 'the people of the country rose in protest [...] saying that it had had enough of universal corruption'.[9] A 'bad' political culture that 'corrupts' the people's spontaneity is the problem, not an exploitative economic system that makes them into wage slaves who must take to the streets in order to meet their basic needs. This is of course the same logic used by the IMF/World Bank, which explains away the contradictions of global capitalism in the global South as local problems of corrupt governance in need of more 'democratic' reforms (by force of arms if necessary), in order to manage the current systemic crisis and normalize exploitation.

The Empire-al Imaginary

Central to the ideological work of giving global capitalism the face of freedom by covering up its basic class inequality and what it makes necessary is Hardt and Negri's manifesto of the new capitalism: *Empire*.[10] It is for this reason that the book was an academic 'best seller'

---

7   Ibid., n. pag.

8   Carlos Gabetta, 'Argentina: IMF Show State Revolts', *Le Monde diplomatique*, January 2002, https://mondediplo.com/2002/01/12argentina.

9   Ibid., n. pag.

10   Antonio Negri and Michael Hardt, *Empire* (Cambridge: Harvard University Press, 2000).

and was celebrated on its publication in 2000 as 'the next big thing' by such official organs of finance capital as *The New York Times* and *Charlie Rose*. Of course, calling the book 'the next big thing' simply repeats, in a popular idiom for those who cannot afford to read the book, its central premise — 'imperialism is over'. It has been displaced by 'empire': a 'new form of sovereignty', where cyber-labor 'creates the very world it inhabits'.[11]

Empire has been so celebrated by the dominant because it is directed against explaining the world as an effect of the economic laws of motion of capital accumulation, which is necessary for transforming it, by announcing a new world free from the past that changes because of changes in rhetoric (freedom of speech). It is rhetoric, for example, to say that 'imperialism is over' because we now live in a world system where 'the economic, the political, and the cultural increasingly overlap and invest one another'.[12] The purpose of this is to make the source of profit in unpaid surplus-labor explained by Marx's labor theory of value a 'fiction'.[13] Without Marx's labor theory, there can of course be no basic contestation of capitalism but only moral condemnation of its more oppressive effects that keeps exploitation intact by immunizing it from critique. *Empire*, in short, does the ideological work of capital by giving it a human face: by displacing Marx's ruthless critique of 'surplus-labor' with the sentimentality of 'affective labor'.

'Affective labor' is one of the phrases for the 'autonomy' of labor, that is, labor as desire rather than praxis in the new order — 'a horizon of activities, resistances, wills, and desires that refuse the hegemonic order, propose lines of flight and forge alternative constitutive itineraries'.[14] 'Affective labor' occults the extraction of surplus-labor by capital that is the source of profit behind the resurgent drive of imperialism in the 21st century and the emergent revolution against it. Moreover, it mystifies the fact that history is at root exploited labor and not a matter of people's desire. Instead, it is the surplus-labor that workers produce for free that is stolen by capitalists, which makes history. Without surplus-labor there can be no capitalism. History will only change when the expropriators

---

11   Ibid., pp. xii, xiv-xv.
12   Ibid., p. iii.
13   Ibid., p. 402.
14   Ibid., p. 48.

of labor are expropriated by the laborers and 'society inscribes on its banner: From each according to his abilities, to each according to his needs!'.[15] To displace surplus-labor, the political economy of need, with affective labor, the symbolic economy of desire, is thus a theory of social change against the workers in complicity with the ruling class.

Behind the premise that 'imperialism' has been displaced by 'empire' is the reduction of history to 'politics' (desire) and the erasure of the primacy of the economic (need). 'Empire' is Hardt and Negri's imaginary of a new time in capitalism free of history that cannot be explained by class struggle. 'Empire' is, they claim, beyond 'the fiction of any measure of the working day'.[16] In actuality 'empire' represents the moment in their analytic when material interests do not enter into consideration on the alibi that labor is no longer economically exploited at the site of production (because, they say, it is 'post-fordist', 'flexible', and 'co-operative'). Whether it is called 'multitude'; 'creative', 'affective' or 'immaterial labor'; or a 'new proletariat', the idealism is the same: a trope of spontaneity and freedom from necessity is meant to signal a basic change in capitalism that makes it impossible to materially explain what makes capitalism and why it changes. Their concept of labor is thus really a trope of cultural resistance, a change of values. As another 'autonomist' marxist puts it:

> labor is for capital always a problematic 'other' that must constantly be controlled and subdued, and that, as persistently, circumvents or challenges this command. Rather than being organized by capital, workers struggle against it. It is this struggle that constitutes the working class.[17]

Labor and class, in this volunteerist logic, are the same as Foucault's idea of 'power' ('power is everywhere' and 'where there is power there is resistance') — only in *Empire*, Foucault's idealist theory of power is masked in a new 'popular' form now that it is impossible to any longer ignore class analysis of the daily.[18] But, it is 'class' as more cultural

---

15   Karl Marx, 'Critique of the Gotha Programme', *Karl Marx/Frederick Engels: Collected Works*, 50 vols (Moscow: Progress Publishers, 1984), 24, pp. 75–99 (p. 87).

16   *Empire*, p. 402.

17   Nick Dyer-Witherford, *Cyber-Marx: Cycles and Circuits of Struggle in High-Technology Capitalism* (Urbana-Champaign: Illinois University Press, 1999), p. 65.

18   Michel Foucault, *The History of Sexuality: An Introduction* (New York: Vintage, 1990),

politics to go along to get along with capitalist inequality, not class as the cause of who is/is not hungry, sick, housed and why.

'Class as struggle', in Hardt and Negri's schema, takes the focus of off production (the social relation in which labor stands in a necessary relation to capital and, therefore, determines what is to be done in the struggle) and puts it on consumption (where labor is 'free' to reproduce itself only to be exploited because of the privatization of the means of production that is the source of profit). This displacement once again makes Marx and Engels' point that 'the ideas of the ruling class are in every epoch the ruling ideas'.[19] By using the 'spontaneity' of 'class as struggle' and 'autonomous labor' as a way to occult how private property makes labor 'free', Hardt and Negri trivialize worker's agency as a matter of desire. Changing 'tastes' and 'values', as in conservative discourses, are represented as just as important as changing property relations. What such a sentimental view of labor and class as cultural change does is blur the line between production (base) and consumption (superstructure) so the class priority of revolutionary praxis is undermined by an opportunist pragmatics that appeases imperialism — the multinational coalition that is raping the global South for the benefit of a few in the global North.

'Affective labor' is in reality a sentimental romanticization of the effects of the falling rate of profit. It portrays the more flexible, and therefore more exploited (i.e., more reliant on capital), workforce of global capitalism as free to (re)make the social. In actuality society changes not owing to the management of workers desire but owing to changes required by the need to make profit in the context of private competition. Worker's 'desire' is itself a matter of need and not free of material history (the law of value). Workers struggle against capital because their needs are not being met. This resistance is what constitutes trade unionism, which is the normal rule of capitalism. Workers' resistance is what Lenin called 'economism': 'arguments that a kopek added to a ruble was worth more than any socialism'.[20] Its social effects can be seen in the multinational

---

pp. 93, 95.

19 Karl Marx and Frederick Engels, 'The German Ideology', *Karl Marx/Frederick Engels: Collected Works*, 50 vols (Moscow: Progress Publishers, 1976), 5, p. 59.

20 V. I. Lenin, 'What Is To Be Done?: Burning Questions of Our Movement', *V. I. Lenin Collected Works*, 45 vols (Moscow: Progress Publishers, 1977), 5, pp. 347–529 (p. 381).

trade-union solidarity against the 'Bolivarian revolution' in Venezuela in 2001. The American Center for International Labor Solidarity, the international arm of the American Federation of Labor and Congress of Industrial Organizations, materially supported the Confederation of Venezuelan Workers whose leaders conspired with the coup plotters. This shows that there is nothing 'autonomous' about workers' struggles. They either support capitalism or socialism. To represent workers' struggles as 'free' to make the world is to conflate them with the agency of capitalism itself that is in power everywhere, including the workers' agencies. This conflation is part of the routine functioning of capitalism needed to manage its contradictions and keep the workers exploited.

Workers will only really be free to change the world when they take power over their own production(s) so no one's needs are unmet because the economy is planned to provide for them. For them to succeed in this there must be advanced for(u)ms of class-consciousness where they can learn to become vanguard fighters for socialism. As Lenin explains:

> Since there can be no talk of an independent ideology formulated by the working masses themselves in the process of their movement, the only choice is — either bourgeois or socialist ideology [...] This does not mean, of course, that the workers have no part in creating such an ideology. They take part, however, not as workers, but as socialist theoreticians, [...] they take part only when they are able, and to the extent that they are able, more or less, to acquire the knowledge of their age and develop that knowledge. But in order that working men may succeed in this more often, every effort must be made to raise the level of the consciousness of the workers in general; it is necessary that the workers do not confine themselves to the artificially restricted limits of 'literature for workers' but that they learn to an increasing degree to master general literature. It would be even truer to say 'are not confined', instead of 'do not confine themselves', because the workers themselves wish to read and do read all that is written for the intelligentsia, and only a few (bad) intellectuals believe that it is enough 'for workers' to be told a few things about factory conditions and to have repeated to them over and over again what has long been known.[21]

In order for workers to succeed in this historical task of acquiring class-consciousness it is necessary to critique the spontaneity of economism, which displaces global class struggle for the good of all with local

---

21   Ibid., p. 384.

struggle for a privileged few. Class-consciousness is the other of the false consciousness of workers' resistance to (and maintenance of) capitalism that is now masquerading as a new 'radical' and 'marxist' theory not only in the writings of the 'autonomist' marxists but the populist left as a whole (as represented by such journals as *Social Text, Monthly Review* and *Rethinking Marxism*).

The North Atlantic left has abandoned a materialist analysis of the world needed to change it, and nothing so much reveals its bankruptcy than the mainstream success of *Empire*. Behind its claim that 'imperialism is over' is a fundamental idealism that says ideas (tropes of desire) shape the world rather than the other way around, which supports the most barbaric imperialism the world has ever seen to date. *Empire* serves imperialism by reiterating the dominant post-al ideology of the end of history in the mode of a tropic performance of resistance where labor is represented as free desire to make the world outside of history.

Not only is the post-al dogma of the end of class struggle found in its assumed premises, but also in its explicit statements. *Empire* reiterates, for example, that the US is 'different' from the rest of the world, not because of what Fukuyama et al. celebrated as its liberal pluralism (which today obviously stands exposed as a cover for world domination) but, using a more philosophical and high-tech idiom, because of its unique 'composition of social forces' which ensures that 'power' is 'effectively distributed in networks' of 'affective labor' that cannot be explained by the working of the law of value central to capitalism.[22]

In place of the logic of profit *Empire* systematically deploys the (a)logic of desire coded as 'immaterial' and 'affective labor'. On this (a)logic what is it that compels the US to back counter-revolution in Venezuela, exploit Argentina through its debt agencies, expropriate the labor and resources in Afghanistan, support Israeli imperialism, engage in nuclear brinkmanship against Russia and China through proxy war in Ukraine and militarist provocations in Taiwan,...? According to Hardt and Negri, it is not the drive to profit from the 'free' labor of the world but 'desire': the old modern national desire to 'police the purity of its own identity and to exclude all that was other' unaware of the new times of 'cooperative' social relations represented for them by the US.[23]

---

22   *Empire*, pp. xiii-xiv.
23   *Empire*, p. xii.

Empire is a religious and therefore reactionary text. Its basic idea is that the world is an expression of an ahistorical essence (e.g., 'labor is a form giving fire'): the 'constitutive power' of affective labor, which is the code for representing the informal high-tech sector in the North as a 'co-operative' social arrangement that makes socialism unnecessary. This agency is ahistorical because it is posited as existing independently of the series of material conflicts over the social relations of property. As in Foucault, 'materiality' is made a matter of desire, 'affective labor' is an 'excess' of history that 'resists' explanation, while its historicity is idealist, only ever considered genealogically, i.e., as a discursive construction. In other words, Hardt and Negri's 'labor' is what Foucault called an 'event': 'the appropriation of a vocabulary turned against those who once used it'.[24] Like all events, it is secondary and superficial. The most important effect of such an ahistorical view of labor is its class opposition to the only consistently materialist theory of labor: Marx's labor theory of value. Marx's theory explains the agency of labor not as spontaneous resistance to causal explanation in the world without borders, which is in actuality a throwback to the 'mechanical' (ahistorical) materialism of the eighteenth century, but as an effect of 'the ensemble of the social relations': i.e., the ongoing class conflicts over the conditions of production.[25]

Against the totally discredited postmodern micro-politics of the past, *Empire* represents a desire-full social totality that tails the popular movements by recognizing the need for systemic change. But because it maintains that the social totality exceeds theory and cannot be reliably explained, it authorizes the immaterial 'stories' of change over materialist theory of change. Change of rhetoric to provide therapy of 'hope' in capitalism is put before red criti(que)al theory for explaining the world so as to change it. Such 'hope' is needed to contain the newer contradictions of the system in which anti-globalization is becoming global anti-capitalism. *Empire* re-news the bourgeois ideology of agency as 'free' by giving it a new life as autonomous labor (which is simply a

---

24 Michel Foucault, 'Nietzsche, Genealogy, History', *Language, Counter-Memory, Practice*, ed. by Donald F. Bouchard, trans. by Donald F. Bouchard and Sherry Simon (Ithaca: Cornell University Press, 1977), pp. 139–64 (p. 154).

25 Karl Marx, 'Theses on Feurebach', *Karl Marx/Frederick Engels: Collected Works*, 50 vols (Moscow: Progress Publishers, 1975), 5, pp. 3–8 (p. 4).

metaphorical embellishment for a trade union-y populism) so as to do what bourgeois ideology has always done: cover up the class antagonism central to capitalism. But, as Lenin said

> there can be no talk of an independent ideology [...] the only choice is —
> either bourgeois or socialist ideology. There is no middle course [...] in
> a society torn by class antagonisms there can never be a non-class or an
> above-class ideology.[26]

In actuality, it is of course the imperialist system of profit that explains why intellectuals in the North can afford to believe the world changes with merely cultural changes while brutal exploitation and unmet need is the daily reality for most people in the world. This reality will only end with the social expropriation of property by the exploited not by affective co-operation with the exploiters. Venezuela most of all proves the impossibility of such cross-class co-operation because there the revolution (in the form of the neighborhood Bolivarian circles) was forced to arm itself in preparation for the next 'bay of pigs' being prepared in the US.

Imperialism certainly is not merely political (sovereignty) as *Empire* claims, but represents, as Lenin theorized, 'the highest stage of capitalism'. It is Lenin's integrated theory of the social, which explains socio-political changes as an effect of class forces, that *Empire* is directed against by announcing a new 'sovereignty' based on cyber ('affective') labor.

Imperialism, however, is the only materialist analysis of global capitalism that explains the contemporary world situation by grasping the rule of necessity (the law of value, or, i.e., the production for profit central to capitalism) underlying the surface events rather than merely (re)describing these events so as to more effectively explain away the social laws that produce them and alibi the ruling class. To fragment such an integrated understanding of the world under the sentimentality of affective labor is, as Lenin explains, 'to sink to the role of a sophist' by substituting for 'the question of the *substance* of the struggle and agreements between capitalist associations' the 'question of the form of these struggles and agreements (today peaceful, tomorrow war-like, the next day war-like again'.[27] In actuality,

---

26 'What Is To Be Done?', p. 384.
27 V. I. Lenin, 'Imperialism, The Highest Stage of Capitalism. A Popular Outline', *V. I.*

the question as to whether these changes are 'purely' economic or non-economic (e.g., military) is a secondary one, which does not in the least affect the fundamental view on the latest epoch of capitalism [...]. [T]he forms of the struggle may and do constantly change [...] but the *substance* of the struggle, its class content, positively *cannot* change while classes exist.[28]

It is only by grasping the essence of history in class that imperialism is explained and thus available to be changed. Why? Because imperialism is that moment in the circuit of capital accumulation when the capitalist must pursue profit and enter into competition with others on a global scale because of the falling rate of profit in their national markets that testifies to the moribund state of the system and its 'ripeness' for socialism. It explains why at its highest stage capitalist

[c]ompetition becomes transformed into monopoly. The result is immense progress in the socialization of production. In particular, the process of technical invention and improvement becomes socialized [...] Production becomes social, but appropriation remains private. The social means of production remain the private property of a few. The general framework of formally recognized free competition remains, but the yoke of a few monopolists on the rest of the population becomes a hundred times heavier, more burdensome and intolerable [...] Domination, and violence that is associated with it, such are the relationships that are most typical of the 'latest phase of capitalist development'; that is what must inevitably result, and has resulted, from the formation of all-powerful economic monopolies.[29]

Lenin's theory of imperialism is explanatory and therefore transformative: it exposes the contradictions of the system and opens space for change by providing a framework for the emergent struggles that takes them beyond the class limits of ideology that accommodates and naturalizes capitalist inequality and points toward what is to be done for social justice for all.

What is needed now is not more of the 'hope'-full stories of 'co-operation' and getting along repeated by *Empire*, but Lenin's red criti(que)al theory as force for change — theory that is radical because

---

Lenin Collected Works, 45 vols (Moscow: Progress Publishers, 1974), 22, pp. 185–304 (p. 253).

28   Ibid., p. 253.
29   Ibid., pp. 205, 207.

it grasps the root of the system in exploited labor and brings it to bear upon the false consciousness of class. This root is radical because it explains the laws of the system that govern its movements, explains why imperialism today is a symptom of decaying capitalism — i.e., capitalism that has lost its viability because it does not meet the needs of the people and is practically ripe for socialist transformation — and why for a new society free of exploitation workers must learn to become what Lenin calls 'socialist theorists' (*teoretikov sotsializma*).[30] This is especially necessary now that workers' struggles have taken up revolutionary tasks against imperialism, while the populist left celebrates these struggles as the rule of spontaneity that fetishizes democracy over revolution and blinds the people: 'The most dangerous people of all in this respect are those who do not wish to understand that the fight against imperialism is a sham and humbug unless it is inseparably bound up with the fight against opportunism'.[31]

---

30   'What Is To Be Done?', p. 384.
31   'Imperialism', p. 302.

CULTURE

4.
Affect

The Pedagogy of Affect

Every year the Modern Language Association of America (MLA), which gives (or denies) legitimacy to ideas and practices in the teaching of the humanities in the United States (which is then followed in most other institutions abroad), publishes a book titled *Profession*. *Profession 2008* is no exception: it is a collection of essays that, in the name of debating various modes of teaching, produces what is in effect a coerced consensus — a consensus that, for example, inhibits critique and contestations of ideas (Rita Felski, Gerald Graff, Peter Brooks), limits experimental modes of knowledge ('Stopping Cultural Studies'), and offers empty talk about humanities and human rights without ever offering a critique that would make it clear that 'human rights' are essentially rights to own and trade in the 'free' market.[1]

Instead of offering a survey of *Profession 2008*, I will focus on the structure which shapes the different discourses and that explains what is behind the consensus — what I will call the pedagogy of affect. The pedagogy of affect represents itself as an open space attuned to difference, positioned as a retreat from which to pragmatically assess what does and does not work in the university so as to manage the contradictions that have arisen therein from the conflict between capital and labor. It represents itself above all, therefore, as a place where these conflicts can be considered 'reasonably', with all its associations of nonpartisan neutrality, and relegates to an 'ideological' past the university as site of commitment to theory for social transformation. *Profession 2008* is telling in the way its contributors all replace sharp conceptualization of the issues with an affective rhetoric that turns the university away from critique for social change into a therapeutic retreat in which to display their class privilege. In affective pedagogy the opposition of concepts to feelings I am invoking here is thought to be an oppressive holdover from the past

---

1   *Profession 2008*, Modern Language Association of America, 1 December.

   https://doi.org/10.11647/OBP.0324.04

that is inherently unstable and prone to slippage, so I need to explain why feelings are really anticonceptual concepts designed to rewrite theory as therapy and reconcile student-citizens to going along with the status quo.

To clarify, by 'explain' I do not propose to 'define' the affective, as any such definition would simply repeat the common sense that subjective experience is self-evidently meaningful by separating it from the social relations which are the cause of our experience. What is considered meaningful is always made sense of by taking sides in the daily struggles that form over the appropriation of material resources. What I do propose to do in the remainder of this text, however, is to provide a conceptual framework for understanding the intellectual conflicts over the affective so as to explain how affect is used to structure the dominant representation of pedagogy in *Profession 2008* and turn what should be an education in conceptual awareness of social relations into ideological training for what is good for big business.

The Materialist Unconscious

Currently, the humanities are undergoing what is called an 'affective turn' away from the discourse of theory and what are considered its uncomfortable and alienating languages, and back to the familiar languages of the experiential and emotional as the basis of commonality above and beyond social inequality (class).[2] The dominant understanding of affect now is an immanent one that traces itself through the writings of Spinoza, Kant, Nietzsche, Bergson, and Deleuze. In this genealogy, the body is made into an opacity that disrupts the dialectic of labor and subverts conceptual abstraction, and it has therefore come under critique as 'matterist' rather than 'materialist'.[3]

In the affective pedagogy dominant today, all concepts are made into modalities of the body, as the arch-conservative Nietzsche taught, and the body is turned into a zone of excess that spontaneously resists all conceptualization. Concepts, in this frame, are elitist constructs imposed

---

2   *The Affective Turn: Theorizing the Social*, ed. by Patricia Ticineto Clough and Jean Halley (Durham: Duke University Press, 2007).

3   Teresa L. Ebert, *Ludic Feminism and After: Postmodernism, Desire, and Labor in Late Capitalism* (Ann Arbor: University of Michigan Press, 1996).

from above that aim to produce 'docile bodies'.[4] Although they cannot finally be done away with they can be made into moments of play, which, as Stanley Fish says, is the apolitical zone of getting things done, as a true academic professional must.[5]

Body matterism is opposed by a materialist understanding of the body, the senses, and the affective that is activated in the writings of Marx, Engels, Lenin, Trotsky, and Kollontai, to name a few, where the body is understood as a site of ideology and theorized in class terms. For Marx, for example, 'the forming of the five senses is a labour of the entire history of the world down to the present'.[6] On these terms, 'the senses have [...] become directly in their practice theoreticians' as they 'relate themselves to the thing for the sake of the thing, but the thing itself is an objective human relation'.[7] In other words, for Marx, the affective, although experienced spontaneously, cannot be understood on its own terms as it is always made in the labor relations that shape both the object and the subject of knowing. In materialist theory the critique of the affective produces the class-consciousness that 'enjoyment and labor, production and consumption, devolve on different individuals'.[8]

In the pedagogy of affect, there are no antagonistic concepts that implicate our thoughts and feelings in the structure of social inequality, but merely more or less affective bodies more or less opportunistically placed for their voices to be heard. What the pedagogy of affect represents is a model of the good society as an empty plurality in which all are entitled to participate, unless they exclude themselves by advancing the struggles for fundamental change. Theory for social change is marked as 'totalitarian' and 'terroristic', and thus made into the other of the compassionate and caring society where differences are accepted and nothing need change. In the pedagogy of affect, it is the intensity of feelings more than providing critique of the system

---

4   Michel Foucault, *Discipline and Punish: The Birth of the Prison*, trans. by Alan Sheridan (New York: Vintage, 1995).

5   Stanley Fish, *Save the World On Your Own Time* (Oxford: Oxford University Press, 2012).

6   Karl Marx, 'Economic and Philosophical Manuscripts of 1844', *Karl Marx/Frederick Engels: Collected Works*, 50 vols (Moscow: Progress Publishers, 1975), 3, pp. 229–346 (p. 302).

7   Ibid., p. 94.

8   Karl Marx and Frederick Engels, 'The German Ideology', *Karl Marx/Frederick Engels: Collected Works*, 50 vols (Moscow: Progress Publishers, 1976), 5, p. 59.

of wage labor and capital that is central to the social. In the affective pedagogy, critique is made to exemplify an uncomfortable and ugly militancy that is relegated to the bad old days of the university that stood for knowing what is to be done to change society (abolish classes).

To make my discussion about the pedagogy of affect more concrete, I will surface its effects in what is a canonical text of the new humanities: *The Political Unconscious* by Frederic Jameson. Jameson's text, of which an issue of the journal *PMLA* has recently been devoted to discussing, provides such an occasion because, while it defends a materialist theory of affect as ideology that normalizes inequality, it proposes using the affective as an ethical response to inequality.[9] The effect of such a move is to underwrite the common sense of consumer culture that makes the affective a therapeutic zone for the subject in which to feel at home within exploitation rather than activate the conceptual against the hegemonic culture industry and its pedagogy of affect.

Central to *The Political Unconscious* is Marx's concept of 'commodity fetishism', which Jameson understands primarily through Lukács' theory of 'reification', the material process of production whereby social relations are depersonalized and seen as relations between things due to the dominance of exchange value (production for profit). Following Marx, Jameson argues that any conception of the autonomy of culture from the economic is 'a symptom and a reinforcement of the reification and privatization of contemporary life' due to the 'universal commodification of labor power'.[10] On these terms, Jameson's materialist theory is in a position to implicate the affective as the commodification of the senses necessitated by private property, in a manner similar to the way he reads Conrad's 'impressionistic' style, for example, which attempts 'to rewrite in terms of [...] sense perception [...] a reality you prefer not to conceptualize'.[11] Jameson's use of commodity fetishism as a theory of affect would seem to show that, far from being a site of resistance to capital, affections, sensations, and feelings are an extension of exploitative relations: the site of ideology. This is significant because he

---

9   *PMLA/Publications of the Modern Language Association of America*, 137.3, May (2022).

10   Fredric Jameson, *The Political Unconscious: Narrative as a Socially Symbolic Act* (Ithaca: Cornell University Press, 1981), p. 20.

11   Ibid., p. 215.

thus establishes the need to read culture and cultural experience (senses, feelings, passion) not in its own terms but in relation to its outside — namely, the class relations that both necessitate such experiences and provide 'ready-made' interpretations that justify social inequality. He shows, in short, that the senses, affects, experience, passion, and so on are not explainable on their own terms (since they are produced under certain circumstances), but require explanation (concepts).

Jameson, however, both in his early and later work, seems to simultaneously undermine this very conclusion in ultimately arguing against the ability to conceptualize economic relations and in suggesting that culture (contrary to what he has already critiqued) should be seen as not only 'semi-autonomous' from class relations but as an (immediate) site of libidinal 'resistance' to class inequality. For instance, he ultimately rejects a materialist theory of ideology which argues that 'superstructural phenomena, are mere reflexes, epiphenomenal projections of infrastructural realities', on the grounds that 'history [...] is inaccessible to us except in textual form, and that our approach to it and to the Real itself necessarily passes through its prior textualization'.[12] There is, in other words, finally no outside to ideology, according to Jameson, and the concept of ideology becomes synonymous with discourse in his writings. By getting rid of the outside, Jameson duplicates the dominant ideology, which reifies the cultural from the class relations in which it is produced. On the discursivist terms Jameson invokes, it is impossible to give a critique of ideology as a false-consciousness of the economic and produce an awareness of the necessity for social change, which is what Marx's labor theory of value does. Because Jameson abandons the critique of ideology, he speculates that, beyond the historical specification of ideology as global commodification that acts as a 'containment' of the awareness of the exploitation of labor in capitalism, culture also provides the individual with a therapeutic 'compensation' for a thoroughly commodified social life in the form of the 'libidinal transformation' of the senses:

> The increasing abstraction of visual art thus proves not only to express
> the abstraction of daily life and to presuppose fragmentation and

---

12   Ibid., pp. 35, 42.

reification; it also constitutes a Utopian compensation for everything lost in the process of the development of capitalism.[13]

In short, as 'compensation' for the 'loss' (theft) of the surplus labor time of the worker by the capitalist at the point of production, the worker receives emotional plenitude in the consumption of art during the time after work.

The increasing abstraction Jameson locates in visual art, which he maintains may act as an affective compensation for exploitation, is itself of course a modality of labor determined by the labor process as the 'secrets which are only disclosed to the eye of the physicist and chemist' — and, subsequently, the artist — is the product of 'industry and commerce' as 'even this 'pure' natural science is provided with an aim, as with its material, only through trade and industry, through the sensuous activity of men'.[14] What this means is that if the development of the senses has reached the point where we perceive a world made up of things as if purely in terms of their natural properties like color and form, as in modern art, this is as much as to say that the senses have become commodified and are therefore only enjoyable at a price. Because the means to enjoyment must first be purchased in order to be consumed, it follows that 'enjoyment and labor, production and consumption, devolve on different individuals' and cannot act as compensation for exploitation.[15] The enjoyment of art, for instance, requires wages not only over and above the means of subsistence to purchase access to art, but also to purchase the education to enjoy it. To hold out a libidinal compensation in consumption and the pleasure of the senses is to conveniently forget that access to consumption and its pleasures is a class matter determined by one's place in production — a 'forgetting', moreover, which is precisely ideological in that it acts to block access to consumption on the part of the exploited (the workers) by normalizing the class privilege of the exploiters (the owners). They, of course, have no need to be compensated as they do not lose anything in the production of commodities, but only gain the surplus labor of others.

13　Ibid., pp. 236–37.
14　Marx and Engels, 'German Ideology', p. 40.
15　Ibid., p. 51.

The Hunt for the Red

Under the dominance of the 'affective turn' in the humanities, *Profession 2008* turns being a professor from being an engaged intellectual committed to the struggle to end social inequality to being someone who just happens to have a job that allows them to profess feelings of what is right and advocate for the good, but that does not mandate them to conceptually establish a basis for achieving it in practice as doing so would assert a mastery of knowledge that violates the sovereignty of differences and marginalizes other voices. It is the dominance of affective pedagogy that explains the rhetorical differences of the contributors to *Profession 2008* and makes it a model of the university for capital at a time of growing social inequality.

What the affective pedagogy does above all is to commodify the effects of class society as cultural differences the better to do away with those practices that have become a structural liability to the accumulation of profit. Take Peter Brooks' essay, 'The Humanities as an Export Commodity'.[16] On the surface it appears to be an argument for the value of the new humanities as a model of democracy and an engaged citizenry, for whom 'reading is a cognitive exercise with real world consequences', that is interested in contesting how the US has entered the ranks of 'rogue nations' by its institutionalized practices of torture in places such as Abu Ghraib, Iraq, which he takes to be 'wholly incompatible with the morality of American democracy'.[17] Actually, however, Brooks' essay is a defense of the pedagogy of affect that has displaced theory with feelings on the grounds that theory went too far and violated the self-evident norms of common sense enshrined in the 'humanistic tradition' and the lessons of 'poetry' which are, pace Shelly, 'the unacknowledged legislators of humankind'.[18] Brooks 'has the feeling that the humanities' big day is over', he says, because 'the body rejected the transplant'.[19] Behind these tropes of affect, with their assumption of a healthy organicism, is the cultural common sense which says that theory is 'ideological' and therefore 'dangerous' because

---

16   *Profession 2008*, pp. 33–39.
17   Ibid., p. 35.
18   Ibid., pp. 35, 38.
19   Ibid., p. 34.

its commitment to 'the instrumental use of language' is 'violent' and 'subversive' of an 'ethical reading' of culture.[20] An 'ethical reading', for Brooks, is one that does not hold out the 'facile' and 'mindless' politics of 'salvation' through 'critique', but the more 'responsible' one that gives to its practitioners 'a clear sense of what their work can and cannot do'.[21] In the pedagogy of affect, one is either in the camp of the 'modest' and 'wise', and possess an innate but unacknowledged sense of right and the good, or you are making a fool of yourself and not to be suffered gladly. How else to read Brooks' earnest desire that, without a trace of irony, wants to 'promote and enforce responsible reading' and 'cleanse' the university of 'ideological flotsam', and the way his rhetoric plays with the discourse of 'border crossing' and 'frontiers' as it seeks to put a halt to 'unmarked vans' with all its violence toward the other?[22] My point in marking such rhetoric is not simply to show how Brooks' 'responsible reading' is itself unethical and antidemocratic ('ideological') on its own terms, because of its instrumental use of poetics, for instance, to diagnose critique-al theory as a pathological contagion on the body politic that needs to be purged, but to explain why the affective is necessary to the university in a time of global capital.

To reproduce the conditions for accumulation, capital must violently displace any limit that stands to protect and promote the material needs of the working class as these come into conflict with the requirements and practices that will increase the production of surplus value from unpaid surplus-labor.[23] For this reason, capital is inherently unstable and crisis prone. On the one hand, it must commodify the needs of the workers by giving them a living wage with which to buy back what they have themselves produced, and, on the other, it must cheapen the value of labor power by increasing the amount of time that workers engage in unpaid surplus labor over the necessary labor time normally required to meet their needs on any given workday. Among other things, this accumulation process 'chases the bourgeoisie over the whole surface of the globe', as *The Manifesto of the Communist Party* says, seeking out pools

---

20   Ibid., pp. 34–35, 38.
21   Ibid., pp. 34–35.
22   Ibid., pp. 33–34, 38.
23   Karl Marx, 'The Working Day', Chapt. 10, *Capital. A Critique of Political Economy*, vol. I, *Karl Marx/Frederick Engels: Collected Works*, 50 vols (Moscow: Progress Publishers, 1983), 35, pp. 239–43.

of cheap labor to exploit with the most advanced productive techniques available.[24] The workers who resist the forces of commodification and fight back to defend their standards of living are marked as criminals and handed over to the state, which has its own ways of exploiting their labor. It is in this global class context that the institutionalization of torture by the United States needs to be seen, not as a moral abomination that tarnishes an otherwise fundamentally just and good society that enshrines human rights and stands for the best of humanity, as in Brooks' rhetoric.

Brooks' attack on theory as a dangerous ideology that violates common sense has also to be read in terms of its class politics. It represents a revanchist attack on the very reforms the university has undertaken since the institutionalization of theory in the 80s to manage the contradictions of global capital which has more and more come to rely on a high-tech and multicultural workforce.

Brooks' 'responsible reading', whose 'proponents speak with a clear sense of what their work can and cannot do', wants to put a halt to 'the free play of the signifier' by demarcating an 'arbitrary and phony [...] parody of a deconstructive reading' from a properly 'ethical' one that calls things 'by their name'.[25] Despite appearances to the contrary, there is in fact no contradiction in Brooks' speaking in the name of an authentic (nonparodic) deconstruction that violently asserts a clear sense of responsibility against which all else is marginalized as arbitrary and ridiculous because the rigors of theory are no longer needed in the corporate university. Theory is to be done away with because the value of deconstruction to create a flexible and compliant workforce that is sensitive to ambiguity and attached to difference with a mystical sense of belonging has already proved itself to capital and now the only theory left is the one that 'goes too far' by uncovering the relation of theory to class — red critique-al theory. The purging of theory in the pedagogy of affect is more than thinly disguised red-baiting; it represents the task of the boss to make production more efficient by cutting the costs that eat into profits. Brooks' defense of deconstruction as 'responsible

---

24 Karl Marx and Frederick Engels, 'The Manifesto of the Communist Party', *Karl Marx/Frederick Engels: Collected Works*, 50 vols (Moscow: Progress Publishers, 1976), 6, pp. 477–519 (p. 487).

25 Brooks, pp. 35, 37–39.

reading' is self-parodic and laughable. It is his defense of poetics as anti-instrumental reason that returns us to common sense that sells in the corporate university where one can only profess the interests of the ruling class, and because these interests are everywhere in crisis and obviously bankrupt and intellectually indefensible, one can only profess them emotionally in sentimental tones that are designed to reassure the public as to the humanity of the wages system.

Profession 2008, by showcasing the affective pedagogy and demonizing the need for sharp conceptual analysis, is saying that the university is not a place of critique for social change, but a feel-good retreat from class conflicts that violently asserts class supremacy.

It is in the space of affect and war on the concept that Graff, for instance, can claim that 'rhetorical proficiency is critical' to those without access to 'money and power' even though 'there's no disputing that money and power often get you access' to the governing institutions that command the social resources.[26] Either this is a feel-good palliative sentiment or it is the height of cynicism. Actually, it is both. On the one hand, Graff shows that he is a realist by acknowledging how the command of wealth distorts democratic institutions by making them into sound chambers for the already rich and powerful while, on the other hand, he represents himself as a caring person who is concerned about this sorry state of affairs and wants to do all that is reasonably possible to help. What is 'reasonable', of course, is to work within the dominant arrangements and not to challenge the ruling consensus, which is why Graff can write that change always comes from within the dominant: 'shared argumentative norms [...] are preconditions of change'.[27] It is the function of the affective pedagogy to replicate the Graffs of the world and produce a layer of feeling managers with a hard-nosed conscience who are capable of getting things done while being attuned to difference. This is the university whose mission is to produce 'well rounded' individuals whose 'clear and distinct' ideas are perfectly receptive to commands and whose 'heart' is in the right place to relay them seamlessly — the university of and for capital.

Even when someone like Kim Emery says in response to Graff that the university should be a place of 'radically democratic' 'critique'

---

26   Gerald Graff, 'Reply', *Profession 2008*, pp. 259–62 (p. 260).
27   Ibid., p. 261.

that 'advances knowledge' beyond the 'current limitations' due to the influence of 'money and power', what is silently assumed is the pedagogy of affect that accommodates difference above and beyond class.[28] She does not need to explain, therefore, why a 'reductive' theory of culture that surfaces how 'culture everywhere and always trumps' the 'different needs, values and purposes' of 'deskilled and deregulated workers' 'support[s] and sustain[s] the status quo', because what is assumed is that class no longer matters.[29] Only cultural differences matter, differences which are, according to her, inherently 'queer' ('neither finite nor fixed') and not to be accommodated or regulated in any way regardless because, after all, isn't 'the secret that our future is unknown' anyway?[30] The 'homogenizing' 'narrow-mindedness' of the 'elitist' university, she says, 'does make me feel queer', and the reader is supposed to take solace in that feeling as 'incoherence is a condition of possibility' of an 'open-ended' democratic society.[31] The pedagogy of affect is indeed a 'radically democratic' space where there is no limit to imagining that the unmet needs of the producers can be explained away as providing a perfect opportunity to reinvent oneself as a more feeling person with deregulated desires who resists 'reductive' knowledge with its presumption that there is some 'predictability', or worse still, 'transparency', about whose needs are and are not being met and what is to de done about it.[32]

In the name of having 'radical' feelings that 'resist' coercive power, these theorists are doing some very reactionary things with theory. Brooks' sentiment that 'how to read poetry' is more 'crucially important [...] now' rather than 'political philosophy and economics' is mirrored by Rita Felski, who feels that a narrowly pragmatic focus on 'how we read' rather than 'why' is truly 'transformative', rather than the 'bigger picture' 'revolutionary' claims of 'theory'.[33] They are joined in these feelings by Emery who 'feels queer' will dismantle the 'homogenizing

---

28 Kim Emery, 'Outcomes assessment and standardization: A queer critique', *Profession 2008*, pp. 255–59 (pp. 255, 257, 259).

29 Ibid., pp. 257–58.

30 Ibid., p. 259.

31 Ibid., pp. 256, 258–59.

32 Ibid., p. 259.

33 Brooks, pp. 33–35; Rita Felski, 'From Literary Theory to Critical Method', *Profession 2008*, 108–16 (pp. 108–10).

standardization' of culture required by 'money and power'.[34] By activating 'feelings' as the zone of effectivity they are opposing theory, which is necessary to reveal the structure of inequality, as 'ideology', which is normatively equated with a 'bad' subjectivity. It seems that joining in the hunt for the red is the only way to have your voice heard in the university now.

---

34   Emery, pp. 255, 258.

5.
Beyoncé

Re: 'The Day Beyoncé Turned Black'. Many of us who teach introductory English courses will more than likely recall this title or something close to it as the subject heading attached to chains of email discussions that followed Beyoncé's Super Bowl half-time performance back in February 2016. It refers of course to the skit that aired on *Saturday Night Live*, that quickly went viral, about 'the day that [white people] lost their damn white minds' after the drop of her 'Formation' video, the song she choose to cover on prime time network television.[1] Her performance of the song to the approximately 111 million live viewers that day, since viewed online by many more, had become, as they say, a 'teachable moment'. The question I would like to investigate here is why? My reason for doing so is to put forward the kind of 'transformative' reading/writing/ thinking that I practice with my students and which, I believe, can empower them to pursue 'lifelong learning and civic participation', as the mission statement of the college where I teach puts it.

Many culturally obvious answers easily come to mind as to why Beyoncé had suddenly become much more 'teachable' the day she 'turned black' that revolve around just what 'blackness' might mean today. Perhaps the most vocal response, at least in the mass corporate media outlets like Fox News or CNN, was from conservative voices who perceived her performance, or, at least, said that they did, as a provocation to attack the police. They claimed to find this call to terrorism embedded in the black power imagery Beyoncé alludes to in her half-time performance (raised fist, black berets, etc.) as well as the video (with the image of a police car sinking beneath flood waters). In these tired discourses, 'black', it goes without saying, is never far from 'violence'.

---

1   'The Day Beyoncé Turned Black', dir. Don Roy King (NBC, 2016), https://www. youtube.com/watch?v=ociMBfkDG1w&ab_channel=SaturdayNightLive.

      https://doi.org/10.11647/OBP.0324.05

I consider it is important to encourage students to investigate this 'reading' of Beyoncé's performance — with which, at the time, they were already familiar from their own media consumption and discussions on social media — because of how it reads Beyoncé's imagery by taking it out of the context of entertainment, where it normally appears to be trivial and unworthy of our sustained attention, and places it within a political one, where things are usually taken more seriously, as a popular composition textbook puts it.[2] In this way the conservative reading, despite its insistence that entertainment be *merely* entertaining and not 'political' and 'controversial', further demonstrates how 'reading' popular culture has become necessary in our media saturated world which is constantly resignifying the signs of culture to serve multiple and conflictual purposes, as Beyoncé's performance itself showed.

In more popular media such as YouTube and Facebook, Beyoncé's performance, it seems safe to say, received a more favorable response, and she was for the most part praised not only for embracing her blackness but also for adding her voice to popular movements such as Black Lives Matter and protesting against police brutality and mass incarceration, what Michelle Alexander calls the 'new Jim Crow'.[3] However, to stop here and simply rehearse this familiar debate — to, in other words, follow the Graffian imperative and 'teach the conflict' — does not, I argue, really get at the underlying question of why the conflict exists, which, to my mind, should be the primary reason for educators to consider such current events as Beyoncé's 'coming out as black' at the Super Bowl half-time performance a teachable moment.[4]

To be clear, I do not disagree that 'teaching the conflicts' has its uses in the composition class, especially because it disrupts the beginning reader's/writer's habit of assuming that the meaning of a text is exhausted by 'what it means to me'. In other words, teaching reading/writing as an engagement with an ongoing cultural 'conversation' or 'debate' at a minimum requires the student to step outside their

---

2   Sonia Maasik and Jack Solomon, *Signs of Life in the USA: Readings On Popular Culture for Writers* (Boston and New York: Bedford St. Martin's, 2015), p. 10.

3   Michelle Alexander, *The New Jim Crow: Mass Incarceration in the Age of Colorblindness* (*Jim Crow: Mass Incarceration in the Age of Colorblindness* (New York: The New Press, 2012).

4   Gerald Graff, *Beyond the Culture Wars: How Teaching the Conflicts Can Revitalize American Education* (New York: W. W. Norton & Co., 1993).

'comfort zone' and see things from the point of view of the 'other', which is of course a primary civic virtue for a democratic culture. The kinds of reading/writing/thinking required by the college composition class should always have as their aim to 'defamiliarize' the student from the 'obviousness' of their own cultural assumptions if only to enable students to become more fully aware of not only what they actually believe but, more importantly, why, and thereby acquire a more articulate and powerful 'voice' in the 'conversations' that they will have in the workplace, the public sphere, and beyond. However, I argue that although 'teaching the conflicts' is necessary, for these reasons it is not in itself sufficient to produce the kind of media literacy that should be the task of the humanities today to advance: what I call 'transformative reading'.

A transformative reading, I argue, is reading beyond the cultural obviousness produced by the dominant media environment in order to uncover the cultural 'unsaid' and thereby not only become a conscious position-taker in the ongoing debates, but also become someone who is able to intervene in them and open up space for change. A transformative reading is necessary for moving beyond the manufactured stalemate of 'they say/I say', as another canonical composition textbook by Graff puts it, in order to show how differences of opinion are really signs of ongoing social conflicts over material resources.[5] In terms of engaging students in a discussion of Beyoncé's Super Bowl half-time performance, this means recognizing that, like all stories, the cultural debate over 'blackness' that it reignited has 'the function of inventing imaginary [...] "solutions" to unresolvable social contradictions'.[6] Transformative reading thereby enjoins the student to take a fresh look at the issues by investigating the roots of the conflicts in social practices and, in so doing, imagine possible real world solutions. My students call this 'thinking outside the box'. My response is always, 'which box'? I'm not being facetious. Thinking outside the box is one thing; thinking about why thinking is 'boxed' another. What I am inviting them to do, hopefully, is investigate the ideological 'framing' of the issues so they

---

5   Gerald Graff and Cathy Birkenstein. *They Say/I Say: The Moves That Matter In Academic Writing* (New York: W. W. Norton & Co., 2014).

6   Fredric Jameson, *The Political Unconscious: Narrative as a Socially Symbolic Act* (Ithaca: Cornell University Press, 1981), p. 79.

may begin to surface what is 'outside' ideology and thereby articulate what normally goes 'unsaid'.

As an example of what I mean by transformative reading, let's return to the 'debate' over Beyoncé's half-time performance that was staged in the media. What seemed to be missing in the framing of the debate over Beyoncé's 'coming out as black' is precisely how 'blackness' disguises inequities of power and wealth as a matter of cultural identity. On the one side, blackness is associated with cultural inferiority and violence by the culturally conservative, while on the other, it is made a source of pride in one's racial heritage and 'speaking truth to power'. However, both 'sides' in the staged media debate are really on the same side when it comes to their shared complicity of silence regarding the underlying ideology of 'Formation' and the way in which it conflates black empowerment with market individualism, as when Beyoncé sings, 'You just might be a black Bill Gates in the making' and 'the best revenge is your paper'.[7] Is this not precisely the 'positive' message of free market individualism the cultural conservatives are always saying needs to be instilled by civil institutions? Its sentiment echoes, for example, Republican Governor Jan Brewer's law that banned ethnic studies in one Arizona school district on the grounds that it was teaching 'resentment toward a race or class of people' rather than that America is an 'opportunity society' in with all are equally empowered to succeed.[8] The conservatives are of course right to recognize that the black power movement generally and the Black Panther Party specifically opposed such libertarian discourse, but not because they were 'un-American', but rather because the commitment to ending racial as well as class oppression requires advancing a socially emancipatory discourse.

On the other side, the 'BeyHive' was right to point out on social

---

7   Beyoncé, 'Formation', *Lemonade* (Colombia, 2016).
8   'Arizona limits ethnic studies in public schools', *CNN*, 13 May 2010, https://www.cnn.com/2010/POLITICS/05/12/arizona.ethnic.studies/index.html. The targeting of class-consciousness has in the time since this chapter was first published become not only the nationwide justification of MAGA fascists but of neofascists everywhere for attacking any socially critique-al pedagogy as 'cultural Marxism', see, 'Defending Our Right to Learn', ACLU/American Civil Liberties Union, 10 March 2022, https://www.aclu.org/news/free-speech/defending-our-right-to-learn, and David Paternotte and Mieke Verloo, 'De-democratization and the Politics of Knowledge: Unpacking the Cultural Marxism Narrative', *Social Politics: International Studies in Gender, State & Society*, 28.3 (2021), pp. 556–578.

media that the song protests racial injustice: it is a call to end, not a call to enact, racial violence. It is 'just a video', after all, and Beyoncé's use of the cultural signs of blackness not only activates the discourse of racial pride, and arguably, commodified 'sexiness', but also represents the kind of cultural politics that has been institutionalized as a result of the civil rights movements since the 60s. In these discourses Beyoncé's use of libertarian ideology must be read ironically, not as a sign of allegiance to the dominant, but in the tradition of a black vernacular that must 'make do' with the master's tools so as to resignify them for black empowerment. In this way, Beyoncé's performance of black pride supports a cultural politics of non-violence as a means to redress racial injustice. However, the equation of blackness with empowerment within the existing social framework through expressions of 'pride' on the master's terms, seems to concede the conservative framing of the issues by silently implying that social movements can at best only ever be protest movements against cultural exclusion that seek inclusion within the ranks of the dominant, rather than radical movements for more fundamental and comprehensive social change seeking to put an end to the mechanisms that produce inequality and injustice in the first place. Beyoncé demonstrates how the cultural appropriation of the signs of black radicalism can serve a culturally assimilationist ideology that, ironically, reiterates and maintains 'blackness' as a mark of 'otherness' that is central to corporatist 'wokeism'. And yet, cultural inclusion within the social arrangements as they are today means the accentuation of cultural 'differences' that elide the fundamental antagonism of class and class ideology between owners and workers, exploiters and exploited.

The shared 'unsaid' assumption of both 'sides' in the media 'debate' that followed Beyoncé's performance seemed to be that if and when social movements become emancipatory and attempt to prepare the people to assume power and establish a society founded on advancing the social good of all rather than individual enrichment, they can only be considered 'violent' because they violate the rule of liberal pluralism that supposedly protects our civil, or, in other words, individuals rights. But, to limit our conception of democracy to the terms of liberal pluralism is to sacrifice democracy to serving the interests of the powerful whose power is furthered by the failure to recognize how the right of the few regularly and systemically disempowers the many. Beyoncé's equating cultural freedom with monetary enrichment is not simply ironic, after all, but a realistic assessment of the way that the private accumulation of social wealth corrupts democracy. It is her equating cultural freedom with advancement within rather than against the structures of wealth and power that is really the problem because of the way it repeats a familiar story that has 'the function of inventing imaginary [...] "solutions" to unresolvable social contradictions'.[9] It seems to me that to be critically empowered to thoughtfully engage such questions — by changing the framing of the cultural debates through transformative reading rather than assuming the pre-established positions in the culture wars staged in the popular media — should be the goal of the college composition class, especially now at a time when our civil institutions are in crisis as they must serve an increasingly polarized citizenry the majority of which are losing the means to access them.

Transformative reading is empowering and encourages 'lifelong learning and civic participation' not only because it provides students with the analytical skills to read the culture, but because it demonstrates how the student is already placed within the ongoing debates by powerful cultural forces, and, as well, asks them to consider how this is so because these forces are tasked with the purpose of keeping things as they are. Transformative reading defamiliarizes the popular culture landscape for student-citizens — from being 'merely entertaining' to being intellectually and politically serious as well — and thereby transforms their image of themselves from being passive spectators to active participants who are able to change how the world will be.

---

9   Jameson, *Politcal Unconscious*, p. 79.

6.
Bartleby

The reading of literature is always also a reading of the world outside literature. Although it is common to make sense of literature as a special language and treat it as a uniquely aesthetic experience separate from daily life, such a canonic view of literature is especially ideological because of the way it suppresses consideration of the way literature is embedded in a society's signifying practices and participates in making sense of the dominant economic arrangements and how they should be understood and changed. Literature, in short, is never about itself; it is always about its outside, which is to say it is an extension of class relations. Even, or perhaps especially, when the outside is declared to be an illusion created by the inside and literature is read politically as having the power to change the real, this reading too is an ideological relay of class. Representing the social relations of production — which, I shall argue, offer the only radical understanding of materialism — as an effect of knowledge assumes that changes at the level of ideas drive history and not the class struggles over wealth. If there is anything 'singular' about literature this has more to do with the amount of resources a society possesses to devote to literary production and interpretation than it does with its 'autonomous potential'. Thus, reading literature becomes more than simply an act of appreciation or of decoding the discourses that surround it: it becomes a means to grasp how different classes narrate the class contradictions — and antagonisms — that are produced in the production relations.

To unpack my point that reading literature is always a reading of class, I will investigate the way Melville's 'Bartleby, the Scrivener: A Story of Wall Street' has become a signpost in cultural theory for a 'new' politics of a 'new' capitalism without borders in which wealth and inequality are assumed to acquire 'materiality' in the circuits of exchange and thus invalidate the classical Marxist critique. Whether understood in terms of a 'refusal of work' (Negri), or as signifying a 'new' form of praxis of

  https://doi.org/10.11647/OBP.0324.06

a 'coming community' (e.g., Agamben, Žižek), contemporary readings of 'Bartleby' serve as a lexicon in which capitalism is represented as having outlived its basic contradiction inscribed in wage-labor/capital relations and therefore the best mode of 'resistance' to capitalism is the 'interrupting' of the flows of exchange value. Against what I shall argue are such accommodationist views — accommodationist in the sense that they all, no matter their surface differences, argue that the time for revolutionary change is over and thus accommodate the domination of finance capital — I propose to read 'Bartleby', along with some exemplary instances of its cyber-left readers, as providing an ideology of capitalism that limits resistance to the realm of circulation and instead will argue for the new not as cultural change in the terms of exploitation but the new as abolishing exploitation.

So let me begin by doing precisely what Bartleby does not, which is to say, give the material basis of his 'preferences' and, in a most un-ethical move, locate them beyond the immanence of his own discourse and outside the walls of Wall Street in the broader logic of capitalism. 'Bartleby, the Scrivener', let me state at the outset, is, at a time of intense class struggles between workers and owners — in the factories as well as on the streets — a text of middle class 'negotiation' between the interests of the bourgeoisie and the interests of the proletariat. Let me explain. On the one hand the story represents the figure of the worker — Bartleby — as primarily a subject of desire who, in refusing the authority of the lawyer in whose offices he is engaged and thus violating 'the natural expectancy of instant compliance' (12) which is the code of 'power', is criminalized, dies, and rises again as a martyr of 'passive resistance' (Melville 16).[1] I will come back to this level of the story as it is central to contemporary readings. What I want to call attention to before I do so are the conditions of legibility of this narrative depicting the worker simultaneously as the subject of oppression and as the ethical model of an absolutely singular resistance, which exceeds and undermines the normative conventions of power by virtue of the worker's unnarrativizable desire. To be more precise, why is this story told by Melville — a story in which the pure instrumentality represented by the lawyer is shattered and the dominant relations of power troubled if not

---

1   Herman Melville, *Bartleby, the Scrivener: A Story of Wall Street* (New York: HarperCollins e-books, 2009).

reversed by the resistance of his subordinate, and in which the moral, logical, and social norms represented by the lawyer are thus shown to be groundless and his categorical 'ought' and 'must' wrecked on the stochastic logic of Bartleby's preference 'not to' — why does this story take place on Wall Street? Why is it indeed a 'Story of Wall Street'? And my argument here is not simply that the real 'secret' of Bartleby's refusal is how it represents capitalism as dependent on the desires of its subjects and thereby occults the economic logic of necessity that in actuality underlies the system — but that the story itself is simultaneously an encoding of the bourgeois economic theory that wealth is produced not on the scene of production but in the circuits of exchange. 'Wall Street', in Melville's tale, is, in other words, neither merely a 'topical' signifier nor a thematic one — it is indeed the ideological foundation upon which the story posits that what is at stake in the relation between the owners and the workers is not 'exploitation' but 'oppression' — it is, in other words, the exemplary signifier of the dematerialization of the relations of production and the class analytic to which it gives rise.

All contemporary readings of 'Bartleby', if not explicitly marxist, put themselves forward as materialist readings. Whether as in Derrida's reading of 'Bartleby' materiality is made synonymous with an ethics of indeterminacy, or whether materiality is contained to the surface of the social as in Negri (*Empire*) and Žižek's readings (*The Parallax View*), where materiality becomes a matter of the performative inversions of power or of ideology, contemporary readers of 'Bartleby' display an underlying ideological sameness in the way they follow Melville's lead and erase production as the zone of the creation of wealth, foregrounding instead the scene of power and the resistance of the singular negation. While they differ in their local understandings of the 'material', they all focus on the slogan of 'I prefer not to' as if it offers a materialist disruption or subversion of the 'logic of capital'. This is, in other words, a 'material' that installs the singular 'desire' — the unexplained and groundless 'preference not to' — as the 'new' mode of resistance in a highly advanced stage of finance capital located in the metropole. (And of course I put 'new' in quotation marks here because, as I have indicated, it is not at all 'new' — it is simply that the ideological languages in which the social relations are narrated need constantly to be updated and revised.) As I have already suggested, 'I prefer not to' is in actuality part of the logic of capital because just as the fiction of Wall Street as the zone of creation of value forms part of its ideological structure, so too does 'resistance' at the secondary level of the cultural — whether conceived as discourse, ideology, power, or consumption, belong to its episteme. These moves of course all focus on emptying out materialism of history and class and making it into a 'language game'. On behalf of finance capital, the 'new' materialisms all negate locating the source of wealth in the exploitation of the worker — that is 'surplus value' as the real material core of capital — and resignify materiality as locally different codifications of ethics. Of the new materialisms, I will briefly rehearse two of the most influential: Hardt and Negri's desire-al materialism and Žižek's materialism of the Real.

Hardt and Negri argue that although Bartleby's refusal 'in itself is empty' and 'completely solitary' it is also a 'refusal of work' and as such 'is certainly the beginning of liberatory politics', that needs only be supplemented with a 'real alternative', which they locate in the so-called 'immaterial labor' — labor, that is, which is engaged in the sphere of circulation — service and other forms of 'emotional labor' — of the high-tech workforce.[2] The assumption here is that 'work', having become primarily a cognitive matter, is ripe for transformation through voluntary acts of subjective refusal that move one out of the realm of material compulsion into an emotionally liberated community without it being necessary to address the structural relations of private property within which work takes place — a displacement that ensures that what is foreclosed as a 'real alternative' is the overthrowing of private property. I leave aside here that the coding of 'non-work' as a 'radical refusal' is itself nothing but a codification of the position of the middle class subjects of the North who are, in the context of the current shift of productive labor to the global South, precisely finding themselves in the 'liberated' position of being jobless. Theirs is an activist materialism that wants to resignify materiality in terms of desire by displacing the logic of necessity in class society with voluntarism.

By contrast, Žižek's reading of 'Bartleby' is put forward as a critique of Hardt and Negri's reading on the basis of reactivating 'dialectical

---

2   Antonio Negri and Michael Hardt, *Empire* (Cambridge: Harvard University Press, 2000), p. 204.

materialism' as 'the philosophical underpinning of Marxism'.[3] He argues that their view is 'precisely […] the conclusion to be avoided' as

> in its political mode, Bartleby's 'I would prefer not to' is *not* the starting point of 'abstract negation' which should then be overcome in the patient positive work of the 'determinate negation' of the existing social universe, but a kind of *arche*, the underlying principle that sustains the entire movement.[4]

For Žižek, capitalism now commodifies all acts, and especially the 'activist' logic that Hardt and Negri exemplify, insofar as they assume that a 'real alternative' can be produced through a positive transformation of the existing. Leaving aside for the moment whether Hardt and Negri actually posit the transformation of capital, at issue here is that, according to Žižek, the only radical act is therefore the act of refusing to act. Thus he writes, Bartleby's 'refusal is not so much the refusal of a determinate content as, rather the formal gesture of refusal as such […] that stands for the collapse of the symbolic order'.[5] It is in fact this (empty) form of the Refusal that underlies all refusals which renders Bartleby's 'presence so unbearable' to capital, according to Žižek.[6] Žižek's 'materialism' therefore posits a neo-Hegelian 'absolute negativity' as the really radical resistance capable of producing the new. Yet while Žižek distances himself from Negri and Hardt as a 'dialectical materialist' he not only reproduces their circulationist logic but articulates it in a form which is in fact beneficial for the strongest fractions of capital. Take for instance Žižek's validation of Karatani's privileging of consumption as the axis of transformation now. For Žižek, following Karatani for whom 'surplus value is realized in principle only by workers *in totality* buying back what they produce', it is also consumption which 'provides the key leverage from which to oppose the rule of capital today [… as] that unique point at which [proletarians] approach capital from the position of a buyer, and, consequently, at which it is capital that is forced to court them'.[7] In other words, the real space of resistance according to Žižek, lies in workers refusing to buy what they have produced and thus

---

3   Slavoj Žižek, *The Parallax View* (Cambridge: MIT Press, 2006), p. 4.
4   Ibid., p. 382.
5   Ibid., pp. 384–85.
6   Ibid., p. 385.
7   Ibid., p. 53.

realizing surplus value for the capitalist. I leave aside that regardless of whether or not surplus value is 'realized' in the circuits of consumption, it has already been extracted at the level of production and that thus materially prior to the sphere of circulation is the fact that the worker is already exploited in the production relations and it is this theft of her unpaid surplus labor that all consumptionist models of resistance work to occlude. In fact, in advancing an economics of 'collapse' at the level of the non-realization of surplus value, Žižek simply upholds the interests of the strongest fractions of big business which have always seen such crises of overproduction not as 'negations' of capital — but as negations of the weakest capitals which are then absorbed by the larger and most productive monopoly capitals.

What is put forth as materialism now are 'surface' readings that propose to find a basis of change in the strange form of Bartleby's refusal ('I prefer not to'), in other words, in the local everyday dissatisfactions and negations that challenge cultural norms, on the assumption that there is no outside basis for the ideology critique of culture and all we can do is await a 'coming community' (Agamben). They thereby abandon a structural analysis of capitalism that reveals its fundamental contradiction in the realm of production and not circulation (which is the sphere of exchange and consumption of commodities). 'I prefer not to' does not disrupt the logic of capital, which is based not on the law of compulsory consumption, but on the economic compulsion on workers to sell their labor power to the capitalists and thus provide the material basis for capital: the extraction of surplus value in commodity production.

7.
Paul

A renewed sense of 'radical' materialism has become the test of one's politics today, but like other historical returns the first time it occurs, such as in the work of Walter Benjamin, it is a tragedy but today, in the work of Slavoj Žižek, Giorgio Agamben, and Alain Badiou, it is a farce. They are all currently involved in repeating Benjamin's performance in his 'Theses on the Philosophy of History' in which he identified, using the language of Paul the Apostle, a 'weak messianic power' in the discourse of historical materialism that more so than any positive and reliable knowledge of inequality, such as provided by Marx's labor theory of value, is what truly makes it radical. The argument that Marx's 'scientific socialism' is secretly a form of the very 'ethical' or 'utopian socialism' that he and Engles never failed to critique for serving to normalize the contradictions of capitalism would seem to call into question the supposed 'radicality' of Benjamin's messianic materialism. And yet, it is precisely Benjamin's messianic interpretation of materialism to which Agamben, Badiou, and Žižek have all turned for addressing the inequalities of capitalism.

The latest repetition of Benjamin's messianic conception of history performs the farce that Paul the Apostle is a 'true Leninist' for announcing that radical change begins as 'a change in you', according to Žižek.[1] On this same logic Paul 'subtract[s] truth from the communitarian grasp [of] social class', for Badiou.[2] Similarly, what Paul teaches us, according to Agamben, is that the true 'revolutionary vocation' today consists of overcoming the 'worst misunderstanding of Marxian thought' of

---

1   Slavoj Žižek, *The Puppet and the Dwarf: The Perverse Core of Christianity* (Cambridge: MIT Press, 2003), p. 9; Slavoj Žižek, 'An Interview with Slavoj Žižek: "On Divine Self-Limitation and Revolutionary Love"', with Joshua Delpech-Ramey, *Journal of Philosophy and Scripture*, 1.2, Spring (2004), pp. 32–38 (p. 36).

2   Alain Badiou, *Saint Paul: The Foundation of Universalism*, trans. by Ray Brassier (Stanford: Stanford University Press, 2003), p. 5.

     https://doi.org/10.11647/OBP.0324.07

identifying the proletariat with the working class rather than with the rhetorical gesture of its own 'autosuppression'.[3]

That such calls for the ideological suppression of class through the exercise of pure faith pass for radical materialism now is related to how they are put forward in opposition to the ludic understanding of the material as the 'materiality of the signifier' that was dominant in the cultural theory of the 1990s influenced by poststructuralist accounts of language (Saussure, de Man, Lacan). The discursive materialism makes social change synonymous with a change in cultural representations and thereby underwrites the cultural common sense that equates freedom with the freedom of speech. Because the inequality and environmental degradation brought about by global capitalism continues to increase and expand despite the freedom of speech, the semiotic democracy announced in poststructuralist theory seems more and more outdated. The increasing inequality has produced an uncomfortable sense of anxiety in cultural theory, and in response it has taken a 'religious turn', as in Derrida's later writings. Derrida's later texts are more concerned with the mystical interpretation of otherness to be found within the traditional framework of Western philosophy from Kant to Heidegger and how this framework may be interpreted as an ethical call of a 'democracy-to-come' that has made his texts more at home in religion departments than on the cutting edge of theory. In response to the religious turn, there has emerged a 'new cultural studies' (Hall) whose central figures are Agamben, Badiou, and Žižek, that claims to reactivate the radical core of materialism as the critique of capitalism from its outside. It is this supposed new radicalism that is the focus of my discussion here.

In different ways all these writers are currently involved in returning materialism to its radical commitment to contest inequality at its root, following Marx's usage of radical. They thus contest the equation of materialism in poststructuralist theory with difference and its allied notion of semiotic democracy as the limit of the radical. Žižek for instance is against the 'Messianic turn of deconstruction [for relying on] a figure of the Other who really believes [so as to justify] the permanent use of the devices of ironic disassociation [toward any radical commitment to the

---

3   Giorgio Agamben, *The Time That Remains: A Commentary on the Letter to the Romans* (Stanford: Stanford University Press, 2005), p. 31.

critique of capitalism]'.[4] Badiou as well argues that the 'contemporary situation consist[s] of [...] a cultural and historical relativism' in public opinion as well as academic philosophy that produces 'identities [...] that never demand anything but the right to be exposed in the same way as others to the uniform prerogatives of the market'.[5] Meanwhile, Agamben has argued that the metaphysical separation of language from the authentic human experience of it to be found in Derrida's writings has become the central political logic of capitalist society today that justifies a condition of 'bare life' in which individuals can be killed outside the coverage of any legal norms that would give their deaths any collective meaning.[6] Using Benjamin's theory of modernity as a permanent 'state of emergency', Agamben argues that democracy today represents the violent curtailment of freedom rather than providing for its realization. And yet, at the same time, their return to a radical materialist critique of the culture of global capitalism is arrived at through Benjamin's messianic materialism which calls into question the radical commitment of the 'new' cultural theory to move beyond the religious turn by providing root knowledge of inequality.

Following Benjamin's messianic materialism, Badiou, Agamben, and Žižek have all in various ways argued that Pauline Christianity, because of its translation of the material into the immaterial, represents the most radical understanding of inequality today — more so than Marx's scientific socialism. In Paul's writings this notion appears as the transcendence of class by a spiritual act of faith in the miracle of Christ's resurrection as having inaugurated a messianic age in which inequality is overcome. What this does to class in his writings can be read in his First Letter to the Corinthians (7:20–22; 24) when he writes

> Let each of you stay in the condition in which you were called. Art thou a slave? Care not for it: but if thou mayest be made free, use it rather. For he that is called in the Lord, being a slave, is the Lord's free man: likewise also he that is called, being free, is slave of the Messiah [...] Let each one remain with God in that state in which he was called.

---

4   Žižek, *Puppet*, p. 6.
5   Badiou, *Saint Paul*, pp. 6, 11.
6   Giorgio Agamben, *Infancy and History: On the Destruction of Experience*, trans. by Liz Heron (New York: Verso Books, 2007), p. 56; Giorgio Agamben, *Homo Sacer: Sovereign Power and Bare Life*, trans. by Daniel Heller-Roazen (Stanford: Stanford University Press, 1998).

For Agamben, Paul's language here represents 'the neutralization [that] social conditions in general undergo as a consequence of the messianic event' which signifies for him 'the expropriation of every [...] substantial social identity [especially in terms of a 'determinate social class'] under the form of the as not'.[7] Žižek agrees with Agamben's reading of the passage adding that it 'has nothing to do with the legitimation of the existing power relations' because it 'suspends the performative force of the 'normal' ideological interpellation that compels us to accept our determinate place within the sociosymbolic edifice', and this through an act of 'pure voluntarism' such that change amounts to 'a change in you'.[8] That such a banal commonplace as that 'change is a change in you' is taken to be the ultra of revolutionary thought today I take quite literally. What Žižek's blurting out of such self-help marketing slogans as radical change shows, is that whatever other radical, philosophical, or Marxist-sounding things he says, his basic assumption remains that change emerges immanently from within the terms of the ideological rather than from outside ideology in the labor arrangements. Far from being a revolutionary principle, 'change is a change in you' is deeply conservative because it underwrites the common sense of class societies that it is ideological change within the terms of exploitation that represents freedom and democracy rather than the abolition of exploitation and the realization of economic freedom from need.

In order to make Paul's belief that 'change is a change in you' appear radical now, Žižek, Agamben and Badiou all make use of the apocalyptic language Benjamin takes from Paul, that Benjamin formalizes as life in a permanent 'state of emergency'. And so one finds Žižek announcing that we are 'living in the end times' of capitalism and that therefore any form of 'fundamental belief' becomes radical because it symbolically contests the privatization of the commons and the cynical 'disavowed form of belief' in the place of the Other to which it gives rise. Agamben of course famously takes the US concentration camp at Guantanamo Bay and the COVID-19 pandemic lockdowns as models of global capitalism today because of how they violently reduce the population to 'bare life' thus justifying the need to recover a belief that change is possible at a time when the idea of common humanity 'threatens to disappear

---

7   Agamben, *Time That Remains*, pp. 13, 31.
8   Žižek, *Puppet*, p. 112; 'Interview', n. pag.

irretrievably', as Benjamin argued.[9]

Benjamin's messianic materialism in which he uses Paul's voiding of class as an image of classless society has proven to be so useful to the new cultural theory because of the way his text makes it seem as if ideology is central to determining the shape of the social rather than economics. As in Althusser's formulation, ideology for Benjamin is not so much a false consciousness of class as Marx argues, but rather 'a representation of the imaginary relationship of individuals to their real conditions of existence' the function of which is primarily political rather than economic, i.e., to produce compliant subjects who find pleasure within the maintenance of the system rather than in opposition to it. In his texts Benjamin separates ideology entirely from the underlying labor relations in a manner similar to Althusser by his reading of history in terms of ethical belief, which has the effect of translating class from an economic antagonism inscribed in production into a cultural clash of values. As a result he produces a conception of history as 'dialectics at a standstill': an image of history as an eternal clash between the belief that human perfectibility lies in the mastery of nature through technological progress and, in eternal opposition to such an ethics of mastery, the weak messianic belief in a classless society that sides with the oppressed. Benjamin's main point of contention in the text would thus seem to be to break with Marx and Engels' historical materialist explanation in *The Manifesto of the Communist Party* for why 'the proletariat alone is a really revolutionary class' because it is the 'special and essential product' of the process of capitalist accumulation, as he claims that 'nothing has corrupted the German working class so much as the notion that it was moving with the current' of history.[10]

According to Benjamin, the 'weak messianic power' that secretly programs historical materialism despite its manifest 'material content' as a scientific socialism lies in its commitment to represent 'history from below' as a repudiation of the conformity to any conception of historical laws, such as he attributes to 'universal history'. Benjamin's history from

---

9   Walter Benjamin, 'Theses on the Philosophy of History', *Illuminations* (New York: Schocken, 1977), p. 255.

10   Karl Marx and Frederick Engels, 'The Manifesto of the Communist Party', *Karl Marx/Frederick Engels: Collected Works*, 50 vols (Moscow: Progress Publishers, 1976), 6, pp. 477–519 (p. 494); Benjamin, 'Philosophy of History', p. 258.

below consists of finding a 'secret agreement between past generations and the present one' in the 'image of happiness' and 'redemption' they project onto us.[11] The messianic power of these images lies in the recognition of their weakness in the face of the ruling class forces intent on mastery and subjugation at a time when happiness 'threatens to disappear irretrievably' under 'the 'state of emergency' in which we live [that] is no[longer] the exception but the rule'.[12] In other words, against the belief that human freedom lies in technological mastery and progress, Benjamin contrasts the belief that what truly makes us human is our weakness and vulnerability in the midst of hardship and oppression, which is what requires us to 'empathize' with each other and in the process find moments of 'happiness' just the same. The use of history from below against universal history he takes to be messianic in its analogy to the Christ myth as it symbolically 'resurrects' the dead and 'redeems' or 'transfigures' the past by siding with the 'weak' and 'vanquishing' belief in the discourse of mastery.[13] He takes the messianic to be radical because it repeats an awareness that he considers 'characteristic of the revolutionary classes at the moment of action', that they are about to 'make the continuum of history explode'.[14]

While Benjamin's text is clearly intent on secularizing the Christ myth in terms of class, at the same time it relies on a mythic image of history as 'dialectics at a standstill' which occults the class inequality and struggle inscribed in the economic base and inverts the material with the immaterial. But there can be no social change without the positive and reliable knowledge of what makes class inequality, and what Benjamin's messianism amounts to in the end, I argue, is the counsel to find happiness in the midst of bare survival, and, as in the re-newed faith of Paul, it represents therefore a therapeutic retreat in cultural theory of learning to live with capitalism rather than overthrowing it.

Making ideology a question of subjective belief and symbolic attachments rather than a false consciousness of class makes it seem as if the primary function of ideology is to provide individuals with a sense of the real that conforms to the dominant social arrangements

---

11 Ibid., p. 254.
12 Ibid., pp. 255, 257.
13 Ibid., p. 255.
14 Ibid., p. 261.

and thus to make change appear in the guise of pure voluntarism as 'a change in you'. Such a view of ideology itself conforms to the dominant cultural politics that makes people's values seem more important than their class position and what the class structure compels them to do. Conversely, Marx's theory of ideology as the false consciousness of class represents a critique of the subject as the locus of agency that is central to the dominant (bourgeois) cultural politics. Whatever one believes, the notion that belief matters in terms of motivating or compelling individuals represents a mystification of 'the real motive forces impelling' individuals, as Engels writes, which is a matter of what Marx calls 'the silent compulsion of economic relations'.[15] The specifics of beliefs are conditioned by the social division of labor and where one stands in relation to capital — whether one owns and controls the wealth of society extracted from the labor of the working class or whether one is without property, having only one's personal labor to sell in exchange for wages. To argue that belief is what really matters under such conditions is to invert the material cause with its immaterial effect as if it were 'the consciousness of men that determines their existence' rather than 'their social existence that determines their consciousness', as Marx argues.[16] The messianic materialism which puts belief over class, far from being radical or even new, represents a revival of the 'opium of the people' which feeds them spiritual illusions about what is to be done to change capitalism and realize a society in which 'from each according to his abilities, to each according to his needs' is the rule.[17]

---

15   Frederick Engels, 'Letters on Historical Materialism', *The Marx-Engels Reader*, ed. by Robert C. Tucker (New York: Norton, 1978), pp. 760–68 (p. 766); Karl Marx, *Capital, A Critique of Political Economy, Volume One*, intro. by Ernest Mandel, trans. by Ben Fowkes (London: Penguin Books, 1990), p. 899.

16   Karl Marx, 'Preface' to *A Contribution to the Critique of Political Economy, Karl Marx/ Frederick Engels: Collected Works*, 50 vols (Moscow: Progress Publishers, 1987), 29, pp. 261–65 (p. 263).

17   Karl Marx, 'Critique of the Gotha Programme', *Karl Marx/Frederick Engels: Collected Works*, 50 vols (Moscow: Progress Publishers, 1984), 24, pp. 75–99 (p. 87).

8.

Occupy

A spectre is haunting Europe — the spectre of communism [...] It is high time to meet this nursery tale of the Spectre of Communism with a manifesto of the party itself.

— Karl Marx and Frederick Engels

The 'Spectre' of Communism

To hear the 'mainstream' corporate media tell it, Occupy Wall Street represents the ghost of communism risen from the dead.

From right-wing commentators like Glenn Beck to liberal establishment news outlets like *The New York Times*, the Occupy movement has been labeled 'communist' because it has raised the issue of class inequality in the US.

Here for example is what Glenn Beck had to say about it:

> You have people on the streets calling for revolution [...] This is a Marxist revolution that is global in its nature [...] The leaders of the movement [...] [are] saying, we're not here to reform, we're going to collapse the system. We're not here to reform it. They're calling openly for revolution.[1]

And what is driving this revolution according to Beck?

It is not the growing inequality in this country that's to blame the fact that real wages have not risen in 40 years, that half the population is in poverty according to the US Census Bureau, that one in seven are 'food insecure', one in six are unemployed and lack health insurance, that millions are losing their homes, and millions struggle with massive student debt.[2] No, what's behind it is the professors: 'We are paying,

---

1   'Glenn Beck: Occupy is SEIU world Marxist movement', YouTube, 14 October 2011 https://www.youtube.com/watch?v=_Dsdofs4lNE&ab_channel=ToddWTIC [accessed 8 June 2024].

2   '99% v 1%: the data behind the Occupy movement, *Guardian* animations', YouTube,

https://doi.org/10.11647/OBP.0324.08

our institutions, our higher learning institutions, to indoctrinate our kids into Marxism', he says.

Echoing Beck's reaction to Occupy, on November 7, *The New York Times* published a piece in its Education section on the occasion of the 94th year anniversary of the Russian Revolution of 1917 that brought the Communist Party to power.[3] In this article they warn their readers that revolutionary social movements that would base themselves on 'Karl Marx's class distinction between "haves" and "have-nots"' have historically 'led to the [...] execution and starvation of millions of people'. The *Times* article then goes on to imply that Occupy is such a movement because the Occupy website says, 'The one thing we all have in common is that we are the 99 percent that will no longer tolerate the greed and corruption of the 1 percent'.

Judging by the panicky reaction to Occupy by the corporate media, it seems that the US has for so long been obsessed with culture wars and identity politics that when a social movement emerges that explicitly addresses the growing class inequality in this country, they imagine it must be Marxist inspired 'terrorism'.

Their fearful reaction, however, exposes their own class bias. In their way of thinking, it is not the injustice and inequality of the system that enriches the few at the expense of the many that's the problem, but the people openly expressing their dissatisfaction with social inequality that is, and the corporate media scapegoats them as dangerous and violent types intent on destroying civilization. Marxism, in their imaginary, operates as a catch-all bogeyman intended to scare the workers into seeing any resistance to capitalism as 'foreign', 'violent', and a threat to the 'American way of life'.

---

18 November 2011 https://www.youtube.com/watch?v=DxvVZe2fnvI&ab_channel=TheGuardian [accessed 8 June 2024].

3 'Nov. 7, 1917 | Russian Government Overthrown in Bolshevik Revolution', The Learning Network, *The New York Times*, 7 November 2011, https://archive.nytimes.com/learning.blogs.nytimes.com/2011/11/07/nov-7-1917-russian-government-overthrown-in-bolshevik-revolution

The 'Nursery-Tale' of Communism

But there is another way too that Occupy is thought to be communist.

As an article in *The Chronicle of Higher Education* explains, many of the ideas that lie behind the Occupy movement can be found in the writings of the academic left, especially those of Michael Hardt, Antonio Negri, and Slavoj Žižek who all openly proclaim themselves communists.[4]

But what kind of communism is this?

Žižek explains at the Occupy encampment in New York City:

> The only sense in which we are communists is that we care for the commons: the commons of nature; the commons of what is privatized by intellectual property; the commons of biogenetics. For this and only for this we should fight. Communism failed absolutely. But the problems of the commons are here. They are telling you we are not Americans here. But the conservative fundamentalists who claim they are really American have to be reminded of something. What is Christianity? It's the Holy Spirit. What's the Holy Spirit? It's an egalitarian community of believers who are linked by love for each other. And who only have their own freedom and responsibility to do it. In this sense the Holy Spirit is here now. And down there on Wall Street there are pagans who are worshipping blasphemous idols.[5]

If communism means Žižek's 'nursery tale' of overcoming our differences through the power of love to defend our common (national) interests against the greedy few who would personally enrich themselves at others' expense, then Glenn Beck has nothing to worry about because what he fears is only a ghost — the 'spirit' of Jesus, not the theory of Marx.

For Marx, on the contrary, communism 'is in no way based on ideas or principles that have been invented, or discovered, by this or that would-be universal reformer' — it is not the nursery tale of how shared beliefs will produce an egalitarian community, which is precisely the kind of 'utopian socialism' that Marx's 'scientific socialism' was

---

4   Dan Berrett, 'Intellectual Roots of Wall St. Protest Lie in Academe', *The Chronicle of Higher Education*, 16 October 2011, https://www.chronicle.com/article/intellectual-roots-of-wall-st-protest-lie-in-academe/

5   'Slavoj Žižek at OWS Part 2', YouTube, 9 October 2011 https://www.youtube.com/watch?v=7UpmUly9It4&ab_channel=visitordesign [accessed 8 June 2024].

a critique of.[6] Rather, it is 'a question of what the proletariat is, and what, in accordance with this being, it will historically be compelled to do' given 'its own life situation as well as in the whole organization of bourgeois society today' that explains the idea of communism according to Marx and Engels.[7]

What Marx's idea of communism requires is the opposite of belief, of only looking at the world the way we would like it to be rather than understanding how it is. What it means is taking a closer look at the 'actual relations springing from an existing class struggle, from a historical movement going on under our very eyes'.[8] According to Marx, communists 'do not confront the world in a doctrinaire way with a new principle: Here is the truth, kneel down before it!' but rather 'merely show the world what it is really fighting for'.[9] Communism, in Marx's terms, is thus 'not a state of affairs which is to be established, an ideal to which reality [will] have to adjust itself' but 'the *real* movement which abolishes the present state of things'.[10]

Take class, for example.

On Marx's terms, class is not merely a problem of the unfair distribution of income between the 'haves' and 'have-nots' that will change by people becoming less greedy and more ethical. Class, for Marx, explains the global division of labor that exists between those who own and control the means of production of social wealth and those who own nothing but their labor power which they must sell to the employers in order to live. Class inequality will only change, therefore, when the workers end their economic exploitation by capital and take control of production and establish a society in which the rule is 'from each according to his abilities, to each according to his needs'.[11]

---

6 Karl Marx and Frederick Engels, 'The Manifesto of the Communist Party', *Karl Marx/Frederick Engels: Collected Works*, 50 vols (Moscow: Progress Publishers, 1976), 6, pp. 477–519 (p. 498).

7 Karl Marx and Frederick Engels, 'The Holy Family, or Critique of Critical Criticism', *Karl Marx/Frederick Engels: Collected Works*, 50 vols (Moscow: Progress Publishers, 1975), 4, pp. 5–211 (p. 37).

8 'Manifesto', p. 498.

9 Karl Marx, 'Marx to Ruge in Kreuznach', September 1843, *Karl Marx/Frederick Engels: Collected Works*, 50 vols (Moscow: Progress Publishers, 1975), 3, pp. 141–45 (p. 144).

10 Marx and Engels, 'German Ideology', p. 49.

11 Karl Marx, 'Critique of the Gotha Programme', *Karl Marx/Frederick Engels: Collected Works*, 50 vols (Moscow: Progress Publishers, 1984), 24, pp. 75–99 (p. 87).

Like the mainstream commentary, Žižek's idea of communism as defense of the idea of community only addresses inequality as if it were a problem of the unfair distribution of wealth and power. While Glenn Beck thinks that any re-distribution of wealth from the rich to the poor would create a violent disruption of an otherwise peaceful, fair, and just society, Žižek thinks that the re-distribution of wealth from the poor to the rich that has been the norm since Reagan's presidency is brutal, unjust, and needs to be made fairer. Communism for Žižek amounts to a fairer distribution of wealth in which we do not sacrifice the common good in order to make a few people rich. If the Occupy protests are communist in the way Žižek argues, however, and what is being protested is only corporate 'greed and corruption' as the Occupy website says, then it is not the cause of the class inequality that lies in the daily exploitation of labor by capital at the point of production that is being opposed, but only the effects of class on culture because of the way the special interests of a tiny minority have been allowed to dominate social and political life.

But by only protesting the cultural effects of class ('greed and corruption'), rather than the cause of the stark inequality that we see, the dominant belief that capitalism may be made 'fair' and 'democratic' is maintained. The effect of this belief is to make it seem as if the daily exploitation of the working class by the capitalist class is normal and therefore acceptable — it's just the way things are and, therefore, ought to be.

By making it seem as if the roots of inequality lie in personal greed and unfairness — and not the law of profit that exploits labor — it becomes impossible to understand and abolish class inequality at its roots. What Žižek and other 'left' theorists promote as 'communism' presumes that if we only make the system a little fairer, with a little more regulation of Wall Street and a little more protection for workers, then everything will go back to the way it was in some mythological past and democracy will be restored.

However, without a basic understanding of class that critiques the dominant ideology that normalizes capitalism by representing it as open to being made 'fair' and 'democratic', it is impossible to change it, and the domination of social and political life by the 1% will continue.

People interested in the Occupy movement have worried that it will be co-opted by the Democrats and diverted from being a movement against social inequality into merely a movement to re-elect Obama and hope for piecemeal reforms. But given the focus on the 'greed and corruption' of corporate rule and given the lack of a critique of capitalism that exposes its basic class inequality and explains why there cannot be democracy while classes exist, it is clear that, at least at the level of ideas, Occupy was always already co-opted into an ideological support of the existing class system. It is for this reason that even the Republicans were able to use the language of Occupy for their own electoral strategies in 2012, as Newt Gingrich and Rick Perry did by attacking the 'vulture capitalism' of Mitt Romney's investment firm during the primaries. This ideological limitation and accommodation to bourgeois norms means that Occupy is yet another reformist attempt to save capitalism at a time of crisis rather than a genuine worker's movement to replace capitalism — which is a system for making profit for a few off of the labor of the many — with socialism — a system whose primary purpose is meeting the needs of the many by abolishing the exploitation of labor by capital.

And yet, what drove people into the Occupy protests, whether or not they realized it — from New York City to Oakland, Detroit and Pittsburgh, to Austin, Charleston, Fort Lauderdale, all over the US and around the world — is not the corruption of democracy by greedy corporations but the crisis of the capitalist system itself.

The ABCs of Communism

Speaking at the Occupy encampment in New York City Richard Wolff reflected on Marx's idea of communism:

> When Marx wrote his critique his image of capitalism's end was not that it was attacked from outside, was not that it was in danger from 'terrorists'. Marx's argument is that capitalism would survive unless and until the internal contradictions, the things about it that undermine each other, make it collapse and make the people who live in that collapse declare that a new and different system has to be begun. That's what's looming here. And Marx if he were here today would have a big grin and probably say, in good German, 'I told you so!'.[12]

---

12   'Richard Wolff OWS of WS', YouTube, 25 October 2011 https://www.youtube.com/watch?v=Q261bPJ-sCo&ab_channel=ChristopherBrown [accessed 8 June 2024].

Leaving aside that the purpose of Wolff's speech was to popularize a messianic vision of a more just society based on workplace democracy, Wolff is right about one thing: Marx's original contribution to the idea of communism is that it is an historical and material movement produced by the failure of capitalism, not a moral crusade to reform it.

Today we are confronted with the fact that capitalism has failed in exactly the way that Marx explained was inevitable.[13] It has 'simplified the class antagonism'; by concentrating wealth and centralizing power in the hands of a few it has succeeded in dispossessing the masses of people of everything except their labor power.[14] As a result it has revealed that the ruling class 'is unfit to rule', as *The Manifesto of the Communist Party* concludes, 'because it is incompetent to assure an existence to its slave within his slavery, because it cannot help letting him sink into such a state, that it has to feed him, instead of being fed by him'.[15] And the slaves are thus compelled to fight back.

Capitalism makes communism necessary because it has brought into being an international working class whose common conditions of life give them not only the need but also the economic power to establish a society in which the rule is 'from each according to his ability, to each according to his needs'.[16]

Unless and until we confront the fact that capitalism has once again brought the world to the point of taking sides for or against the system as a whole, communism will continue to be just a bogeyman or a nursery-tale to frighten and soothe the conscience of the owners, rather than what it is — the materialist theory that is an absolute requirement for our emancipation from exploitation and a new society freed from necessity! As Lenin said, 'Without revolutionary theory there can be no revolutionary movement'.[17]

We are confronted with an historic crisis of global proportions that demands of us that we take Marxism seriously as something that needs

---

13   Nouriel Roubini, 'Karl Marx Was Right', WSJ/Video, 12 August 2011 https://www.wsj.com/video/nouriel-roubini-karl-marx-was-right/68EE8F89-EC24-42F8-9B9D-47B510E473B0.html [accessed 8 June 2024].

14   'Manifesto', p. 485.

15   Ibid., pp. 495–96

16   Marx, 'Critique of the Gotha Programme', p. 87.

17   V. I. Lenin, 'What Is to Be Done?: Burning Questions of Our Movement', *V. I. Lenin Collected Works*, 45 vols (Moscow: Progress Publishers, 1977), 5, pp. 347–529 (p. 369).

to be studied to find solutions to the problems of today.

Perhaps then we can even begin to understand communism in the way that *The Manifesto of the Communist Party* presents it as 'the self-conscious, independent movement of the immense majority, in the interest of the immense majority' to end inequality forever.[18]

---

18   'Manifesto', p. 495.

9.
Twin Peaks

In order to address the question why *Twin Peaks* is 'happening again' in 2017 after 25 years it is useful to consider why the melodramatic and campy murder mystery had such popular appeal — at least among the mostly white college educated audiences for whom the catchphrase 'Who killed Laura Palmer?' could be taken as a kind of cool and ironic riposte to the libertarian trope 'Who is John Galt?' — when it originally aired in 1990. To do that requires reading it against the socioeconomic and ideological background of the last quarter century.

The original series first aired during the early years of the neoliberal period of global capitalism heralded by neoconservative and Reagan administration functionary Francis Fukuyama as the 'end of history'. What that meant in neoliberal sociology was the superiority of 'free markets' over the ideological driven politics of the past. What the end of the Cold War entailed for the former Soviet Union was a blueprint for what has since come to be known as the 'shock doctrine' (Klein): the use of a manufactured financial crisis as a thin justification for a kleptocratic elite to pillage public resources and carve up the USSR into warring neoliberal fiefdoms. In the US, the capitalist triumphalism launched a new imperialism of endless wars against external and internal 'others' (the drug war, the crack down on 'illegal' immigrants, union busting, the 'war on terror',...) that was justified in the 90s under a pragmatic post-political Third Way approach to governance by 'new democrats' like Bill Clinton who presided over the dismantling of the 'welfare state' and the build up of the reigning warfare state. In cultural theory, class was no longer taken to be the operative division in society on the view that in the 'knowledge economy' all have equal access to 'cultural capital'. Discourse theory dominated the academy and echoing Thatcher's claim that 'there is no such thing as society' limited its analyses to the 'micropolitics' of everyday life on the argument that the universal 'grand narratives' of the past such as class struggle no longer

 https://doi.org/10.11647/OBP.0324.09

compelled belief. *Twin Peaks* reflected its time. It presented the vision of a world in which material conflicts are resignified as cultural differences and inverts causal explanations into the undecidable play of endless interpretations.

On the surface, a murder mystery told with campy and melodramatic excess featuring the many off-beat and quirky characters that populate the small town of Twin Peaks, on another level, the show tells the noirish story of the ruthless Pacific Northwest border war between the Horne and Renault brothers over the drug trade and prostitution ring centered on the Canadian brothel One-Eyed Jack's that included plans for the scrapping of the local lumber mill and destruction of forest preserves for the commercial development of the region. In most readings of the Lynchian universe, this doubling of the world is taken to be a critical gesture that defamiliarizes the cozy and quaint appearance of rural, small town America by exposing the seedy underworld of rape, incest, and sadistic criminality that sustains it. In this sense the story centers on how beneath the perfect facade of high school student and homecoming queen Laura Palmer, whom everyone thought they knew and loved, there lurked the terrible secret of traumatic rape and abuse at the hands of her father and the local business leaders who ruthlessly exploited her suffering. By its structure the show suggests that the multitudinous pleasures and tragicomic narratives that make up everyday life are but coping mechanisms that distract us from the true misanthropic horror of a world ruled by the alogic of patriarchal power and desire. *Twin Peaks* personifies its cynical double vision of the world in the gleeful visage of the otherworldly character of Killer BOB — 'He is BOB, eager for fun. He wears a smile, everybody run!' — the evil entity who, when he is not possessing Laura's father Leland, takes on the appearance of a homeless indigenous man. More important than whatever doubtful and confused feminist message the show may seem to be telegraphing, however, is how its bifurcated narrative structure privatizes public explanations based on economic causes and limits intelligibility to the emotional and affective in the manner typical of melodrama, as Marx explained in his critique of Eugene Sue's *The Mysteries of Paris*.[1] *Twin Peaks* performed

---

1   Karl Marx and Frederick Engels, 'The Holy Family, or Critique of Critical Criticism', *Karl Marx/Frederick Engels: Collected Works*, 50 vols (Moscow: Progress Publishers, 1975), 4, pp. 5–211.

the ideological legitimation of the politics of neoliberal austerity by renarrating class antagonism as cultural differences, putting the thick description of endless cultural negotiations over meanings in place of root explanation of the social totality.

The 'twinning' of the world in *Twin Peaks* (from the eponymous 'peaks' themselves, to Laura's two deaths, the White vs. the Black Lodge, doppelgängers, mirrors,) represents the 'negation of the negation' of the material world by the spiritual. In other words, because the world produced by the triumph of global capitalism over actually-existing socialism is a class divided world and its appearance as a series of material conflicts gives the lie to all idealist interpretations and ideological justifications: such materialist knowing must be actively suppressed in public discourse. *Twin Peaks* serves this reactionary function by representing the social conflicts as the after effect of a spiritual division, if not exactly the good/evil dichotomy of Christian theology, whose tropes also feature in the show, then more so the division of the world between those who value 'love' (supported by the White Lodge) over 'fear' (the denizens of the Black Lodge), as more in line with the vedantic derived TM woo of the David Lynch Foundation. In short, in the original *Twin Peaks*, class does not divide people, values do.

Perhaps the most articulate reason for this inversion of material causes into spiritual 'values' given in the show is delivered by Annie, the ex-catholic nun and love interest of Agent Cooper in season 2, when in her acceptance speech for the crown of Miss Twin Peaks she proposes a spiritual solution to the corporate destruction of the environment by quoting Chief Seattle, the leader of the Suquamish tribe after whom the city is named,

> 'Your dead [...] are soon forgotten and never return. Our dead never forget the beautiful world that gave them being' [...] We tell ourselves the world is not alive so that we won't feel its pain. But instead we feel it all the more. Maybe saving a forest starts with preserving the little feelings that die inside us every day. Those parts of ourselves we deny. Because if that interior land is not honored, then neither will we honor the land we walk.[2]

---

2   *Twin Peaks*, 'The Night of Decision'/'Miss Twin Peaks', dir. Tim Hunter, s2.e21/28 (Lynch/Frost Productions, 1991).

In the world of *Twin Peaks*, the dead never really die (they go to the red lined Waiting Room) and their haunting of the living is a way to signal opposition to a dualistic materialist worldview held to be responsible for the deadening of the world. The 'loving' (those representing the ecological values of the White Lodge) interpret this mystification of the material into the 'interior land of feelings' as a 'beautiful' thing needing to be 'preserved' so as to overcome materialistic division by the embracing of difference as self-same. Those of the Black Lodge, on the other hand, like BOB and Windom Earle, the despised and dishonored in Annie's discourse, who return to the living in order to feed on their 'garmonbozia' (pain and sorrow), have a different interpretation. As Windom Earle puts it

> Once upon a time, there was a place of great goodness, called the White Lodge. Gentle fawns gamboled there amidst happy, laughing spirits. The sounds of innocence and joy filled the air. And when it rained, it rained sweet nectar that infused one's heart with a desire to live life in truth and beauty. Generally speaking, a ghastly place, reeking of virtue's sour smell. Engorged with the whispered prayers of kneeling mothers, mewling newborns, and fools, young and old, compelled to do good without reason [...] But, I am happy to point out that our story does not end in this wretched place of saccharine excess. For there's another place, its opposite.[3]

Through this spiritual division *Twin Peaks* represents the world as a culture 'clash of civilizations' between rival interpretations of hegemonic capitalism that either imagine its negation as the absorbing of differences into the logic of the same (White Lodge) or promote the acceleration of its rapacious drive against any and all ideological limitations (Black Lodge). In either case it is a world without an 'outside' alternative to capitalism grounded in class and thus perfectly in line with the neoliberal ideology of the end of history.

The spiritualization of conflicts is clear in the opening credit sequence as well which opposes images of nature (robin, trees, waterfall) against industrial production (smokestack industry) which, significantly, appears to be completely automated. It encapsulates the depiction of a world without labor or class struggle where 'values' divide people. The

---

3   Ibid.

'spiritual' polarization of the world in *Twin Peaks* functions as a moral condemnation of the 'externalities' of capitalism that immunizes its root in exploited and alienated labor from materialist critique.

The nineties version of Twin Peaks is a post-racial allegory as well. Although it reproduces familiar stereotypes of people of color as 'exotic' (Josie, Hawk,...) and 'violent' (Killer BOB, Josie again,...) it renarrates race as merely cultural difference — the division of the world into 'fearful' vs. 'loving' types, Black (Lodge) against White (Lodge). The iconic black and white zig-zag pattern of the Waiting Room floor itself serves as an allegory of the color line in the US as a shifting slippery one open to playful reversals rather than a ruthless and oppressive binary. If this sounds like a stretch, consider that upon his first entry into the show at the end of season 2, Cooper confronts Jimmy Scott, the famous jazz vocalist playing the Black Lodge Performer, singing 'Sycamore Trees' (written by Lynch) in a haunting style that evokes Billie Holiday's rendition of 'Strange Fruit', except in this version it's the black man who tells the white man, 'I'll see you in the branches that blow, In the breeze, I'll see you in the trees'. Then there is the 'comedic' subplot of season 2 in which Ben Horne, the hotel magnate/crime syndicate boss, becomes obsessed with the Confederacy, implying that because nostalgia for a racially polarized past is a coping mechanism for white anxiety in a world of cutthroat competition from 'others' (the Renault family), it should be indulged. The Bookhouse Boys club that local law enforcement forms to keep the 'darkness of the woods' at bay (shape-shifting beings like Killer BOB, played by the Native American actor Frank Silva), as well as to torture suspects, is another way that the show plays with racist tropes. It what may perhaps be a knowing wink of acknowledgment of the ludic cultural politics of the show, in much the same way as the soap opera Invitation to Love that plays in the background is a reflexive commentary on the show within the show, there is the subtle allusion to what appears to be a copy of The Marx-Engels Reader in Sheriff Truman's office that suggests by its placement in the Bookhouse Boys library that 'class' is just white identity politics writ large to be taken as a sign of fear and resentment toward 'others' (see Fig 1).

Fig. 1. David Lynch, *Twin Peaks* (1990–1991), Viacom/CBS.

It is significant to the racial politics of the show that the Agent of the FBI
Internal Affairs Unit to whom Cooper must turn over his badge in season
2 because he has violated FBI jurisdiction by crossing the Canadian
border to save Audrey from the Renault crime syndicate is played by a
black actor (Clarence Williams III). The Agent is, incidentally, the only
black character in the entire original Twin Peaks universe who is not a
demon from the Black Lodge (which on my count amounts to three).
This is significant for the same reason that Dennis/Denise, the Special
Agent who first appears in season 2 played by David Duchovny and
returns as FBI Chief of Staff in season 3, is a transgender person. What
is being suggested by the placing of culturally marginalized figures
in positions of power is that race and gender are no longer divisive
categories — even the bigoted Agent Rosenfield turns out really 'loves
everybody' as he choses to live his life 'in the company of Gandhi and
King' — but that the Law of the land is post-racial and post-sexist. And
yet, Cooper's disregard for the Law, not only in his roaming outside its
geographic jurisdiction but with his 'Tibetan method' too that allows
him to border cross into the spirit world and glean from his dreams
and visions clues and insights into suspects' characters, is yet another
of the ways the story argues that it is necessary to violate the Law in
order to save it. What makes Coop a hero we are being told is how even

in his disregard for the Law, he preserves its spirit, in contrast to those who in their privileged bureaucratic complacency subvert its force. Cooper's appearance in the town of Twin Peaks as an Agent of the Law explains why he is so often referred to by the townies as the foreign element causing the weird events that are besieging their homeland. At the same time, Cooper's violations of the Law and his wish to join their gated community (most especially, the Bookhouse Boys) also suggests another unconscious reason for his golly-gee-whiz enthusiasm for the small town simplicity of Twin Peaks to begin with: 'white flight' from the big city overrun by overbearing PC multiculturalism. This may also explain why already upon his entry into Twin Peaks in the pilot episode he says to Diane that he would 'rather be here than in Philadelphia', where his Bureau office is stationed, which is where, as was revealed in the 1992 prequel to the show, *Twin Peaks: Fire Walk with Me*, we saw that he had recently had the disconcerting experience of encountering the border jumping Agent Phillip Jeffries (played by the gender bending David Bowie), with his 'exotic' shirt, inexplicably teleported in from Buenos Aires without a Law or wall in the world able to prevent it, questioning his identity (see Fig. 2). From the episode with Jeffries in the prequel which propels him to Twin Peaks, to his encounter with the androgynous Black Lodge Performer in the last episode of the original series, Cooper comes full circle, as can be seen by the same hurt and confused expression he wears in reaction to the same accusatory gesture that questions his sure sense of himself and renders him speechless and immobile (see Fig. 3). Cooper's symbolic castration, represented by the flaccid and infantile Dougie Coop in season 3 (2017), functions in the same way as does the sacrifice of MIKE's arm as a sign of his 'goodness' in contrast to a world given over to the mindless pursuit of narcissistic enjoyment represented by BOB. Cooper's strange adventures in the spirit world give an inverted reflection of the multicultural landscape he must navigate as a white man that indicates and alludes to feelings of inadequacy and anxiety regarding the loss of his privilege. What the cultural politics of the original show normalized, however, was the repression of class from public awareness. What is signified in the new season in its very title, *Twin Peaks: The Return*, is the return of the repressed symbolized by the ghost army of blackfaced homeless men.

Fig. 2. '*Who do you think that is there?*' David Lynch, *Twin Peaks: Fire Walk with Me* (1992), MK2 Éditions (France).

Fig. 3. David Lynch, *Twin Peaks* (1990–1991), Viacom/CBS.

Twin Peaks has returned to television after a quarter century when the domestic cost of the US's endless wars in the form of inequality, austerity, and insecurity has embedded itself in the public consciousness while its economic causes remain a politically taboo topic foreclosed from public debate that displaces and distorts people's anger and frustration onto 'others' (Muslims, Black Lives Matter, immigrants, Antifa, Russia, China,...). Someone born after the 'end of history' would be coming of age now and not have experienced a world with any alternative to capitalism and its endless wars, nor even a radical critique capable of producing class-conscious explanations and solutions to the social immiseration and climate destruction produced by unfettered and borderless capital.

In line with the contemporary historical moment, *Twin Peaks: The Return* presents a much darker vision of the world. In stark contrast to the New-Age-y lifestyle politics of the original series, we find characters confronting their problems with a much more materialist mind set, as when Janey-E Jones, the suburban housewife played by Naomi Watts, dresses down the gangsters extorting her husband Dougie by informing them that, 'We are not wealthy people. We drive cheap, terrible cars. We are the 99 percenters. And we are shit on enough. And we are certainly not gonna be shit on by the likes of you!' Sure it's opportunistic boilerplate not to be taken seriously — leaving aside the cliché rhetoric and melodramatic delivery, we know that he's in debt because of gambling and that she's trying to keep the bulk of her husband's winnings — but still the discourses the show relies on register what has become the new populist common sense since the 2007–08 crash. Because the old ideological mechanisms for suppressing the centrality of class relations as the shaping determinant of capitalism no longer work, popular culture is forced to talk about class, but the way that it does relieves the pressure of class awareness on the common sense by representing class as 'classy', as lifestyle differences based on income and access to 'cultural capital' rather than the exploitation of labor. The blackfaced homeless horde that emerges in episode 8 of season 3 marks the equation of class with the possession of 'cultural capital' such that 'lower' class is signaled as the lack of whiteness, cleanliness, domesticity, privacy, individuality, etc.

Fig. 4. David Lynch, *Twin Peaks* (1990–1991), Viacom/CBS.

The show itself suggests an explanation for the new populist common sense in the way that the season premier of season 3 repeats the penultimate Waiting Room scene of season 2 which features the enigmatic gesture Laura Palmer presents to Cooper by way of characterizing the intervening quarter century (see Fig. 4). Although one interpretation of the gesture is that it is the mudra of 'fearlessness' found in Hindu and Buddhist iconography, this is perhaps more its prescriptive meaning for how the past 25 years ought to be dealt with, according to the spiritual ideology of the show's creators, in contrast to its more descriptive meaning as a sign of the dominance of the market logic *über alles*, as suggested by its similarity to the commercial hand gesture of retro advertising (see Fig. 5). What the sequence suggests is that the 'waiting room' period of the 'end of history', the last quarter century dominated by neoliberal economics and culture wars, has in the meanwhile allowed the dark forces of 'materialism' to run rampant: materialism as mindless consumerism.

Fig. 5. Ivanka Trump. Instagram (14 July 2020).

If in its original iteration *Twin Peaks* presented the dark forces of the Black Lodge threatening to engulf the heartland of small town American values, today it depicts a world where the Black Lodge has most decisively triumphed, and the show now reveals the rapacious spirit of BOB to be a technologically wired and borderless power (moving from Las Vegas to Los Angeles, South Dakota to Buenos Aries), served by a reserve army of unemployed that New York City billionaires are seeking to harness through science (with the Glass Box device). What's on TV is no longer a litany of saccharine soap operas but a toxically metastasized much more nasty, brutish, and Hobbesian version of *Animal Planet* lacking any trace of cultural value. The quirky local characters have been transformed too. Dr. Jacoby is no longer the pathetic hippie figure with a quaint out-of-date vision of free love, but has become Dr. Amp, the raving host of a conspiracy theory podcast denouncing global corporate dominance and climate destruction, while opportunistically hawking gold painted shovels to 'dig yourself out of the shit and into the truth for only $29.99!'

In the meanwhile, Coop has transformed from the epitome of moral rectitude as FBI Special Agent Dale Cooper from season 1, to the more down to earth-toned sheriff's deputy of season 2, to become a Chauncey Gardiner type character (Dougie) totally at the mercy of shrill, gold-digging, domineering women, such as his 'wife' Janey-E and Jade, the black sex worker Dougie frequents. The question is: Will Cooper be able to reassert the power of White Law and return to the real world to defeat the Black forces of materialistic desire and greed that have run rampant in the meanwhile (See Fig. 6)?

Fig. 6. David Lynch, *Twin Peaks* (1990–1991), Viacom/CBS.

In any case, beyond the surface difference of a shift from postmodern cultural politics to a new 'materialist' populist politics, what has not fundamentally changed in *Twin Peaks: The Return* is the basic way that the show performs the ideological function of occulting the class relations that alone explain the state of the world by projecting the cause onto demonic 'others' — a secret cabal of evildoers now represented by the 'swarthy' doppelgänger of Cooper himself.

10.
Trump Speak

Trump bragged about how the US has done a 'beautiful job' because, at the time of his speech, 'only' upwards of 120,000 and counting had died of coronavirus. Although this particular example of Trump Speak had been widely commented on because the commenters did not analyze its class politics, the commentary itself was a diversion that served to normalize the prevailing cynicism of Americans toward politics so perfectly captured in Trump's 'mission accomplished' speech. To understand how such a comment could be so normalized that despite the 'buzz' it generated it is treated as hardly worthy of serious analysis and critique requires an investigation into the cultural politics of interpretation.

Such an investigation, however, requires the use of abstract concepts that in the mainstream commentary are widely taken to be irrelevant as well as elitist. A thoughtful approach to daily life that goes beyond its constructed obviousness is thought to be irrelevant because it speaks an alienating language that is 'out of touch' with the people. It is this populist rule of ignorance that treats people as know nothing actors that goes some way toward explaining why Trump Speak is so effective: it panders to a deep insecurity about abstract ideas that has been put into the minds of Americans by a steady consumerist diet which has taught them to regard ideas as foreign to pleasure and to embrace their spontaneous feelings as signs of personal freedom and authenticity. It does not seem to bother them that what they take to be spontaneous (and therefore true and authentic) has been manufactured by corporations who use a sensationalized and relentlessly emotive language to construct a cultural obviousness that rejects analysis and self-reflection to the point that the average person is unable to question the underlying class relations in which they live, making them all the more easily exploitable. For this reason, although many will find my text abstract, alienating, and thereby irrelevant, such language is nevertheless unavoidable in

    https://doi.org/10.11647/OBP.0324.10

order to penetrate the ideological purpose of Trump Speak which aims to maintain the cultural obviousness and rule of ignorance, thereby immunizing the existing social order from critique.

In this instance, when Trump declares victory over the virus and minimizes the death toll, it is not that anyone literally believed the deaths are to be celebrated, as the Liberal interpretation would have had us believe. The Liberal reading of Trump Speak is what the cultural critic Roland Barthes calls 'readerly' (S/Z) as it takes the text to have an obvious transparent meaning.[1] On this reading, Trump is the leader of a death cult that all rational people find abhorrent. In the Liberal ideology, 'ideology' is always for 'those' dogmatic types, whereas 'we' are 'open minded' and 'clear thinking', as in, 'don't those people know that rational governments like those of Western Europe have flattened the curve without massively increasing unemployment?' On this view, America would 'return to normal' when it elects an enlightened and responsible administration.

Another popular (mis)reading of Trump Speak is what Barthes calls the 'writerly' interpretation, which is given by right-wingers who, in the words of cyber-libertarian Peter Thiel, 'take Trump seriously but not literally'.[2] On this interpretation, Trump Speak makes the pandemic seem like something Americans should be proud to take part in 'fighting', as if it were a great patriotic war in which the dead sacrificed their lives to protect the homeland from a foreign invader. Like the old postmodernists, right-wingers reject the readerly transparency of meaning as a totalitarian imposition and focus instead on the interpretive pleasures to be found in the performative aspect of Trump Speak, in 'how' it says, rather (more) than 'what' it says. This is simply the obverse of the Liberal ideology except instead of 'ideology' being defined 'negatively' as 'bad' ideas 'those people' naively believe, it is defined as the 'good ideas' we rightly 'value', as in religious discourses. On this view America will 'return to normal' when it truly and sincerely believes in its founding beliefs.

---

1   Roland Barthes, *S/Z*, trans. by Richard Miller (Oxford: Blackwell Publishing Ltd., 1974).

2   Although widely attributed to Thiel, the phrase seems to have been taken from Salena Zito's article, 'Taking Trump Seriously, Not Literally', *The Atlantic*, 23 September 2016, www.theatlantic.com/politics/archive/2016/09/trump-makes-his-case-in-pittsburgh/501335.

There is an alternative writerly interpretation found in left discourses that also understands ideology as performative speech, but on this reading, the meaning of Trump Speak is found neither in its literally irrational content nor in its affirmative tone, but in its political implication in justifying the 'return to work' policies that benefit the elites while sacrificing the lives of the American people. Here the 'return to normal' is the problem and America must learn to value the 'other' America of the dispossessed and dehumanized.

In the leftist interpretation, Trump Speak is what Foucault called an 'event': 'the appropriation of a vocabulary turned against those who once used it'.[3] Trump Speak is 'event-al' because, as one *New York Times* commentator put it, he has 'stolen philosophy's critical tools' and deconstructed objective facts for the 'post-truth era'.[4] On this view, 'the Trumpian version of reality' conforms to the same theory of knowledge associated with celebrity postmodern academics like Derrida, Foucault, and Latour, who claim that 'truth is not found, but made, and making truth means exercising power'.[5] (Truth, however, is neither objectively found nor opportunistically made. It is an historical effect.)

The above are all localizing readings of Trump Speak that allow the readers to continue to believe that how one reads (the cultural politics of interpretation) matters more than why one reads (the outside of interpretation). Reading, however, is always the cultural effect of class.

Reading, in other words, is not an isolated act of interpretation (discovering 'the truth'), nor is it an ethical performance (making 'truth'). Reading is a social process that is needed to train the workforce to submit to being exploited by capital. Truth, historically considered, is that which is socially necessary to believe in order to reproduce the class relations. In other words, language is neither an object of 'readerly' transparency or 'writerly' performativity, as discourse theorists claim, but a 'speecherly' medium, what Marx and Engels call 'practical, real consciousness', which 'only arises from the need, the necessity, of

---

3   Michel Foucault, 'Nietzsche, Genealogy, History', *Language, Counter-Memory, Practice*, ed. by Donald F. Bouchard, trans. by Donald F. Bouchard and Sherry Simon (Ithaca: Cornell University Press, 1977), pp. 139–64 (p. 154).

4   Casey Williams, 'Has Trump Stolen Philosophy's Critical Tools?', *The New York Times*, 17 April 2017, https://www.nytimes.com/2017/04/17/opinion/has-trump-stolen-philosophys-critical-tools.html.

5   Ibid., n. pag.

intercourse with other men', and that ideologically mediates the class relations in such a way as to re-secure them at a time of crisis when they are being called into question by newer and more advanced forms of socially productive labor.[6] This is why Marx, in *The Eighteenth Brumaire*, calls counter-revolutionary speech 'farcical' and proletarian revolution the 'poetry of the future'.[7]

None of the 'interpretations' of Trump's bragging about the US's failure to contain the COVID-19 pandemic are able to uncover the 'speecherly' dimension of Trump Speak as an ideological reflection of what Marx called the contradiction between the 'forces of production' (science and technology) and 'relations of production' (private ownership and class inequality). What is rarely commented on and never focused on in any sustained way is the fact that the US should be in the forefront of fighting COVID-19 given the country's historic accumulation of wealth and advanced scientific knowledges and the fact that the only reason it is not is because its ruling class regressively prioritizes what is profitable for the owners as the sole measure of the social good and, therefore, considers market forces the only mechanism of real solutions.

The result is that whatever is seen as necessary for the production and accumulation of private wealth, such as corporate bailouts, tax cuts on the wealthy, and reopening the economy, is made into the standard of 'liberty' and freedom while everything that stands to cut into the private appropriation of social wealth, such as government health care, socialized public utilities like education and housing, and a federal jobs guarantee, is made to seem 'un-American' and tyrannical.

But the side-show of who or what is or is not American is itself a diversion because none of the proposed 'socialist' reforms will change the underlying class relations which explain why in a capitalist system the needs of workers for nutritious food, adequate housing, easily accessible health care, an advanced and worldly education, a meaningful cultural life, and so on, cannot be met despite the material and technical

---

6   Karl Marx and Frederick Engels, 'The German Ideology', *Karl Marx/Frederick Engels: Collected Works*, 50 vols (Moscow: Progress Publishers, 1976), 5, p. 44.

7   Karl Marx, 'The Eighteenth Brumaire of Louis Bonaparte', *Karl Marx/Frederick Engels: Collected Works*, 50 vols (Moscow: Progress Publishers, 1979), 11, pp. 99–197 (pp. 103–06).

capability of doing so, which the workers have themselves produced, being abundantly available. Instead we get the ritualized outrage over Trump Speak. The circus without the bread.

The 'speecherly' meaning of Trump Speak, the fact that what he is saying by bragging about the criminal US response to the pandemic is that Americans must be proud to sacrifice their lives on the altar of Capital, is a reflection of the brutal reality of high-tech multinational capitalism in which the workers of the world have no alternative but to submit to having their labor exploited to make profit for the owners or die.

But, Trump understands, as all good managers do, that to be an effective boss requires not only authority but also respect for authority and that to instill such respect, it is necessary to speak to working people in an obsequious and patronizing way to make it easier for them to accept the reality of what is required by the law of profit. This explains the jokey 'upbeat' tone and child-like cadence of Trump Speak as well as the diversionary Liberal focus on its arrogant stupidity. Both, in different idioms directed to different audiences, are ways of making the brutal abject misery of capitalism more emotionally tolerable.

The 'writerly' meaning of Trump Speak, its boorish smugness and goofy out of touch tone, reflects the ideological subjectivity required of the workforce so as to reproduce the class relations of production. His Liberal readers simply find his performance ineffective for doing the job of being the boss of America. They want a 'real' (no malarkey!) boss that makes them feel like he's really listening.[8] What they fear is the loss of respect for the boss. They fear the boss being a joke because they require a rational public sphere to institute their 'reasonable' and 'realistic' proposals to 'save' capitalism. Meanwhile, the rural and suburban so-called 'middle class' Americans who sacrificed their educations to their careers in serving the bosses feel less insecure about their life choices when the boss acts the fool, so long as he threatens the others who don't see the funny in the fascism.

The fact that Trump can brag about the necronomics of the US so openly and it is not exposed for what it is at bottom — the failure of capitalism — is a testament to the underlying consensus between Trump

---

8   'No Malarkey' was the name of a campaign tour undertaken by Joe Biden for the 2020 Democratic presidential primaries.

Speak and his American audience. Beyond whatever surface differences that exist, all are already in agreement that there is no alternative to capitalism and we must learn to live with it by making its brutalities more tolerable. This explains why, despite the fact that no one can take Trump seriously or believe anything he says, there is no real interest in contesting the class ideology Trump Speak represents. It is this underlying class consensus that gives American 'culture' its perverse medieval backwardness that is shunned by modern democratic people to the point that Americans were banned from travel to most parts of the world during the pandemic. Outside the backwater playground of American politics, Trump Speak is neither funny nor stupid — it is capitalist barbarism.

CRITIQUE

11.
Capital

The New Global Intellectual

Transnational capitalism has, as *The Manifesto of the Communist Party* says, 'simplified' the question of social inequality by dividing the world between a class of 'haves' whose material needs are met only because the majority 'have not' the means to do so as these means have been privatized.[1] This ruthless binary of class in global capitalism has produced a new wave of anti-capitalist struggles that has given renewed urgency to the question: what is the place of the intellectual in contemporary social relations? It is as one answer to this question that a new global intellectual has emerged, featured most prominently in the writings of Pierre Bourdieu. The global intellectual as found in Bourdieu's texts seeks to go beyond the dominant notion of the 'local intellectual' required by an earlier, more regulated, phase of capital accumulation that traces itself in the writings of Foucault, Lyotard, and de Certeau, to name a few.

The local intellectual, according to Foucault, is not a 'totalizing' and 'theorizing' intellectual, someone who demystifies the mystique of commodity culture by speaking for truth and justice and providing the oppressed and exploited with emancipatory knowledges.[2] Rather, he is a 'specific' intellectual who, in the name of getting things done, separates and self-encloses the local from the global by focusing on the experiences of the oppressed as sites of spontaneous 'resistances' to 'power', which is itself considered primarily cultural by Foucault and unconnected to global class forces. The specific intellectual is an intellectual who is not really an intellectual because he uses the rhetoric

---

1   Karl Marx and Frederick Engels, 'Manifesto of the Communist Party', *Karl Marx/ Frederick Engels: Collected Works*, 50 vols (Moscow: Progress Publishers, 1976), 6, pp. 477–519 (p. 485).

2   Michel Foucault, 'Intellectuals and Power: A Conversation Between Michel Foucault and Gilles Deleuze', *Language, Counter-Memory, Practice* (Ithaca: Cornell University Press, 1977), pp. 205–17.

    https://doi.org/10.11647/OBP.0324.11

of theory to merely re-describe the common sense and support a rather traditional empiricism. He is a post-al intellectual who uses anti-theory *theory* to obscure the division of labor by positing an ideal commonality across class lines for ethical and pragmatic reasons. The conclusion of such a cynical practice is the banality that, as Foucault put it, 'the masses no longer need [the intellectual] to gain knowledge: they know perfectly well, without illusion; they know far better than he' and can 'speak for themselves'.[3] Foucault posits a merely semiotic freedom as the limit text of the political that, like all bourgeois freedoms, is empty because it occludes the class relations of production which in actuality divide the powerful from the powerless. This ideological occlusion of class relations is necessary to normalize the freedom to exploit labor-power at the center of capitalism, the freedom to work or starve for the majority in order to produce wealth for a few. Foucault's specific intellectual provides a familiar alibi for capital in making the freedom of speech more important than economic freedom in the regime of wage-labor by occluding the global division of labor. Yet it is this division of labor between capital owners and propertyless workers that actually determines why for the many the merely formal democracy of bourgeois society secures their exploitation by the few. In short, the local intellectual speaks for those who already have their material needs met who can afford to see politics in terms of what is possible within the existing institutions of capitalism and already have the power to project that interest as universal.

As I have suggested, in the current climate of a growing anti-capitalist movement which is seeking to address the actions of big business on a global scale, the merely semiotic democracy of the 'specific' intellectual appears too readily corporatized to be legitimate because it performs a reification of power that authorizes the volunteerist subjectivity required by the free market to normalize its rule as the social good. By fetishizing discursive 'resistance' in the cultural everyday where all appear equal in relation to speech, Foucault's discourse theory of the social underwrites the bourgeois fiction that wage-labor is a 'lifestyle choice'. As this pan-culturalism can no longer cover the contradictions of global capitalism, newer legitimations of wage-labor have emerged that take the form of

---

3   Ibid., p. 207.

a critique of the ludic cultural politics of postmodernism. Bourdieu's writings are central to this cultural shift in the ruling discourses.

Bourdieu has directly critiqued the dominant knowledges as complicit with social inequality by arguing, for instance, that the local intellectual's exclusive focus on the cultural has ignored 'the highest achievements of civilization [...] living and active in people's lives' that 'govern their everyday existence', such as 'the right to work, a health and welfare system'.[4] He has opposed the local intellectual for presenting 'the defense of these entitlements' as 'a form of conservatism', thereby serving the reigning neoliberal orthodoxy by helping to create 'a climate favorable to the withdrawal of the state and, more broadly, its submission to the values of the economy' that are making 'the consumer [...] the commercial substitute for the citizen'.[5] In the interests of speaking broadly to a growing international counter-hegemony, he has proposed a new 'collective intellectual' who is capable of recognizing that 'the state also exists in the minds of the workers' as an 'attachment to "established rights"' and who will reactivate this sense of justice so as to 'invent new forms of collective political work capable of taking note of necessities, especially economic ones'.[6]

And yet, Bourdieu's concept of a collective intellectual, while breaking rhetorically with Foucault's specific intellectual, returns in the end to the same reformist conclusions that alibi capitalism. On these reformist terms, the function of the intellectual, whether 'global' or 'specific', is to pluralize the social into localities and normalize a merely superstructural politics by occulting knowledge of the material base — the structure of conflicts over the rate of exploitation inscribed in what Marx calls the capitalist 'working day'.[7] As for Foucault, Bourdieu's intellectual similarly remains a pragmatist who takes his performance of ignorance as a model for the social good: he is thus someone who will not 'provide answers to all questions about the social movement and its future' but an activist who can 'help to define the function of meetings'

---

4   Pierre Bourdieu, *Acts of Resistance: Against the Tyranny of the Market*, trans. by Richard Nice (New York: The New Press, 1998), p. 61.

5   Ibid., pp. 6–7, 25.

6   Ibid., pp. vii, 26, 33.

7   Karl Marx, 'The Working Day', Chapter 10, *Capital. A Critique of Political Economy*, vol. I, *Karl Marx/Frederick Engels: Collected Works*, 50 vols (Moscow: Progress Publishers, 1983), 35, pp. 239–43.

under the ethical alibi of putting aside the privilege of his 'cultural capital' and letting others 'speak for themselves'.[8] Leaving aside the immanent (logical, ethical) contradictions of an intellectual who makes the figure of the intellectual a populist who puts himself in the place of 'the people' as a zone of knowing without theory, the fact that this is not a disinterested but a partisan practice undertaken on the side of capital and directed against the workers is clear when the 'cultural capital' of the intellectual being singled out for erasure is 'Marxist theory' because of its commitment to 'provide answers to all questions about the social movement and its future'.[9]

Bourdieu makes the intellectual into a symbolic designation whose knowledges, her cultural capital, make her an 'elite' dominating over others whose knowledges have less status in the market and who can only unite with these others, therefore, by de-privileging her knowledges and becoming a pragmatic activist. Although Bourdieu takes the narrowing of intellectual horizons resulting from such a move — from discussing 'the social movement and its future' to 'defining the function of meetings' — as globally consequential and essential for a 'new collective intellectual' capable of inventing 'new collective forms of political work', a 'new division of labor' and a 'new internationalism', it is nothing of the kind.[10] In actuality the intellectual as anti-theorist activist represents the global privatization of the intellectual as someone who refuses to become a traitor to the ruling class by raising themselves 'to the level of comprehending theoretically the historical movement [of class society] as a whole'.[11]

It is only such a scientific knowledge of social totality as provided by classical Marxism that can produce an understanding not only of the effects, but also of the causes of inequality in capitalism and therefore of what needs to be done to change it. By merely contesting the political dominance of capital and its symbolic mystique through ethical performances of symbolic disinvestments in 'cultural capital' while failing to provide a scientific (i.e., materially causal) knowledge of the social, the figure of the new global intellectual in Bourdieu's writings

---

8   *Acts*, p. 56.
9   Ibid, pp. 53, 56.
10   Ibid, pp. 26, 41, 57.
11   Marx and Engels, 'Manifesto', p. 494.

merely reinscribes the ruling ideas that, as a totality, make cultural changes at the level of the superstructure more important than meeting the need for what Marx calls theory as a 'material force': 'theory [...] capable of seizing the masses' because it 'grasp[s] things by the root'.[12] The 'root' of social inequality is not 'knowledge' but 'labor'.

The differences in knowledges available in a society reflect differences in labor, especially the amount of time people have available after performing the socially necessary labor required for them to survive. For the majority, time is mostly spent in performing unpaid surplus-labor for the capitalist who realizes a profit from it. This class division of labor between the many who are wage-slaves for the few who own the means of production will not change with changes in lifestyle and knowledge, by the voluntary sacrifice of the cultural prestige that comes with performing intellectual labor for example. It will only change when 'the expropriators are expropriated' by the working class and form 'an association, in which the free development of each is the condition for the free development of all'.[13] Because of the high technical level of development of the productive forces, such a revolution presupposes workers who have already become class-conscious, i.e., 'raised themselves to the level of comprehending theoretically the historical movement [of class society] as a whole'.[14] In other words, the historical materialist theorization of class-consciousness in classical Marxism presupposes that 'the time [...] of revolutions carried through by small conscious minorities at the head of masses lacking consciousness is past' as capitalism itself has already produced a proletarian vanguard; the 'most advanced and resolute section' of the 'proletariat [that] is already conscious of its historic task and is constantly working to develop that consciousness into complete clarity' in the social movements.[15] What

---

12 Karl Marx, 'Contribution to the Critique of Hegel's *Philosophy of Law*. Introduction', *Karl Marx/Frederick Engels: Collected Works*, 50 vols (Moscow: Progress Publishers, 1976), 3, pp. 175–87 (p. 182).
13 Marx, *Capital*, I, p. 750; 'Manifesto', p. 506.
14 Ibid., p. 494.
15 Frederick Engels, 'Introduction to Karl Marx's *Civil War in France*', *Karl Marx/ Frederick Engels: Collected Works*, 50 vols (Moscow: Progress Publishers, 1990), 27, pp. 506–524 (p. 520); Marx and Engels, 'Manifesto', p. 497; Karl Marx and Frederick Engels, 'The Holy Family, or Critique of Critical Criticism', *Karl Marx/Frederick Engels: Collected Works*, 50 vols (Moscow: Progress Publishers, 1975), 4, pp. 5–211 (p. 37).

is required of the intellectual due to these conditions is not to perform exemplary actions but to take sides in the ongoing class struggle at the level of theory where '[t]he only choice is — either bourgeois or socialist ideology [for] in a society torn by class antagonisms there can never be a non-class or an above class ideology'.[16]

Despite the call for reinvigorating the demands of class justice against a capitalist monolith, what is deployed as the social totality and a global alternative to inequality in Bourdieu's writings is merely opposition to the cultural domination of capital and not its basic class arrangements. Bourdieu's writings are so popular now not because they contain a radical critique of the knowledge industries of capitalism, such as postmodernism and globalization, but because, despite their critique of the dominant knowledges, they serve to contain the social contradictions and maintain capitalism by limiting the critique to reforming the culture of capitalism rather than contesting its basic class arrangements. Bourdieu reveals as much when he naively blurts out that in the end he is not so much against capitalism as a global regime of exploitation but only 'unfettered capitalism without any disguise' because of the 'total costs' to society incurred in terms of 'the logic of enlightened self-interest' itself, such as 'the insecurity of persons and property, the consequent policing costs, etc'.[17] He protests, in short, undisguised capitalism for one with a better disguise. In other words, one with a government that directs the social wealth of workers more effectively in terms of reconciling them to their own exploitation by normalizing more efficient police forces so that capitalism as a whole is less vulnerable to the emerging social revolution. It is because of this basic acceptance of capitalism that Bourdieu does not contest the underlying exploitation of labor that makes capitalism — the extraction of surplus-value from propertyless wage-workers that must be central to any radical critique for social change — but instead what he calls 'flexploitation', 'a mode of domination of a new kind'.[18] As Mas'ud Zavarzadeh has theorized of post-ality generally, 'flexploitation' too 'posits, a rupture, in capitalism:

---

16   V. I. Lenin, 'What Is To Be Done?: Burning Questions of Our Movement', *V. I. Lenin Collected Works*, 45 vols (Moscow: Progress Publishers, 1977), 5, pp. 347–529 (p. 384).

17   *Acts*, pp. 35, 40.

18   Ibid., p. 85.

one that severs the past of capitalism from what is regard[ed] to be its radically different and 'new' present (which unlike its past is now free from exploitation)'.[19]

On this post-al logic, the object of the 'new' capitalism (flexploitation), Bourdieu argues, is more the disciplining of the workers in the fixed idea that 'economic forces cannot be resisted' and creating in them a 'sense of unworthiness' than their exploitation at the site of production.[20] The very 'economic necessity' Bourdieu uses to critique the merely cultural politics of postmodernism is, it turns out, itself merely cultural and more concerned with the 'worker's belief[s]' rather than, as Marx and Engels put it, in 'what the proletariat is in actuality and what, in accordance with this being, it will historically be compelled to do'.[21]

Furthermore, in taking what is a constant feature of capitalism in general — the alienation of the worker that comes from her separation from the means of production and lack of control over her own labor/ life — and making this feature the basis for positing a new mode of domination (flexploitation) that posits a break in capitalism, Bourdieu returns social theory to an economism characteristic of bourgeois sociology and political economy generally which always locates the motive forces of history in individuals conceived as essentially free of the social relations of production. On this view, 'cause' and 'effect' are reversed and as a consequence Bourdieu is in effect arguing that if workers simply felt differently about themselves, the contradictions of the social, and in particular the inequalities produced by capitalist relations of exploitation, could be resolved. Such culturalism is in fact the *arche*-logic of economism despite the sentimentalism, because economism in essence denies that social inequalities are determined by the mode of production. Thus, it posits that all that is necessary in order to resolve the social contradictions of capitalism is to address the inequities as a self-enclosed issue of what Weber called 'life chances on the market', in other words, as matters of the distribution of resources rather than of the general conditions that shape the social. What else is this in practice

---

19 Mas'ud Zavarzadeh, 'Post-Ality: The (Dis)Simulations of Cybercapitalism', *Transformation 1: Marxist Boundary Work in Theory, Economics, Politics and Culture* (Montreal: Maisonneuve Press, 1995), pp. 1–75 (p. 1).

20 *Acts*, pp. 31, 99.

21 *Acts*, p. 87; 'Holy Family', p. 37.

but a call for an 'ethical' capitalist who is not so 'greedy' because he has been moved by the spectacle of an 'empowered' worker who has found self-esteem in her work? What such sentimentalism leaves out, of course, is that production for profit over meeting and cultivating social needs is structurally necessary within capitalism and not in actuality a free choice for capital or labor.

It is this fundamental idealism in Bourdieu's writings that has made him so popular. One of the tasks of this text is to show how this idealism surfaces in his major concepts and throughout his writings, from the more sociological to the more activist. Because some of these concepts, such as 'capital' and 'class', are appropriated from political economy in order to transform them into tropes whose only substance is ideological, Bourdieu must oppose the orthodox Marxist critique of these concepts as 'bad' epistemology, and thus I also place the texts of revolutionary Marxism in active contestation with Bourdieu's writings throughout this text. Not only does this reveal the class struggle being waged in contemporary theory in which the texts of revolutionary Marxism are totally suppressed by the dominant knowledges but it also advances Marxist theory so as to address the common sense objection that this theory is unable to explain the contemporary which is assumed to be post-exploitation and therefore post-revolutionary.

Take the concept of 'capital' for example. Capital, as only Orthodox Marxism explains, is precisely what divides the working class from the capitalist class and is specific to capitalism as a mode of production premised on the commodification of labor-power. Capital is the accumulated surplus-value extracted by the capitalists who, having monopolized the means of production, as happened in early modern England during the eighteenth century when the common lands of the peasants were privatized, have forced the majority of people to engage in unpaid surplus-labor in order to survive. According to Bourdieu, however, capital is anything capable of being culturally valued by people in general and whose possession establishes group distinctions and thus motivates competition and rivalry over the 'symbolic profits' accruing around accumulated and habitualized social status markers. In short, his is not a 'new' theory of 'capital' (and thus 'class') for 'new' times as is claimed, but a re-writing of the old Weberian theory of class as social status or stratification, in which concepts that have historically been produced from within capitalism to criti(que)ally explain its mode of production are taken as having a transcendental validity for all and for all time. As in all forms of economism, capitalism is thereby naturalized by being de-historicized and universalized. On this logic, ending social inequality is impossible since all that can be done is to change the composition of classes. As is the case in all bourgeois ideology, the point is the same — don't even think of changing capitalism.

What makes Marxism *Marxism*, and what is contested by all the post- and neo- marxisms, is its theorization of what Marx and Engels call the 'actuality' of class.[22] In Orthodox Marxism the actuality of class explains the movement of history. This actuality is the historical unity of the material interests of a class and its agency that must be secured in the context of nature and society at a particular stage of development. 'Class-consciousness' names the actuality of class in Orthodox Marxism and is what constitutes the other of 'false consciousness' or 'ideology', the 'selfish misconception' of the capitalists that 'induces [them] to transform into eternal laws of nature and of reason, the social forms springing from [their] present mode of production and form of property'.[23] As Marx and Engels explain, class-consciousness

> is not a question of what this or that proletarian, or even the whole proletariat, at the moment *regards* as its aim. It is a question of *what the proletariat is*, and what, in accordance with this *being*, it will historically be compelled to do. Its aim and historical action is visibly and irrevocably foreshadowed in its own life situation as well as in the whole organisation of bourgeois society today.[24]

What is class in actuality? It is not a subjective identity or self-enclosed discourse but the social antagonism in production itself between 'the class of modern wage-labourers who, having no means of production of their own, are reduced to selling their labour-power in order to live' to the capitalists, and 'the class of [...] owners of the means of production and employers of wage-labour' who make a profit off the unpaid surplus-labor of the majority.[25] What has made Bourdieu such

---

22 Karl Marx and Frederick Engels, 'Alienation and Social Classes', *The Marx-Engels Reader*, ed. by Robert C. Tucker (New York: Norton, 1978), pp. 133–35 (p. 134).
23 'Manifesto', p. 501.
24 'Holy Family', p. 37.
25 'Manifesto', p. 482.

a popular figure is the symbolic displacement of the class antagonism at the base of capitalism in his writings: the fact that he makes 'the symbolic order [...] the condition of the functioning of the economic order' rather than the other way around and therefore expects that he is resisting class by opposing Marxism because on such an (ideo)logic, 'class as it is observed is [...] the product of the theoretical effect of Marx's work'.[26] So popular has Bourdieu become because of this displacement of class-consciousness that he was eulogized in a *New York Times* obituary as an 'iconoclastic' and 'provocative' thinker who has led the way for 'all those fighting against perceived injustices wrought by unfettered capitalism'.[27] His popularity in short comes from the support he provides for the dominant ideology of cyber-capitalism that *The New York Times* represents, as can be seen in the writings of its columnists — not only the neoliberal Thomas Friedman, but the liberal democrat Paul Krugman, who concluded in a lead article about 'class' in its magazine that it was, echoing Judith Butler, Ernesto Laclau, Slavoj Žižek,... merely cultural.[28] Bourdieu's reduction of political economy to symbolic economy is central to the dominant ideology of global capitalism that posits 'the source of wealth in post-al societies as "knowledge" rather than "labor"'.[29]

The ideological function of symbolic economy is to immunize capitalism from critique by placing its wrongs on secondary and supposedly separate and contingent cultural features so as to normalize the daily exploitation in the base of existing society. As for Bourdieu being a 'provocative' and 'iconoclastic' figure who 'fights against the injustices of capitalism', *The New York Times* refers to Bourdieu in such terms at a time, of course, when capitalism has already had its legitimacy massively shaken around the world, not only in places like Indonesia and Argentina, which were supposed to have proven the superiority of the free market for ending the poverty of the global South but which clearly

---

26   *Acts*, p. 82; Pierre Bourdieu, *In Other Words: Essays Toward A Reflexive Sociology*, trans. by Matthew Adamson (Stanford: Stanford University Press, 1990), p. 18.

27   Alan Riding, 'Pierre Bourdieu, 71, French Thinker and Globalization Critic', *The New York Times*, 25 January 2002, https://www.nytimes.com/2002/01/25/world/pierre-bourdieu-71-french-thinker-and-globalization-critic.html.

28   Paul Krugman, 'For Richer', *The New York Times*, 20 October 2002, https://www.nytimes.com/2002/10/20/magazine/for-richer.html.

29   Zavarzadeh, 'Post-Ality', p. 10.

has rather exacerbated it, but also in the US itself as became evident to all after the bubble burst on the cyber-economy and revealed it to be a speculative fiction of growth maintained only by the massive loss of jobs and outright theft of workers' benefits, as the Enron scandal showed. Capitalism is experiencing a falling rate of profit, and it is showing itself capable of doing anything to counter it.[30] In fact, celebration in the elite publications of big business of loyal critics of capitalism like Bourdieu, who do not simply ignore its class contradictions but pluralize class and so diffuse it as lifestyle politics, goes hand in hand with advancing the new imperialist wars around the world that in practice help to 'simplify' the class antagonism.

What *The New York Times* failed to specify in its recognition of Bourdieu as a 'globalization critic' is that, according to Bourdieu, 'globalization is a myth' that has only come to seem obligatory to people through reiteration and which will change when people change their minds about economics.[31] Global capitalism, in other words, is not a mode of production whose central law of motion is the pursuit of profit from the exploitation of labor, but a matter of the 'doxa' that 'economic forces cannot be resisted' and it is incorporation of this doxa in the minds of the workers, according to Bourdieu, that has deprived them of their agency to change the world — especially the orthodox Marxist 'doxa' of 'class'.[32] In Bourdieu's social theory, history is a matter of 'habitus' — a 'social necessity turned into nature, converted into motor schemes and bodily automatisms'.[33] This reduction of history to the terms of the affective and experiential leads to the recurrence of a constant theme in his writings that would seem to call into question their usefulness as serious social theory and radical practice after discourse theory — the idea that 'social classes do not exist' and are as 'observed [...] the theoretical effect of Marx's work'.[34] The fact that despite the theoretical and political incoherence of his position — which

---

30 Michael Roberts, *The Long Depression: Marxism and the Global Crisis of Capitalism* (Chicago: Haymarket Books, 2016).

31 *Acts*, p. 29.

32 *Acts*, p. 31; Pierre Bourdieu, 'Doxa and Common Life. In Conversation: Pierre Bourdieu and Terry Eagleton', *New Left Review*, January/February 1992, pp. 111–21 (p. 114).

33 *Logic*, p. 68.

34 Pierre Bourdieu, *Practical Reason: On the Theory of Action* (Stanford: Stanford University Press, 1998), p. 12.; *Other Words*, p. 18.

critiques as merely cultural the politics of postmodernism, while at the same time makes 'globalization' and class matters of belief, argues for a passionate 'attachment to "established rights"' as a mode of 'resistance' to 'globalization' and says goodbye to the proletariat as a revolutionary critique of capitalism as a totality — his writings have come to occupy a privileged space in the knowledge industry as the text-acts of an engaged intellectual is directly related to the fact that Bourdieu's concept of 'class' is most of all directed against the orthodox Marxist theory of class as the social articulation of historical necessity.[35]

Bourdieu makes 'class' an outcome of struggles over 'capital' in a plurality of 'fields' that exceed conceptual reduction. What Bourdieu's 'field' theory of class struggle does is segregate the social into autonomous zones lacking systemic determination by the social structure of private property so that everyone is considered to be equally in possession of 'capital'. Not only does this repeat the petty-bourgeois dream of the democratization of ownership through a discursive ruse, but it is also an argument that makes social(ist) revolution unnecessary and, in the end, serves the ruling class. What the reduction of 'class' and 'capital' to the self-evidency of different lifestyles cannot explain is the systemic primacy of the production of surplus-value in unpaid-labor, the basic condition of the global majority, which determines that their needs are not being met and which economically compels them into engaging in collective class struggles. According to Bourdieu, however, the global class struggle is an effect of Marxist theory: in other words, it is discursively rather than economically constituted, which then makes socio-historical change dependent on changing people's ideas and appealing to their morals as in conservative discourses.

Bourdieu opposes Marx's labor theory of value with a (Nietzschean) value theory of class that posits class as an after-effect of the past symbolic struggles of intellectuals over 'cultural capital'. His notion of class is therefore totally ahistorical: it can be applied to any stage of production in history regardless of the specific form of the production and consumption of social wealth. He claims that

---

35 *Acts*, p. 33.

Every state of the social world is [...] no more than a temporary equilibrium, a moment in the dynamics through which the adjustment between distributions and incorporated or institutionalized classifications is constantly broken and restored. The struggle which is the very principle of the distribution is inextricably a struggle to appropriate rare goods and a struggle to impose the legitimate way of perceiving the power-relations manifested by the distribution, a representation which, through its own efficacy, can help to perpetuate or subvert these power-relations.[36]

On such a theory of the social, there can be no historical transformation of labor relations, only historical change of the performances of social actors who occupy fixed class positions relative to a given accumulation of goods (what Bourdieu anachronistically calls their 'economic capital'). Bourdieu's economic theory is the essence of economism and not a critique of it as he claims because it blurs the class antagonism in production that is historically specific to capitalism by positing a commonality of social agency in the market, in the continual accumulation and redistribution of what he calls (economic, cultural, symbolic, etc.) 'capital', thereby naturalizing bourgeois social relations across history. Bourdieu's theory of capital is, again, totally ahistorical because it is based on a distributionist theory of value rather than a labor theory of value which takes into account the historicity of the mode(s) of production: how men and women have organized their collective labor time under particular conditions of production. What has made Bourdieu so successful in the bourgeois media is that he has taken Marx's historical concepts of 'class' and 'capital', which lay bare the social totality, and turned them into floating 'categories' and self-reflexive cultural 'classifications' that can be formally applied to any social practice because these concepts have been cut off from their historical determination, their connection to the global relations of production, what Marx in his 'Theses on Feuerbach' calls 'the ensemble of the social relations'.[37]

Class, as explained by Marx, is determined by the mode of production of material life as a totality and is not a reification of the productive forces from social and political forces, as Bourdieu claims causes him to reject

---

36 *Logic*, p. 141.
37 *Practical Reason*, pp. 10–11; Karl Marx, 'Theses on Feurebach', *Karl Marx/Frederick Engels: Collected Works*, 50 vols (Moscow: Progress Publishers, 1975), 5, pp. 3–8 (p. 4).

Marxism as 'economism'.[38] He opposes orthodox Marxist theory on the grounds that it 'fetishiz[es...] the productive forces' and thus normalizes the neoliberal social policies of globalization by de-politicizing the social under an 'economic fatalism'.[39] Bourdieu conveniently forgets that not only was Marx the first criti(que)al theorist of 'globalization' but that Orthodox Marxism is a systematic critique of 'economism' that comes from Marx's critique of bourgeois political economy (among other places, in *The Economic and Philosophical Manuscripts of 1844*, the *Grundrisse* and *Capital*). It is only in the texts of Orthodox Marxism that the other of 'economism' is explained and not 'categorized' so as to pluralize the social into separate self-enclosed areas labeled 'the political', 'the social', etc., and subjectively 'valuing' one or another of these over and above 'the economic'. Such a positivist approach is the essence of economism, which always consists of analytically separating what in actuality is concretely united in a particular social formation so as to make the unity of these areas appear only a matter of ideological generality. Making the totality merely an instance of epistemic generality only assumes the social at root to be an expression of some ideal norm of humanity as constituted by the 'eternal laws of nature and of reason' that Marx and Engels find specific to the 'selfish misconception' of the bourgeoisie and its form of private property.[40] When Bourdieu totalizes what he otherwise analytically separates as 'social fields' under the general principle that 'the symbolic order [...] is the condition of the functioning of the economic order', his assumption reflects in such a way so as to naturalize what in actuality is the self-justifying norm of private property in bourgeois economics.[41]

What Bourdieu wants to throw away as useless economism is the orthodox Marxist critique of bourgeois ideology that alone has explained why differences in the social distribution and consumption of surplus-value — the differences in income, for example, which determine class position in bourgeois sociology and the dominant cultural studies whose position he shares — presuppose the material production of value

---

38 *Acts*, pp. 50–51.
39 Pierre Bourdieu, 'A Reasoned Utopia and Economic Fatalism', *New Left Review*, I/227, Jan/Feb (1998), pp. 126–54.
40 'Manifesto', p. 501.
41 *Acts*, p. 82.

through the expenditure of surplus-labor.[42] Before there can be social inequality in consumption and political inequality in distribution, there must first be the economic exploitation of labor in production which generates the surplus-value. What the dominant ideology of capitalism is constitutively unable to explain and that marks its class interest is the production of social inequality through the extraction of surplus-labor central to capitalism: the fact that before having a position of social 'status' as an intellectual, a black, latino, queer, or trans subject, one is inserted into class relations as either a worker whose labor produces surplus-value for another, or a capitalist, whose ownership of the means of production allows one to exploit the labor of others. Without Marx's labor theory of value, it is impossible to critique capitalism at root and Bourdieu's rejection of it as economism reflects the interest of the ruling class in social theory to occult the source of wealth in capitalist society — the exploitation of labor.

Not only is Bourdieu's idea that 'class' is an effect of Marx's writings a reiteration of the central ludic dogma of poststructuralism which makes the social an effect of the free-play of discourse, but it is the dominant ideology of post-al capitalism in general, which can be seen turning to its more familiar everyday articulations. Calling 'class' a theory-effect of Marxism is like when the Republicans in the US accuse those who seek to politically address class inequality of engaging in 'class warfare' as if class warfare depends on a rhetoric of class for its existence and is not materially determined by the objective antagonism in production between labor and capital, between production for profit over production for meeting people's needs. Bourdieu participates in the same red-baiting practices, which is odd for someone who claims 'social classes do not exist' while at the same time claiming to speak for the economically oppressed. Bourdieu's argument against Orthodox Marxism is that it is essentially an economism because it posits the objectivity of classes and their historical struggle as existing independently of the consciousness and will of individuals and thereby causes people to believe in class as real and forget about the symbolic activity of their own values in doing so. For Bourdieu, like the conservatives, it is these values that are central

---

42   On class in the dominant social theory see, *Class and Its Others*, J. K. Gibson-Graham, Stephen A. Resnick, and Richard D. Wolff (eds), foreword by Amitava Kumar (Minneapolis: Minnesota University Press, 2000).

to the social and that are more important than economic necessity.

Bourdieu's theory of class proves to be very useful to the ruling class because without a materialist theory of class that uncovers the objective source of material antagonism in production, one cannot, as Marx says, explain what the working class 'will historically be compelled to do' as a result of its position in the economy — the actuality of class. Proof of this usefulness to big business is Bourdieu being featured as a 'new' economic thinker in the *Financial Times* of London.[43] It is through the troping and reversal of the question of inequality as symbolic that Bourdieu proposes as a precondition for a 'genuine democracy' not that class-consciousness (the knowledge of exploitation that explains why workers and owners are in a relation of irreconcilable antagonism) be developed, but that 'the logic of intellectual life, that of argument and refutation [be] extended to public life' so as to 'reconstruct a universe of realist ideals' that will lead toward greater 'social harmonization'.[44] Realist ideals, in short, are a code for pragmatic change, change which does not fundamentally change anything, but merely works to smooth the harsh contradictions of exploitation and which thus enables the global barbarism of capitalist exploitation to continue with a 'human face'. The coding is needed to oppose revolutionary knowledge of the social as 'utopian' and normalize capitalism as the end of history. But the rule of ignorance enshrined in the pragmatism of Bourdieu's intellectual as activist is most utopian because he does not see the impossibility of reforming capitalism: as Marx says, 'It is not the *radical* revolution, not the *general human* emancipation which is a utopian dream [...] but rather the partial, the *merely* political revolution, the revolution which leaves the pillars of the house standing' that is, because it fails to change the underlying social conditions which are bringing about explosive contradictions in transnational capitalism, especially the contradiction between the global socialization of wage-labor as the norm in production and the bourgeois form of consumption of the social wealth that excludes the majority from meeting their needs.[45] What else is behind the 'anti-

---

43 Michael Prowse, 'So you think you make your own choices?', *Financial Times*, 25 November 2000, p. 26.

44 *Acts*, pp. 8–9, 67.

45 Karl Marx, 'Contribution to the Critique of Hegel's *Philosophy of Law*. Introduction', *Karl Marx/Frederick Engels: Collected Works*, 50 vols (Moscow: Progress Publishers, 1976), 3, pp. 175–87 (p. 184).

globalization' protests but precisely how a tiny handful of capitalists are able to command the wealth and control the lives of millions just to maintain profits for a few?

As Marx was the first to explain, because history is class struggle — i.e., about how changes in the mode of production determines 'the respective power of the combatants' and their ability to make history according to their needs — the dominant ideology through which class relations are maintained must change to keep up with the changing labor relations.[46] Today, the most effective way ideology mystifies class and maintains the bourgeois hegemony over the productive forces is to appear to be contesting class inequality. The interests of the dominant class, however, determine the mode of how class is contested, and so the class analysis focuses on differences of consumption (unequal distribution of social wealth) over production (unequal access to the means of production). The writings of Bourdieu are exemplary of today's containment of class to the limits set by the dominant ideology because of his reduction of class to the differential distribution of social wealth on the one hand, and, on the other, his defense of the discursive idealism which makes class an effect of incommensurable symbolic practices.

As do conservative discourses generally, Bourdieu's theory saves capitalism by positing the social as comprised of knowledge and not labor, thereby holding out the false hope that social change will come with a change in people's values. Thus, the role of the intellectual in the process of social change is not to uncover the *material* root of social inequality in the exploitation of wage-labor and produce awareness of what is to be done to change it for a new society where the needs of all are met, but the invention of 'new forms of symbolic action', a 'change of language', that does not really change anything.[47] What Bourdieu's new 'global' intellectual in the end proves is not what is needed to lead the emerging struggles to 'fight against the injustices of capitalism', but, rather, Lenin's theory of opportunism in the working class movement, especially his explanation of how 'when the working class movement has grown a little stronger, [the liberals] dare not

---

46   Karl Marx, 'Value, Price and Profit', *Karl Marx/Frederick Engels: Collected Works*, 50 vols (Moscow: Progress Publishers, 1985), 20, pp. 101–49 (p. 146).

47   *Acts*, p. 57.

deny the class struggle but attempt to narrow down, to curtail and emasculate the concept of class struggle'.[48] Bourdieu's version of the collective intellectual is precisely such a figure of opportunism who does not deny but curtails class struggle to what is possible within capitalism for the benefit of a few.

The Intellectual as Socialist Theorist

As Marx and Engels explain, the necessity of the intellectual in the process of social change is determined by the laws of motion of capitalism, specifically in terms of how the competition over surplus-value has as its effect the accumulation of greater concentrations of social wealth alongside a growing proletariat — 'a class of labourers, who live so long as they find work, and who find work only so long as their labour increases capital'.[49] Because of the technical development of production and the concentration of capital required to set it in motion, it is inevitable that as capitalism grows 'entire sections of the ruling classes are [...] precipitated into the proletariat' because 'their diminutive capital does not suffice for the scale on which Modern Industry is carried on' and they are 'swamped in the competition with the large capitalists'.[50] The proletariat is thus 'recruited from all classes of the population'.[51] It is this process of 'simplification' of the class struggle that enabled Marx and Engels to critique the 'utopian socialism' of their day with their own 'scientific socialism' and prove that 'communism' is 'in no way based on ideas or principles that have been invented, or discovered by this or that would-be universal reformer' but rather is 'the *real* movement which abolishes the present state of things'.[52]

A precondition of this real movement is the way in which, as capitalism unfolds, it unites 'the man of science' — that 'portion of

---

48   V. I. Lenin, 'Liberal and Marxist Conceptions of the Class Struggle', *V. I. Lenin Collected Works*, 45 vols (Moscow: Progress Publishers, 1977), 19, pp. 119–24 (p. 122).

49   'Manifesto', p. 490.

50   Ibid., p. 492–93.

51   Ibid., p. 492.

52   Ibid., p. 498; Karl Marx and Frederick Engels, 'The German Ideology', *Karl Marx/ Frederick Engels: Collected Works*, 50 vols (Moscow: Progress Publishers, 1976), 5, p. 49.

the bourgeois ideologists, who have raised themselves to the level of comprehending theoretically the historical movement as a whole' and whom capitalism has 'converted [...] into its paid wage-labourers' — and 'the revolutionary class, the class that holds the future in its hands' that is the 'special and essential product' of capitalism.[53] It is 'the bourgeoisie itself therefore [that] supplies the proletariat with its own elements of political and general education' and brings to them the consciousness of their historic mission to form 'an association, in which the free development of each is the condition for the free development of all' from outside their merely political struggles to reform capitalism in its localities.[54] It is for this reason that Marx and Engels say that the historic mission of the proletariat they outline is not based on any 'sectarian principles [...] separate and apart from those of the proletariat as a whole', but rather comes from the conditions of its formation itself, especially as 'it becomes evident, that the bourgeoisie is unfit any longer to be the ruling class in society, and to impose its conditions of existence upon society as an over-riding law'.[55] It is 'unfit to rule'

> because it is incompetent to assure an existence to its slave within his slavery, because it cannot help letting him sink into such a state, that it has to feed him, instead of being fed by him. Society can no longer live under this bourgeoisie, in other words, its existence is no longer compatible with society.[56]

The function of the opportunist intellectuals of the bourgeoisie is to place under erasure the historical materiality of the intellectual whereby she becomes transferred into the proletariat and a traitor to her class by joining the class whose interest lies in uniting the many in the fight for socialism. To be clear, Bourdieu meets this requirement by making the intellectual into a symbolic figure whose knowledge makes her an 'elite' who dominates others because of her knowledge and who can only unite with others by divesting herself of them by becoming a pragmatic activist. He thus occludes through an ethical ruse that 'the *only* choice is — either bourgeois or socialist ideology [for] in a society torn by class

---

53 'Manifesto', pp. 481, 487, 494.
54 Ibid, pp. 493, 506.
55 Ibid, pp. 495, 497.
56 Ibid., pp. 495–96.

antagonisms there can never be a non-class or an above class ideology'.[57]

Because Bourdieu articulates his social theory as primarily a political critique of a hegemonic economic essentialism that deprives workers of agency and does not foresee the need for revolutionary theory to provide a guide for the emergent class struggles, his writings mark a return to a traditional social democratic reformism on the left after the bankruptcy of 'radical democracy' and the 'new social movements'. The problem with reformism is that it does not challenge the existing division of labor and thereby silently underwrites the agency of the bourgeoisie rather than fighting on the side of the working class that is 'alone', as Marx says, 'a really revolutionary class' because 'as the lowest stratum of our present society, [it] cannot stir, cannot raise itself up, without the whole superincumbent strata of official society being sprung into the air' and 'along with these conditions [...] the conditions for the existence of class antagonisms and of classes generally'.[58] The preservation of classes is reflected in Bourdieu's writings in the way that the work of the intellectual is considered in a totally idealistic manner as a constitutive activity that creates the agents of the struggle themselves out of 'inventive' discursive practices conceived as 'symbolic' redistributions of 'cultural capital'. As in all reformism the aim is to install social policies to redistribute the wealth from the 'haves' to the 'have nots'. Redistribution of wealth, however, is neither radical nor transformative. 'Redistribution' does the work of containing social struggles by occulting the need to produce knowledge of the root of class inequality in production relations which is needed to end social inequality. In fact, the argument for addressing class inequality through an activist redistribution of resources under capitalism is a bourgeois politic because its practical effect is to accommodate bourgeois economism which always reduces politics to competition between 'special interests' over already-accumulated surplus-value. Dissolving class-consciousness in a spontaneous activism that takes the reified politics of capitalist civil society as a given only helps normalize the interests and policies of big business that are designed to stimulate demand by subsidizing consumption of its overproduced commodities. Redistribution policies are a means to bolster the falling rate of profit

---

57   Lenin, 'What Is To Be Done?', p. 384.
58   'Manifesto', pp. 494–95, 506.

and save monopoly capital rather than transform the class relations of production and inaugurate a society freed from need (socialism) — the first priority of which is to make the working class the ruling class. Bourdieu fails to seriously consider the failure of welfare state policies in helping to bring about the present need on the part of capital to transform the nation-state into a transnational neoliberal warfare state because he has abandoned the Marxist analysis of social production as reactionary 'economism' and put in its place a symbolically activist version of neo-Keynesian economics which reifies market distribution as separate from its basis in production.

What Bourdieu's work shows is that without the orthodox Marxist theory of class as the economic determination of history, the focus invariably shifts to conceiving the role of intellectual work as that of 'inventing' formal models of the social that simply re-describe in a self-enclosed language the self-evidency of capitalist ideology rather than change the world. What this revisionary move does is dis-articulate the social into a voluntarism that naturalizes the status quo.

Contrary to the imaginary of the new global intellectual found in Bourdieu's writings, I argue that the only effective theory of the intellectual in global capitalism is to be found in the writings of Orthodox Marxism, notably the writings of Lenin. This is because Lenin extends Marx's theory of the self-negation of capitalism through its own laws of motion to explain the contemporary and thus provides the revolutionary critique of the opportunist politics of the new global intellectual represented by Bourdieu. It is Lenin who explains the basic 'connection between imperialism and opportunism' that is currently masquerading as a radical anti-capitalism and rethinking of Marxism for the present.[59] Opportunism, as Lenin explains, is the 'defense of imperialism in a somewhat veiled form' that 'strive[s] to push specific and secondary details into the forefront [...] to distract attention from essentials by means of absolutely ridiculous schemes for "reform"'.[60] Central to opportunism is the reformist attempt to 'contrast imperialism with free competition and democracy' while failing to recognize 'the

---

59   V. I. Lenin, 'Imperialism, The Highest Stage of Capitalism. A Popular Outline', *V. I. Lenin Collected Works*, 45 vols (Moscow: Progress Publishers, 1974), 22, pp. 185–304 (p. 301).

60   Ibid., p. 286.

inseverable bond between imperialism [...] and the foundations of capitalism'.[61] Lenin's critique of the basic opportunism of reformism in global capitalism recognizes the tendency of imperialism 'to create privileged sectors also among the workers, and to detach them from the broad masses of the proletariat' by occulting the fact that capitalism has realized 'the partition of the world, the exploitation of countries [...] which means high monopoly profits for a handful of very rich countries' that 'makes it economically possible to bribe the upper strata of the proletariat'.[62] At the same time, Lenin never loses sight of the fact that 'the distinctive feature of the present situation' is how the same global economic forces are increasing 'the irreconcilability between opportunism and the general and vital interests of the working class' which are not capable of being met by capitalism and can only be realized in a global socialist society.[63] His writings therefore provide an integrative approach to the social that engages in the ongoing ideological struggles with knowledge of their outside in labor arrangements — a global political economy based on the necessity of economic equality in a world divided by capital and wage-labor masked as a world where knowledge matters more than praxis for a new society. They provide, in short, a guide for workers to become what Lenin calls 'socialist theorists': persons in collectivity capable of providing *outside* knowledge of the global struggles on the terrain of wage-labor and capital that break with the ideas of the ruling class and explain what is needed to end exploitation and emancipate all from the regime of necessity imposed by the rule of profit.[64]

---

61   Ibid., pp. 287–88.
62   Ibid., pp. 281, 283.
63   Ibid., p. 284.
64   Lenin, 'What Is To Be Done?', p. 384.

12.
Critique

The material force of critique comes from its explanation of the actual and phenomenal in terms of the cultural unsaid of class lying 'outside' the dominant ideology. Class, that is, not as a floating signifier or a 'feeling in common' as it is in the culture wars, but class as the material antagonism in the workday over the hidden unpaid surplus-labor of workers that the owners privatize as profit. The agony over materialist critique in the (post)humanities today represents an inversion of the material force of critique that comes from outside ideology into the immanent vibrancy of matter and the vitality of life as resistant to the conceptual. On these terms, the critique of ideology, because of its foregrounding of class as a product of unpaid surplus-labor in the economic base of society, is rejected, for example, by Michael Hardt for its 'negative' stance toward the 'positive project to generate an ontology of ourselves and create a new social world' in common.[1] On this account, because ideology critique produces an authoritative knowledge of class as the exploitation of labor by capital and thereby explains why there can be no common while classes exist, it denies the 'autonomy of those it is aimed to help', and thus has no place in the process of social change.[2] Against the radical negation of the existing that comes with 'grasping things by the root' in exploited labor, as in Marx, Hardt argues that cultural theory should instead become more affirmative, by having 'the courage not only to speak the truth to and about ourselves but also to live in a way harmonious with that truth'.[3] The harmonious 'truth' of the autonomous subject is 'beyond critique', according to Hardt, because it 'seeks to change social life while being a part of it', rather than

---

1   Michael Hardt, 'The Militancy of Theory', *The South Atlantic Quarterly*, 110:1, Winter (2011), pp. 19–35 (p. 26).
2   Ibid., p. 26.
3   Ibid., p. 30.

    https://doi.org/10.11647/OBP.0324.12

'stand above the lives of others [...] as a vanguard'.[4] Thus, the problem with critique, in this framing, and precisely because of its insistence on producing class-consciousness of the objective material 'outside' of ideology lying in unpaid surplus-labor, is its ethical blindness to the desire of the other, who he represents as in 'voluntary insubordination' of global knowing.[5] In place of critique, which negates the ideological 'inside' by bringing to bear upon it the 'outside' of class that in actuality explains why the task of critique is to expose the false-consciousness of the economic, Hardt puts forward what he takes to be the more 'positive' idea that a 'new mode of life' comes from within, by a change in 'moral attitude' by anyone who so desires it.[6]

At a moment of growing class polarization, poverty, and un-/ underemployment in which ever vaster populations are excluded from all social goods, Hardt's framing of critique as the other of the spontaneous voluntarism of the multitude represents not a new social ethics of solidarity but rather a further privatization of knowledge for the benefit of the ruling class. Critique is necessary for connecting the poverty of the many, including their lack of class-consciousness, to the obscene levels of wealth of the few, in whose interest alone it is to privatize knowledge and celebrate the ignorance of the underlying material conditions of production. The rejection of critique in the name of defending the spontaneity of the multitude is, therefore, part of the larger ideological attack on critique-al knowing as the enemy of the people to make the workers more easily exploitable. By marking critique — which is an investigation of the underlying terms of the capitalist system which are foreclosed from common sense ideas and beliefs — as unethical, the anti-critique-al theory of the (post)humanities not only breaks with the historical role of critique-al thought in transforming social reality — because to do so requires confronting the powers that be — but theoretically underwrites the regressive populism of prideful ignorance which has now been legitimated as the official culture by Trumpism. On the terms of this regressive populism — which in fact is a product of a decades long ideological campaign by corporate institutions — the common sense idea of many rural workers that

---

4   Ibid., pp. 29, 33.
5   Ibid., p. 22.
6   Ibid., p. 31.

'immigrants' and the urban poor are the source of their social problems, for instance, should not be critiqued as a product of racist propaganda to deflect attention from the ongoing class war in the US, but should be, if not applauded, at least propitiated because it provides them with a feeling in common.

In the manufactured post-factual cultural environment, postcritique, which is really anti-ideology critique, has become the mantra of the (post)humanities advanced by the critical theorists themselves who appear as more reasonable than regular right-wingers because their opposition to critique takes the form of a defense of the common and all that is vital and redemptive in the culture against the rationalizing 'spirit' of capitalism (in Weber's sense). Against the disenchantment and re-enchantment with the spirit of capitalism that underwrites the agony of critique in the (post)humanities now, I argue that what is urgently necessary for transformative social change is to reconnect the spirit with its material body: the systemic exploitation of labor by capital that alone explains the roots of ideology and the necessity of critique as essential to the ongoing praxis of social change.

The dominant attack on ideology critique — whether from the right or the left, from above or below, in the academy or in the popular culture — relies on a sentimentality, which is itself the product of the anti-intellectualism of popular media, that makes complex thinking out to be the other of life itself. The result is to discourage inquiry into the root cause of critique in the social — where, as Marx says, 'critique [*Kritik*] represents a class' whose dehumanized condition stands as the 'ruthless critique of all that exists' — and to direct the focus instead to the alien appearance of critique in the everyday because of its defamiliarization of the 'normal' (in the Kuhnian sense) mode of sense-making.[7] The popular image of critique as a foreign disruption of normal, everyday life inverts the class basis of critique so that rather than it representing the side of the propertyless in the social struggles — the class, as Marx writes, who 'have no ideals to realize' but whose objective social

---

7   Karl Marx, 'Afterword to the Second German Edition of *Capital*', *Karl Marx/Frederick Engels: Collected Works*, 50 vols (Moscow: Progress Publishers, 1996), 35, pp. 2–20 (p. 16); Karl Marx, 'Marx to Ruge in Kreuznach', September 1843, *Karl Marx/ Frederick Engels: Collected Works*, 50 vols (Moscow: Progress Publishers, 1975), 3, pp. 141–45 (p. 142).

position in the division of labor itself stands as 'the negation of [the class] system' — it is instead turned into a cultural sign of the 'classy': a sign of social superiority and status rather than an act in solidarity with the oppressed.[8] The conflict over critique in the (post)humanities is thus really about opposed theories of class which are rooted in the daily conflicts of capitalism: Is 'class' a structure of exploitation, the unpaid surplus-labor inscribed in the workday, that necessitates critique because the profit system is 'based on the unconsciousness of the participants' who are subject to it, or, is 'class' simply a constantly shifting 'rhizomatic assemblage' (Deleuze) of desires that provides a sense of common belonging to the multitude 'beyond' capitalism?[9]

The class basis of anticritique in the (post)humanities is clarified by turning to the writings of Bruno Latour — which are widely credited along with those of Quentin Meillassoux, Graham Harman, and Claire Colebrook — with effecting a 'new materialist' turn in contemporary theory. Yet, what is taken to be material in the new materialism is a vitalist conception of life held immanently in common, by human and nonhuman alike, that opposes critique as 'correlationism', the analytical opposition of thinking and being.[10] On these terms, because being exceeds the conceptual, the object world cannot positively and reliably be known but only endlessly interpreted. According to Latour, the radical project of critique has 'run out of steam' because the binary organization of power that gave 'critique its steam and modernism its impetus' has been displaced by a new 'flat' world; a 'biological and cultural network' composed of 'billions of people and their trillions of [nonhuman] affiliates and commensals' collectively engaged in 'composing' a 'common world' with 'the certainty that this common world has to be built from utterly heterogenous parts that will never make up a whole'.[11] For Latour, this means that Thatcher had it right when she claimed

---

8   Karl Marx, 'Civil War in France', Address of the General Council of the International Workingmen's Association, 30 May 1871, *Karl Marx/Frederick Engels: Collected Works*, 50 vols (Moscow: Progress Publishers, 1986), 22, pp. 307–59 (pp. 335, 504).

9   Frederick Engels, 'Outlines of a Critique of Political Economy', *Karl Marx/Frederick Engels: Collected Works*, 50 vols (Moscow: Progress Publishers, 1975), 3, pp. 418–43 (p. 434).

10   Quentin Meillassoux, *After Finitude: An Essay on the Necessity of Contingency*, preface Alain Badiou, trans. by Ray Brassier (London and New York: Continuum, 2010).

11   Bruno Latour, 'An Attempt at a "Compositionist Manifesto"', *New Literary History*, 41. 3, (2010), pp. 471–90 (pp. 472, 474, 477).

'there is no such thing as a society' because the 'social' is constantly being reconstituted, whether by 'a new vaccine [that] is being marketed, a new job description [...] offered, a new political movement [...] being created, a new planetary system [...] discovered, a new law [...] voted, [or when] a new catastrophe occurs', as in each instance, he claims that 'we are no longer sure about what "we" means' as we are forced 'to reshuffle our conceptions of what was associated together because the previous definition has been made somewhat irrelevant'.[12] It is of course telling that on these terms, cultural theory must abandon even the 'mere invocation of the word capitalism' as a way to systematically connect and explain such cultural events as part of the global series of struggles over social resources: a fact which proves my larger point that without a concept of 'capitalism', as its beneficiaries and defenders well know, there is no class system to transform, and thus systemic change is invalidated in advance by an objectless proceduralism oriented on localities.[13]

Latour claims that because the proletariat has 'passed away' in the contemporary that the critique of capitalism has lost its 'political relevance' to make sense of the daily.[14] Leaving aside Latour's own correlationism here, in which theory must reflect the existing, in fact the direct opposite is the case and the reality that knowledge claims always reflect class is indicated by Latour's discourse itself. It is not because class no longer exists that Latour argues that the critique of capitalism no longer has relevance — if anything the proletariat has grown worldwide and the objective divide between the owning class and those compelled to sell their labor in order to live is undeniable — but because Latour, like other postcritique ideologues, has no interest in surfacing the contradictions of capitalism which leads him to deny the existence of, as he puts it in the mock tone of a conspiracy theorist, 'powerful agents hidden in the dark acting always consistently, continuously,

---

12 Bruno Latour, *Reassembling the Social: An Introduction to Actor-Network-Theory* (Oxford: Oxford University Press, 2005), pp. 5–6.

13 Bruno Latour, 'On Some of the Affects of Capitalism', lecture given at the Royal Academy, Copenhagen, 26 February 2014, p. 4, http://www.bruno-latour.fr/sites/default/files/136-AFFECTS-OF-K-COPENHAGUE.pdf

14 Bruno Latour, 'Why Has Critique Run out of Steam? From Matters of Fact to Matters of Concern', *Critical Inquiry*, 30, Winter (2004), pp. 225–48 (p. 226); 'Affects', p. 4.

relentlessly'.[15] This is clear when Latour at other moments reveals, despite his claims to the contrary, that critique of capitalism is more relevant than ever before, as when he acknowledges, for instance, what he takes to be the 'worrisome' and 'troubling' fact that a 'gullible sort of critique' of capitalism in which 'Everything is suspect... Everyone is for sale... And nothing is what it seems' has become so popular today.[16] His discourse itself thus inadvertently reveals that it is not because the proletariat has 'passed away' that critique has lost its 'political relevance' for him, but because critique threatens to become, as Marx argues, 'a material force when it has seized the masses', that is causing him to be concerned with critique and precisely because it delegitimates capitalism.[17]

Latour argues that critique represents the dominant today because by reducing 'matters of concern' to 'matters of fact' it marginalizes the voices of 'new unexpected actors' who 'make up their own theories of what the social is made of'.[18] In a parodic reversal, to be 'radical' now, he claims, means to 'abstain from falling into the trap of fighting a system' because it can only stabilize belief in capitalism, which '[l]ike God [...] does not exist'.[19] And yet, the narrative that the scientific critique of capitalism dominates over other voices is contradicted by Latour's own academic celebrity and the rewards accorded to his followers who are busy marginalizing critique-al culture in the academy and beyond. Rita Felski, for instance, a close supporter of Latourian descriptivism and phenomenalism in such texts as *The Uses of Literature* (2008), *The Limits of Critique* (2015), and *Critique and Postcritique* (2017), which argue that the historical enterprise of the critique of the literary as a mediation of extra-literary relations of power prevents literary studies from finding new aesthetic pleasures in the text and furthers cultural disenchantment with the literary tradition, was awarded a 4.2 million dollar grant to further apply Latour's anti-critique-al arguments to literary studies.[20]

---

15 'Critique', p. 230.
16 Ibid., pp. 229–30.
17 Karl Marx, 'Contribution to the Critique of Hegel's *Philosophy of Law*. Introduction', *Karl Marx/Frederick Engels: Collected Works*, 50 vols (Moscow: Progress Publishers, 1976), 3, pp. 175–87 (p. 182).
18 *Reassembling*, p. 22.
19 'Affects', p. 10; *The Pasteurization of France*, trans. by Alan Sheridan and John Law (Cambridge: Harvard University Press, 1993), p. 173.
20 Lorenzo Perez, 'UVA English Professor Lands Large Danish Grant to Explore

Such projects are so richly rewarded not because of a need to 'save the literary tradition' but because the humanities remains the last redoubt of critical intellectual culture and are thus under increasing social attack by the ruling class which, in times of systemic crisis, is unwilling to tolerate any opposition to its rule. Anti-critique is the umbrella under which the critical humanities of the twentieth century is dismantled in order to ensure a twenty-first century anodyne Arnoldian 'disinterested criticism' of social reenchantment by the dominant ideology.

Critique, in the Latourian discursive universe, because of its 'gesture' of exposing a 'true world of realities lying behind a veil of appearances' has 'the immense drawback of creating a massive gap between what [i]s felt and what [i]s real' that authorizes a 'totalitarian' conception of society as a system.[21] On this reading, the only 'good' interpretation is therefore one embedded in the local domain which accepts without question that the 'actors […] have their own elaborate and fully reflexive meta-language' and 'know very well what they are doing'.[22] Yet this is, as I have suggested, a populist rhetoric which in fact denies knowledge of class exploitation to social actors and blocks access to any 'outside' to the hegemony of ruling class culture which actually shapes people's supposedly 'spontaneous' beliefs, values, and feelings. The celebration of the 'popular' as an index of the freedom of the self-determination of ideas by people themselves is a mechanism by which not only is the denial of access to intellectual resources and independent and critical thought to the masses underwritten, but this denial is itself then put forward as their means to empowerment.

In the end, the current onslaught of the discursive purging of the critique of capitalism from the humanities is not ideologically very far from how Republican operatives in this country argue for purging the words 'capitalism' and 'class' from public discourse as contrary to the libertarian spirit of the people, or, from how Trump surrogates defend the falsifications of their leader from critique by arguing that they are not 'really lies, because facts themselves no longer exist' as 'everybody

---

Literature's Social Use', *UVA Today*, 25 March, 2016 news.virginia.edu/content/uva-english-professor-lands-large-danish-grant-explore-literatures-social-use [accessed 8 June 2024].

21 Latour, 'Compositionist Manifesto', pp. 474–5.
22 *Reassembling*, pp. 4, 30.

has a way of interpreting them to be the truth or not true'.[23] But the task of the humanities — if they are to live up to the urgent requirements of the present moment — is to resist the encroaching authoritarianism of this manufactured faux populism and take a stand on the unrelenting necessity of critique against the brutality of class. It is to resist the privatization of the social and the devolution of change into endless local processes cut off from their decisive relation to the global class system, which is now threatening the future of humanity itself. Latour, of course, knows this, and his response would no doubt be yet another ironic comment to suspend critique for the pleasure of the ruling class, as when he says, 'Thesis 11: Economists have hitherto only changed the world in various ways, the point is now to interpret it'.[24]

---

23   Chris Moody, 'How Republicans are being taught to talk about Occupy Wall Street', *Yahoo News*, 1 December 2011, http://news.yahoo.com/blogs/ticket/republicans-being-taught-talk-occupy-wall-street-133707949.html; Max Greenwood, 'Trump's Lies Aren't Lies Because "There's No Such Thing" As Facts Anymore, His Surrogate Says', *Huff Post News*, 1 December 2016, https://www.huffpost.com/entry/trump-surrogate-claims-no-facts_n_58408f8ee4b0c68e047fd952.
24   'Affects', p. 10.

13.
Covid

The global COVID-19 pandemic is not a causeless 'event', nor a return of repressed 'nature', but the intensification of the underlying conflict between the global organization of labor and private ownership for profit. Millions have lost their jobs and health care as companies downsize or go bust from what was not only a foreseeable but foreseen global health problem because of an economy that puts profits before needs. Such a crisis would not have been allowed to occur in a centrally planned socialist society run by the workers, who are becoming all too aware of the dangers posed by the commodification of human needs for profit. And yet, the revelation of this basic economic truth in the wake of the pandemic is occulted by the post-al left, who use an 'event-al' logic that disconnects effects from their underlying causes lying in the exploitation of labor by capital, to make the pandemic seem a break from the 'normal' order rather than its inevitable result.

The War Against the Virus is a Class War

Alain Badiou, for example, who in his 'new communist' writings turns orthodox Marxist theory into a 'State-fiction' that tries to contain 'the rupture of the revolutionary event' (35) defined as the 'aleatory, elusive, slippery, evanescent dimension' of the 'political real', now says that the pandemic has revealed 'a major contradiction of the contemporary world', showing how the global 'mechanisms of Capital' exceed the power of any one nation-state.[1] And yet, confronted by a social reality that pressures his belief that social transformation occurs as a result of

---

[1]   Alain Badiou and Peter Engleman, *Philosophy and the Idea of Communism*, trans. by Susan Spitzer (Boston and New York: Polity Press, 2015), pp. 35, 239; Alain Badiou, *The Communist Hypothesis* (New York: Verso Books Books, 2010), p. 247; Alain Badiou, 'On the Epidemic Situation', *Verso Blog*, 23 March 2020, https://www.versobooks.com/blogs/4608-on-the-epidemic-situation.

    https://doi.org/10.11647/OBP.0324.13

the spontaneous eruption of events rather than by the revolutionary praxis of workers who have acquired global class-consciousness, he cynically dismisses the idea that the epidemic situation might be the 'founding event of an unprecedented revolution' on the grounds that the connection between ending capitalism and 'the extermination of a virus remains opaque'. Instead, using 'simple Cartesian ideas', he declares that the pandemic is 'a nature-society intersection', between 'ill-kept markets that followed older customs' in Wuhan, China in which at 'a certain moment the virus found itself present, in an animal form itself inherited from bats, in a very dense popular milieu, and in conditions of rudimentary hygiene', and, 'a planetary diffusion of this point of origin borne by the capitalist world market'. In other words, what one learns from Badiou's cynical viral ontology is that this crisis is not a cause for revolution because the 'traditionally' regulated market (of the cultural other) is its cause and thus future prevention simply requires more 'hygienic' regulations.

Leaving aside the dubious science behind Badiou's tabloidy rhetoric, this is how Badiou's 'event-al' logic simply reinscribes bourgeois common sense as the limit of knowing by disconnecting the social and political effects from their underlying economic causes.[2] In place of an analysis which uncovers the historical and material conditions which produce pandemic, Badiou ontologizes these now causeless effects as novel 'events' that emerge spontaneously and without class-conscious direction as a disruption of the existing. This is why he says without a trace of irony that while the cause of the crisis is not an unprecedented event, it is still 'event-al' in that while its cause remains 'opaque' ('a certain moment the virus found itself present in an animal') it has 'transversal' effects ('planetary diffusion of this point of origin borne by the capitalist world market').[3] In other words, the 'real' can only be known at the level of its effects and the causal world-in-itself is 'absent'. On this logic, the event-al origins of the virus are, at best, only known in their local manifestations and therefore cannot be connected to the global logic of capitalism inscribed in the law of value.

---

2   Jon Cohen, 'Wuhan seafood market may not be source of novel virus spreading globally', *Science*, 26 January 2020, https://www.science.org/content/article/wuhan-seafood-market-may-not-be-source-novel-virus-spreading-globally.

3   'On the Epidemic', n. pag.

The pandemic, however, should be understood as fundamentally an indictment of the global capitalist system. Leaving aside the fact that zoonotic epidemics have and will break out in more regulated markets — just look at the numerous well-documented violations of New York City's 'wet markets' — the conditions found in Wuhan are not due to 'older customs' or Badiou's thinly veiled racist pandering about 'dangerous dirtiness' and 'rudimentary hygiene' in China.[4] Rather, the conditions there are due to emerging contradictions between the tremendous productivity of labor in China — which is resulting in urbanization and development on a historic scale — and the introduction into the country of the most modern forms of 'market regulation' that are designed to keep the costs of labor in China low in order to attract the biggest capitalist firms of the global North. Economics, to spell it out, is not about 'markets', which is where commodities are exchanged after they have been produced from exploited labor, but the mode of production. Market regulations are merely 'rules' for distributing the surplus-value added to the commodity by the labor-power of workers into the hands of the biggest transnational capitalists, and their implementation is determined by their effects on the rate of profit. Making the cause of the crisis seem like a contingent local event, as Badiou does, fails to explain why the commodification of nature for profit, no matter how it is regulated, always serves the law of value which puts profit before need. While advances in science, medicine, technology, and agriculture make it possible for everyone in the world to have access to safe (and nutritious) food, the commodification of food production means that profit always comes before safety. As Badiou echoes the imperialists' displacement of their own failed response to the pandemic on the 'ill-kept' food markets in Wuhan, even workers in the United States, the most advanced of capitalist markets, are also subject to deplorable working conditions while food-borne illnesses are on the rise and are said to 'cost' the US economy $3 billion dollars a year.[5] The connection

---

4   'Not Just China, New York Too Has Over 80 "Wet Markets" That Sell & Slaughter Live Animals', *india.com*, 3 April 2020, https://www.india.com/news/world/not-just-china-new-york-too-has-over-80-wet-markets-that-sell-slaughter-live-animals-3989281; 'Origin of 2009 H1N1 Flu (Swine Flu): Questions and Answers', *CDC.gov*, 25 November 2009, https://www.cdc.gov/h1n1flu/information_h1n1_virus_qa.htm.

5   Laura Reiley, '2018 saw the most multistate outbreaks of foodborne illness in

between ending the pandemic and ending capitalism that Badiou says is too 'opaque' because it violates his 'simple Cartesian ideas' is not a more or better regulated capitalism, but the replacement of the anarchy of capitalist market regulation with socialist economic planning according to need not profit. And the only class that is materially positioned so as to advance such a global revolutionary project is the working class, led by workers who have become 'socialist theorists', in other words, the workers 'of every country' who 'bring to the front the common interests of the entire proletariat, independently of all nationality' because 'theoretically, they have over the great mass of the proletariat the advantage of clearly understanding the line of march, the conditions, and the ultimate general results of the proletarian movement'.[6]

Because Badiou has established his leftist credentials by defending the 'idea of communism' (which is just an idealist desire for abstract equality in his discourse), he has to disguise his support of capitalism under the guise of 'new communism'. This he does by, on the one hand, cynically mouthing that President Macron 'is correct [...] the state is compelled [...] to undertake practices that are [...] more authoritarian [...] while remaining within the established social order', while, on the other, claiming that in order to effectively 'manage the situation', French imperialism is 'integrating the interest of the class whose authorised representative it is with more general interests'.[7]

How to explain Badiou's faith in the bourgeois state as guarantor of the 'general interest' given that it stands in direct contradiction to his own 'event-al' theory that the state cannot reconcile 'two into one' because it must subsume 'the truth of the collective' under some 'identitarian assignation' of a 'racial or sexual [...] or [...] social status' nomination?[8] It is because Badiou's 'new communist hypothesis', in which all radical

---

more than a decade, CDC says', *The Washington Post*, 25 April 2019, https://www.washingtonpost.com/business/2019/04/25/cdc-releases-its-annual-report-card-foodborne-illness-did-not-have-passing-grade.

6   V. I. Lenin, 'What Is To Be Done?: Burning Questions of Our Movement', *V. I. Lenin Collected Works*, 45 vols (Moscow: Progress Publishers, 1977), 5, pp. 347–529 (p. 384); Karl Marx and Frederick Engels, 'The Manifesto of the Communist Party', *Karl Marx/Frederick Engels: Collected Works*, 50 vols (Moscow: Progress Publishers, 1976), 6, pp. 477–519 (p. 497).

7   'On the Epidemic', n. pag.

8   Alain Badiou, *Metapolitics*, trans. by Jason Barker (New York: Verso Books, 2005), pp. 81, 93–94.

politics are 'event-al', is really a way to make bourgeois apologetics seem 'radical'. How else to understand his dismissing the revolutionary communist idea of turning the pandemic into the 'founding event of an unprecedented revolution' as merely the 'apocalyptic' rhetoric of 'revolutionaries' while still embracing bourgeois hegemony as the precondition for making an 'epidemic interlude' necessary for thinking about 'new figures of politics, on the project of new political sites, and on the trans-national progress of a third stage of communism'?[9]

It might be laughable that the philosopher of the event, in encountering what is by his own parameters an 'event', declares it uneventful. But, it is a manifestation of the wider left's abandonment of revolutionary theory and praxis, the consequences of which have been devastating for the struggle to abolish the class relations that prioritize profit over social need.

Badiou's empty radicality is the event-al replication of market logic at the level of ideas. It argues for the spontaneous 'desire' for the 'new' that emerges out of an 'interlude' from the normal made possible by the well-regulated background provided by the violent dictatorship of capital. What makes the 'interlude' as well as the 'normal' possible of course is the ongoing exploitation of labor, the disruption of which is precisely what is causing the crisis of capitalism Badiou dismisses as the 'apocalyptic' rhetoric of 'revolutionaries'.

Mourning in America, with Judith Butler

The COVID-19 pandemic has, among other things, provided American intellectuals with a new political opportunity to affirm the order of things while criticizing it. This has, of course, always been their main strategy: to criticize capitalism's culture from the left and thus acquire ethical and political authority for leaving its economic order intact.

The pandemic has provided a unique cultural target: it has become almost routine for the left friends of capital to say that communities of color have suffered more from the pandemic and the suffering shows that there is a need for a new direction in social justice. The communities of color in the left narrative suffer more, in other words, because race is

---

9   'On the Epidemic', n. pag.

the determining factor in who is affected by the pandemic and who gets care. But communities of color do not exist in an economic vacuum: they are affected more not because of race (although that is not irrelevant), but they suffer more because of lack of resources — from loss of work, to absence of health care, to lack of information about the pandemic, to..., to simply the lack of inexpensive disposable masks. The communities of color suffer not because of race but because of class.

To make my argument more inclusive, more explaining of the American social relations now, I will read the article by Judith Butler, 'Why Donald Trump will never admit defeat'.[10] Here Butler updates her anti-transformative social theory, the basic elements of which she articulated in her essay, 'Merely Cultural'.[11] In that essay she argued that class is not the primary source of social relations but race is. Class, she argued, is 'lived' (i.e., it is basically a subjective fact) through 'race'.[12] In her article in *The Guardian* she reiterates this idea by writing that COVID-19 is not a class issue that affects all workers who must work to live and lack workplace protections and health care, but a racial one as 'communities of color are most adversely affected' because 'white supremacy has now resumed an open place in US politics'.[13]

In this familiar narrative, which appears under different signatures across the spectrum of corporate media outlets, the class politics of the pandemic are racialized and the recognition that white working class people die in the same way and for the same reasons as workers of color — because the 'war against the virus' is a class war and, as in every country, the needs of the owning class take precedence over the needs of the working class — is taken to be a denial of the difference of black lives that underwrites an hysterically racist fear of whites 'being "replaced" by black and brown communities, by Jews'.[14] Butler's 'solution' to the social inequality she has racialized is to psychologize it and in a pop-Freudian language she says that whites must learn to properly 'mourn'

---

10   Judith Butler, 'Why Donald Trump will never admit defeat', *The Guardian*, 20 January 2021, https://www.theguardian.com/commentisfree/2021/jan/20/donald-trump-election-defeat-covid-19-deaths.

11   Judith Butler, 'Merely Cultural', *New Left Review*, I/227, January-February (1998), pp. 33–44.

12   Ibid., p. 38.

13   'Donald Trump', n. pag.

14   Ibid., n. pag.

the 'historical reality' of the death of white supremacy and give up the 'political fantasy' it represents. What is considered 'social justice' here is ending discrimination in the market, in other words, the equalization of the conditions of exploitation, which is how the left friends of capital serve to maintain the basic class oppression of workers by owners whose property allows them to extract profit from their unpaid surplus labor.

But clearly Butler's own argument perpetuates the 'fantasy' of 'white supremacy' by psychologizing it as a racist refusal to face the 'reality' of the death of whiteness. Neither 'blackness' nor 'whiteness' are ontological conditions (essences), but are produced historically under specific material relations through which they come to appear as 'natural' and essential justifications for unequal access to the conditions of life. Unequal access to social wealth between whites and blacks in the US, for example, as evidenced in the unemployment rates and family income of these groups, among other things, are due not to 'extra-economic' factors such as 'white supremacy', but due to the economics of production for exchange in which technological innovation cheapens the value of labor by putting workers in competition with each other over fewer jobs at less pay. The cause of the disparities of outcomes in the market is not explained by race but by the rule of profit over production which insures that not everyone will have access to the means to live.

The difference between the employed and unemployed workers that is historically produced by the mechanism of exploitation is used by pro-capitalist intellectuals to explain (away) the appropriation of social wealth by the owners from its primary producers, the multicultural working class, by deflecting attention onto how the wealth is unequally distributed among the workers as 'cultural capita' (Bourdieu), or, more commonly, lifestyle differences. Although racial difference is physically apparent, it is not natural but social and no longer has 'any distinctive social validity' when 'all are instruments of labour, more or less expensive to use'.[15] Cheap labor has always been racially stigmatized under the property relations of capitalism irrespective of the skin color of the workers so as to keep wages at subsistence levels and block the political solidarity of the workers against the owners. This is why revolutionary

---

15   Karl Marx and Frederick Engels, 'The Manifesto of the Communist Party', *Karl Marx/Frederick Engels: Collected Works*, 50 vols (Moscow: Progress Publishers, 1976), 6, pp. 477–519 (491).

Marxists have always argued that 'labor cannot emancipate itself in the white skin where in the black it is branded'.[16]

Because the social labor of workers is appropriated by property owners in the form of profit and workers are forced to compete with each other for access to wages to live, not all people can be provided with jobs, despite the democratic promise of equality and opportunity for all. The capitalist system therefore requires an explanation for why, despite the inability of everyone to receive the same opportunity, the wages-system is still the best possible system. Such an apologetic 'explanation' must be grounded in an 'extra-economic' reason for it to justify the class structure of the wages-system, and, in effect, it must blame the workers for the failures of capitalism. Race is one such non-explanatory 'explanation' for why, in a society where there is no objective reason everyone's needs for health care, housing, physical and cultural sustenance, etc., cannot be met, there is yet mass hunger, mental and physical suffering, and millions go houseless, and which instead gives the nonsensical cause that some are more deserving than others because they are made of better 'stuff'. This 'stuff' is the ontological 'matter' whose origin is made 'extra-economic' in bourgeois theory — whether the essentialized 'blackness' of the afro-pessimists (Saidiya Hartman, Frank Wilderson), or, the mysterious 'objects' of the object-oriented ontologists (Graham Harman, Timothy Morton), or, the microbial 'actants' of the transspeciesists (Bruno Latour, Donna Haraway) — to argue for the incoherence of social explanation.

The extra-economic 'matter' that is supposed to immunize capitalism from critique by explaining away its inequalities as natural differences has changed in form historically: from being the 'spiritual' matter of a 'heart' devoted to a god against which some hearts have hardened in the early modern period, to the 'biological' matter that shaped one's physical being as more 'evolved' for survival in the late nineteenth century, to the 'cultural' matter of 'values' as manifest in communal practices that constitute pride in one's identity, as in Butler's (post)modern writings, to the 'vital' matter of today's (post)humanists in which identity is made out to be an effect of a desire immanent to the transspecies commons

---

16   Karl Marx, 'The Working Day', Chapt. 10, *Capital. A Critique of Political Economy*, vol. I, *Karl Marx/Frederick Engels: Collected Works*, 50 vols (Moscow: Progress Publishers, 1983), 35, pp. 239–43 (p. 305).

that one is expected to 'affirm' or be branded as a 'speciesist' enemy of all those historically 'excluded' by Western anthropocentrism. The 'extra-economic' matter that is meant to elude reduction to the calculus of value by the logic of capital has at every turn reflected that logic in how it divides the social into conflicting moral orders and cultural identities and occulted the base-ic economic arrangements (class) that explain the material history of humans in relation to nature.

'White supremacy' is not a shared 'fantasy' that makes white people 'feel' different from non-white people, as Butler's outdated culturalist framing makes it out to be, but the ideology of a ruling class that can no longer afford to justify its rule as being universally good and so must resort to the violence and authoritarian ideology historically most associated with fascism. The fascist coup attempt of January 6 was after all bankrolled by capitalists and composed of the petty bourgeoisie — 'business owners' and those with 'white-collar jobs [...] CEOs, shop owners, doctors, lawyers, IT specialists, and accountants' — who oppose the 'lockdowns', masks, and social distancing as 'communism' because such measures limit their ability to live off the exploitation of wage workers.[17] Fascism of course is not an aberration of capitalism but one of its most brutal extensions that emerges when the regular periodic crises of capitalism threatens to turn the working people against capitalism, as evidenced by the renewed interest in socialism and Marxism since the 2007–08 crash and even more so during the COVID-19 crisis in the growing strike wave around the world. As Butler's essay shows, however, it is much easier and popular in bourgeois media to pin the fascist tail on the ignorant white (m)asses who have not read enough cultural theory (Freud) and therefore do not know how to properly manage their emotions and need to be trained to do so, rather than critique the roots of fascism in the logic of capital. It alleviates the need to address the social relations which allow the exploitation of the labor of the other and which naturalize it by naturalizing the other's difference.

---

17   Rebecca Ballhaus, Alexandra Berzon, and Shalini Ramachandran, 'Jan 6 Rally Funded by Top Trump Donor, Helped by Alex Jones, Organizers Say', *The Wall Street Journal*, 1 February 2021, https://www.wsj.com/articles/jan-6-rally-funded-by-top-trump-donor-helped-by-alex-jones-organizers-say-11612012063; Robert A. Pape and Keven Ruby, 'The Capitol Rioters Aren't Like Other Extremists', *The Atlantic*, 2 February 2021, https://www.theatlantic.com/ideas/archive/2021/02/the-capitol-rioters-arent-like-other-extremists/617895.

Recently when Butler has turned to address Marx's theory of class, which it has become impossible to ignore any longer, she makes Marx speak Freud to justify her performative theory of 'class' as 'lived' (race).[18] She hollows out Marx's theory of class as the exploitative social relation inscribed in the production process by turning the proletariat, which is the 'special and essential product of modern industry' that explains the source of profit and the end of capitalism, into the 'precariat', which is a merely descriptive sociological category for 'the collective for whom work is elusive, temporary, and debt has become unpayable'.[19] Here again cultural differences among workers that have arisen in the market are used to obscure the social being of the proletariat as the propertyless class which must sell its labor for wages to live so as to increase the value of capital. Despite what Butler says in defense of critical theory against Latour et. al. in this essay she reconfirms their anti-critique-al social theory with her own descriptive cultural theory which remains on the surface of the social as 'lived' while refusing to inquire 'into the hidden abode of production', what Latour dismisses as 'the deep dark below'.[20] One of the consequences of her rejection of Marx's critique-al theory, which explains the experience of oppression in relation to its roots in the daily exploitation of working people, is a surface-al theory of capitalism. For example, in 'Capitalism Has its Limits' she argues that because 'the virus demonstrates that the global human community is equally precarious', it shows that the 'limits' of capitalism are 'spatial' (i.e., demographically discriminatory).[21] There is in short no core problem with capitalism as the root cause of inequality in production relations (class), only local problems in its unequal distribution of outcomes in the market (race). The unequal distribution of 'life chances on the market' (Weber) do not of course have an extra-economic source in ideology ('white supremacy'), but an economic cause in the logic of exploitation — the law of profit — of class relations. The

---

18 Judith Butler, 'The Inorganic Body in the Early Marx', *Radical Philosophy*, 2.06, Winter (2019), pp. 3–17.

19 'Manifesto', p. 494; Butler, 'Early Marx', p. 10.

20 Karl Marx, *Capital, A Critique of Political Economy*, vol. I, *Karl Marx/Frederick Engels: Collected Works*, 50 vols (Moscow: Progress Publishers, 1983), 35, p. 186; Bruno Latour, 'Why Has Critique Run out of Steam? From Matters of Fact to Matters of Concern', *Critical Inquiry*, 30, Winter (2004), pp. 225–48 (p. 229).

21 Judith Butler, 'Capitalism Has its Limits', *Verso Blog*, 30 March 2020, https://www.versobooks.com/blogs/4603-capitalism-has-its-limits.

end of 'whiteness' that results from the equal immiseration of whites alongside non-whites in the US will not end racial injustice, which is a means to regulate the workforce among competing nation-states to insure the global supremacy of capital over labor. The cultural form of social inequality has and will change, so long as its function in the totality to maintain class rule remains. Racial justice therefore demands international socialist revolution, as Marx was the first to argue.

At the core of Butler's recourse to universal precarity and mourning lessons is the ontologizing of 'loss' that is produced in the relations of wage labor. The only way to adequately respond to the present crises, she suggests, is to accept the loss of 'white privilege' as part of the wider 'precarity' of 'all'. There are those who 'accept' loss and appropriately 'mourn' and those who do not and are subsequently filled with resentment. Loss, however, is not ontological nor psychological but historical and material. People lose family and friends unnecessarily due to COVID-19; they lose the ability to pay their mortgages and feed their families; they are deemed 'essential' workers and then denied the basic safety equipment to protect themselves as they save the lives of others, etc. — not because loss is the condition of life, as in religious discourses, but because life is conditioned by material relations (property). The people who lose are working people; what they lose is an outcome of their relation to the means of production. Under the relations of wage labor, the lives of those who do not own the means of production are put at the material mercy of those who do. Butler's gospel of mourning preaches acceptance of economic precarity to the white working class as the precondition for social justice among the already equally immiserated.

Butler appeals to the ontology of loss because that which 'appears in the worker as an *activity of alienation, of estrangement*, appears in the non-worker as a *state of alienation, of estrangement*'.[22] To make material loss the state of loss is of course to affirm the negation of the lives of working people, which is another way of saying that to insist that the most radical way to address race is to treat it experientially and affectively is to perpetuate the conditions of racism lying in the division of workers

---

22   Karl Marx, 'Economic and Philosophical Manuscripts of 1844', *Karl Marx/Frederick Engels: Collected Works*, 50 vols (Moscow: Progress Publishers, 1975), 3, pp. 229–346 (p. 282).

into productive (currently employed) and unproductive (contingently unemployed) on a global scale.

Butler's story in *The Guardian* about the racial fragility of the white precariat is part of the manufacturing of the new affective condition of capital in crisis. Her writing absorbs class relations into moods and feelings, and reproduces class divisions in its mood(y) cultural politics. It divides the social not according to a material logic (class, exploitation, profit, etc.), but according to an immaterial desire (affect, values, race,…), between those who attend to and 'affirm' their moods (i.e., accept 'loss' by reaffirming faith in bourgeois democracy's commitment to diversity) and those who refuse to do so, 'negate' them and become 'destructive'. In the new moody cultural divisions, mourning, joy, and reconciliation represent the progressive moods, while anger is a right-wing mood. There is no place for class critique in Butler's woke capitalism except as a form of white *ressentiment* (Nietzsche). No basis, in other words, for grasping class as an objective social category that explains the universal interest of the global working class in ending their common exploitation by capital.

Butler explains Trump's fascism in terms of Freud (libidinal economy) not Marx (political economy) because Freud psychologizes class contradictions and turns them into the human condition beyond history, beyond transformation and preaches abnegation and mourning, which sells at a time of crisis when millions are forced into poverty, hunger, and death so as to profit the few.

But affect has in Butler's writings become even more spiritual — less 'bodily' and more 'ambient' — it is 'in the air' she says — the 'atmospheric' condition of 'spirit' that mediates the social. She has moved from *Bodies That Matter* (1995) — the matter of language and signification — to bodies that feel — the matter of sensation and impression — now that the old discourse theory has lost its cachet with the fading of neoliberalism. 'Matter' of course represents the 'outside' of the social as 'beyond' comprehension and transformation, the bare reality with which we must learn to live. What it denies is the social as historically produced through labor from which is manufactured the 'limits' of the 'real' in ideology.

The discursive play of what 'matters' that traces itself through Butler's writings are badges of class distinction that are taken as signs that she is a 'subtle' and, above all, a 'non-dogmatic' thinker which proves that she can be reliably called upon to provide the up-to-date ideological cover for what capital requires. Under the sclerotic measures proposed by the Biden administration to monetize solutions to the health and economic crisis through deficit financing while 'raising' the minimum wage to poverty levels under the most diverse cabinet the US has ever seen, this means representing such measures as socially progressive acts of 'healing' the nation through the public performance of cultural reconciliation while failing to do what is minimally required to prevent the loss of millions of lives, by, for example, instituting a federally guaranteed jobs program and federal lockdowns at full pay while raising taxes on those grown obscenely wealthy from their immiseration of the workers.

Butler's writings on the pandemic therefore display her class allegiance by refusing to penetrate to the root of the issues in class — the economics of the pandemic and the fascist policy of 'herd immunity', actually 'social murder', favored by capital as a whole to force the workers back to work — and instead set the requisite tone of mourning and melancholia in the lite tabloid style of the popular genre of 'woke' storytelling.[23]

What explains Butler and Badiou's reversals is of course nothing new — they are what Lenin called the 'hysterical impulses' of the 'petty bourgeois driven to frenzy by the horrors of capitalism'.[24] The true communist response to the opportunistic vacillations of these left thinkers can be found in Lenin's slogan against the first world war:

'TURN THE WAR [AGAINST THE VIRUS] INTO A CIVIL WAR!'

---

23   Kamran Abbasi, 'Covid-19: Social murder, they wrote—elected, unaccountable, and unrepentant', *BMJ*, 372:n314, 4 February 2021, https://www.bmj.com/content/372/bmj.n314.

24   V. I. Lenin, '"Left-Wing" Communism – An Infantile Disorder', *V. I. Lenin Collected Works*, 45 vols (Moscow: Progress Publishers, 1966), 31, pp. 17–118 (p. 32).

14.
Communism

'The final variant is called Communism' — meme

The 'Return' of Marx

The global economic crash of 2007–08 — as well as the subsequent government bailouts of the dominant bourgeois institutions responsible for it and their continued commitment to a program of social austerity in its wake around the world since — has dramatically revealed what is normally hidden behind the everyday glare of consumerism in the global North: capitalism systematically sacrifices the livelihood of the many to serve the interests of a privileged few. Suddenly millions were forced to confront the fact that capitalism is failing in exactly the way Marx and Engels predicted in *The Manifesto of the Communist Party* because it is 'incompetent to assure an existence to its slave within his slavery, because it cannot help letting him sink into such a state, that it has to feed him, instead of being fed by him'.[1] As more and more people are finding that capitalism is unable to 'assure their existence' even in the midst of the superabundant wealth of the western democracies, it is no surprise to see that 'class' has once again returned to the popular lexicon and there is a renewed interest in Marx, Marxism, and communism as workers begin to struggle to make sense of their immiserated lives and to investigate why the political means to address these conditions is so severely delimited.[2] However, as I will explain, the contemporary engagement with Marx is predominantly 'writerly' as it reinterprets

---

1   Karl Marx and Frederick Engels, 'The Manifesto of the Communist Party', *Karl Marx/Frederick Engels: Collected Works*, 50 vols (Moscow: Progress Publishers, 1976), 6, pp. 495–6.

2   Jason Barker, 'Happy Birthday, Karl Marx. You Were Right!', *The New York Times*, 30 April 2018, https://www.nytimes.com/2018/04/30/opinion/karl-marx-at-200-influence.html.

    https://doi.org/10.11647/OBP.0324.14

class as a spectral presence in the circuits of the daily, rather than a serious engagement with the 'speecherly' truth of class found in Marx, i.e., class as a matter of how 'the mode of production of material life conditions the general process of social, political and intellectual life'.[3]

What will be of particular importance in the contemporary encounter with the intellectual and political legacy of Marx today, I argue, is to engage with Marx's speecherly theory of communism found in his speeches on the Paris Commune of 1871. Marx in his addresses, circulars, and correspondence during and after the Commune speaks as a founding leader of the first international workers' party and the most intransigent defender of the seizure of State power by the Parisian proletariat. In them he focuses his critique of the Commune on what he calls the 'infantile' communism of the anarchists, whom he holds as largely responsible for its defeat because of how their doctrine of the 'equality of classes' led them to support class collaborationist policies and to subvert the international solidarity required for its success.[4] An engagement with Marx's critique of the infantile communism of the anarchists is necessary because if the emerging social movements of the twenty-first century are to abolish class inequality, they need to counter the 'writerly' conception of communism dominant on the North Atlantic left today in the writings of the 'new communists' (such as Badiou, Negri, and Žižek, to name a few), which subtract class from communism so as to affirm an egalitarian idea of the 'common' without the need of revolution. The 'new communism' is writerly because by subtracting class from communism it turns communism into 'an ideal to which reality will have to adjust itself', as Marx and Engels put it in *The German Ideology*, rather than grasp it as 'the real movement that abolishes the present state of things'.[5] The communism of Marx and Engels, by contrast, is 'speecherly' in that it emerges out a close examination of *'what the proletariat is*, and what, in accordance with this *being*, it will historically be compelled to do', given the irreconcilable antagonism between owners and workers due to the exploitation of wage-labor by

---

3   Karl Marx, 'Preface' to *A Contribution to the Critique of Political Economy, Karl Marx/ Frederick Engels: Collected Works*, 50 vols (Moscow: Progress Publishers, 1987), 29, pp. 261–65 (p. 263).

4   See note 459.

5   Karl Marx and Frederick Engels, 'The German Ideology', *Karl Marx/Frederick Engels: Collected Works*, 50 vols (Moscow: Progress Publishers, 1976), 5, p. 49.

capital.[6] As I will explain, the speecherly, because it reveals how conflicts over the social real are produced out of the dialectical series of class struggles over social wealth, is the suppressed other of the readerly/ writerly opposition found in Roland Barthes' theorization.[7] What I am calling Marx's speecherly communism, I argue, is the other of Barthes' 'readerly' transparency, on the one hand, which takes the meaning of communism to be fixed in its relation to the real in the form of a Platonic Ideal of 'equality', or, on the other, of 'writerly' inventiveness, in which communism is made into a floating signifier whose relation to the real is purely contingent, the effect of a desire. It is in Badiou's writings most of all that communism today is dissolved in the play of the readerly/ writerly in opposition to its speecherly connection with class, as in Marx's speeches on the Paris Commune.

The speecherly in Marx is a matter of the way in which Marx intervenes in the daily struggles and demonstrates in concrete practice why the materialist theory of class as the motor of history is necessary to change it. Marx's speecherly approach is evident, for example, in such early texts as *The German Ideology*, where he and Engels oppose to the common sense of class as inequality, which cannot see beyond the obviousness of the proletariat as 'a crowd of scrofulous, overworked and consumptive starvelings', its connection to 'the necessity, and at the same time the condition, of a transformation both of industry and of the social structure'.[8] These different visions of the proletariat as self-evident object ('class-in-itself') versus dialectical agent ('class-in-and-for-itself') testify to a class conflict at the level of theory, between a 'readerly' approach to class as a conventional understanding of 'a structure of signifieds' that 'imitates' an original, and a 'speecherly' one that moves beyond the common sensical appearance by laying bare the material cause that produced it.[9] As an example of the readerly approach to class, take the way 'working class' is normally represented in the US with its association with such signifiers as 'blue collar, manual labor,

---

6   Karl Marx and Frederick Engels, 'The Holy Family, or Critique of Critical Criticism', *Karl Marx/Frederick Engels: Collected Works*, 50 vols (Moscow: Progress Publishers, 1975), 4, pp. 5–211 (p. 37).
7   Roland Barthes, *S/Z*, trans. by Richard Miller (Oxford: Blackwell Publishing Ltd., 1974).
8   'German Ideology', p. 41.
9   Barthes, *S/Z*, p. 4.

low skill', and, as is more often the case today, 'white, rural, poor, Trump supporters', or, as one right-wing commentator put it, 'dysfunctional, downscale communities' that are 'in thrall to a vicious, selfish culture, used heroin needles' and 'cheap theatrical Bruce Springsteen crap', who as 'economically negative assets' are 'morally indefensible' and 'deserve to die'.[10] On Barthes' theorization, such a text is readerly as it seeks to close down interpretation by attaching the meaning of working class to a 'principle of determination', or, a 'logic' that 'can be authoritatively declared to be the main one', which is of course in the above example, the logic of the market ('economically negative assets').[11] The writerly, by contrast, seeks to liberate the 'galaxy of signifiers' from 'any constraint of representation (of imitation)' to show how the meaning of the text is 'reversible' and 'indeterminable'.[12] In the example of the right-wing commentator above, this would entail our abandoning the impulse to 'accept or reject the text' so as to instead appreciate the sheer 'pleasure of writing' on display, which even despite the writer's conservative moral panic about the culture of the working class yet represents it as 'the image of a triumphant plural' that exceeds and resists closural meaning ('vicious', but into Springsteen, 'selfish', but sharing needles, 'dysfunctional', yet needing to be put down), which just goes to show that 'nothing exists outside the text' and its meaning is undecidable.[13] The writerly in the end is not opposed to the readerly as they are simply different 'interpretations' of the real that disconnect the meaning of the text from its speecherly source of production in the historical series of class conflicts over meanings.[14]

On Marx and Engels' theorization in *The German Ideology*, as the 'readerly' description of class is intellectually and politically indefensible because of its deviation from the 'ideals' of the culture, it necessitates a middling 'writerly' mode of addressing class by re-interpreting it, in the way, for example, they demonstrate how Feuerbach, despite his

---

10   Kevin D Williamson, 'Chaos in the Family, Chaos in the State: The White Working Class's Dysfunction', *National Review*, 17 March 2016, https://www.nationalreview. com/2016/03/donald-trump-white-working-class-dysfunction-real-opportunity-needed-not-trump.
11   *S/Z*, pp. 5–6.
12   Ibid., pp. 5–6.
13   Ibid., pp. 4–6.
14   Ibid., p. 5.

materialist inversion of Hegel himself, 'relapses into idealism' when confronted with the material reality of the proletariat and 'take[s] refuge' in the "higher perception" that the proletariat finds its "compensation in the species".[15] On the writerly logic, when Feuerbach describes the working class as 'a crowd of scrofulous, overworked and consumptive starvelings', what he is actually doing in a moment of sheer writerly pleasure is de-inscribing the connection of the material to the Hegelian Idea so as to re-inscribe the meaning of class by attaching it to his own materialist concept of the species.[16] Marx, conversely, implicates the writerly in supporting the readerly against the speecherly when he argues in his *Theses on Feuerbach* that the 'species' is in reality an effect of 'the ensemble of the social relations' and not an abstract 'essence'.[17] It was to oppose the 'writerly' negation of idealism in post-Hegelian German philosophy for the way it conflated critique with the agent of change by merely 'interpreting the existing world in a different way' rather than inquiring into 'the connection of German philosophy and German reality' that led Marx to formulate his famous eleventh thesis about how the philosopher's only 'interpret' the world rather than struggle to change it.[18] The way to actually change class entails a speecherly negation of the one-sided writerly negation of the readerly common sense appearance of class as 'inequality' that is committed to speaking the truth about '*what the proletariat is*, and what, in accordance with this *being*, it will historically be compelled to do'.[19] The speecherly approach to class represents the dialectical negation of the readerly/writerly, which explains why grasping the real of class requires understanding how the 'aim and historical action' of the proletariat is inscribed 'in its own life situation as well as in the whole organisation of bourgeois society today'.[20] Class, in short, is a material relation of economic exploitation that generates political and ideological antagonism not simply social inequality and cultural difference.

Although Marx's commitment to the speecherly as a critique of the

---

15   'German Ideology', p. 41.
16   Ibid., p. 41.
17   Karl Marx, 'Theses on Feurebach', *Karl Marx/Frederick Engels: Collected Works*, 50 vols (Moscow: Progress Publishers, 1975), 5, pp. 3–8 (p. 4).
18   'German Ideology', p. 30.
19   Marx and Engels, 'Holy Family', p. 37.
20   Ibid., p. 37.

readerly/writerly mode of sense making is evident even in his early writings, it is most forcefully manifest in his 'speeches', i.e., in the many circulars, addresses, pamphlets, meeting minutes, and international correspondence that Marx generated in his organizational engagement with the day to day struggles of the proletariat that make up roughly half of the fifty volumes of Marx and Engels' *Collected Works*. It is in these texts more so than the more transdisciplinary theoretical writings with which Marx and Engels are canonically identified — produced during periods when workers' militancy was low — that we can see most clearly demonstrated the need for the speecherly in the daily struggles so as to counter the readerly/writerly in the workers' movement and produce the class solidarity required for international communism. Feuerbach's theory of class is readerly: he takes the passivity of the proletariat as a self-evidency in need of no explanation, and because he abhors its misery, attempts to negate it in the only way that he can as an isolated individual, through a writerly act of re-interpretation. This is understandable given that Feuerbach was writing before the emergence of a politically organized working class movement capable of challenging bourgeois hegemony. In this period Marx and Engels themselves could only argue for the speecherly in general terms as the negation of philosophical idealism and advocate for 'making the critique (*Kritik*) of politics' tantamount to 'participation in politics' by identifying critique with ongoing '*real* struggles' on the grounds that consciousness of the meaning of political action is something that must be acquired, 'even if [the world] does not want to'.[21] In the mid-1840s Marx had already grasped the need for the speecherly so that the masses would not blind themselves to the content of their own movement, but he had not yet formulated the necessity of a revolutionary organization especially dedicated to this task in an ongoing way, which would not be until the founding of the Communist League in 1847, and more significantly, the First Communist International, the International Workingmen's Association, in 1864. In between these dates lies the continental revolutions of 1848 and the discovery that the proletarian revolutions of the nineteenth century would not simply extend or

---

21   Karl Marx, 'Marx to Ruge in Kreuznach', September 1843, *Karl Marx/Frederick Engels: Collected Works*, 50 vols (Moscow: Progress Publishers, 1975), 3, pp. 141–45 (p. 144).

complete the bourgeois revolutions of the eighteenth in the way implied by Hegel's idealist dialectic in which political events are symbolically codified and philosophically ratified only through their historic repetition. In *The Eighteenth Brumaire of Louis Bonaparte* of 1852, what Hegel 'forgot to add', Marx argues, is that historical repetition is not necessarily the raising of the spontaneous act of the initial event to the principle of 'self-consciousness' on its reoccurrence, but inevitably 'farcical' because of how it mystifies in the imaginary of the actors the material causes of their actions lying in the existing social relations.[22] It is an irony of history, on Marx's account, that precisely during times of 'revolutionary crisis' when 'men seem engaged in revolutionising themselves and things, in creating something that has never yet existed' that they 'anxiously conjure up the spirits of the past [...] in order to present the new scene of world history' in a 'time-honoured disguise and [...] borrowed language'.[23] The irony is due to the fact that the bourgeois revolutions Marx is discussing have had to 'dull themselves to their own content' as the capitalist relations they sought to establish entail the subjugation of the working masses whose emancipation they must promise so as to enlist their enthusiastic participation. Marx therefore argues that, by contrast, the social revolutions of the nineteenth century will have to 'critique themselves constantly' so that the workers may draw the necessary lesson that the content or object of their revolutionary movement to abolish class far outstrips the revolutionary phrases of the past that have promised but failed to do so.[24] It is not until Marx's speecherly engagement with the Paris Commune of 1871 that we see Marx put this historical lesson into practice in his critique of anarchism for its regression back into the writerly idealism of socialism's infancy through its preaching of 'the equality of classes'.

In Marx's speeches on anarchism given during and after the Paris Commune, later published as *Fictitious Splits in the International* (1872), he argues that the anarchist interpretation of communism as the 'equality of classes' represents a return to the infantile phase of the socialist movement, when the proletariat 'had not yet developed sufficiently

---

22 Karl Marx, 'The Eighteenth Brumaire of Louis Bonaparte', *Karl Marx/Frederick Engels: Collected Works*, 50 vols (Moscow: Progress Publishers, 1979), 11, pp. 99–197.

23 Ibid., p. 104.

24 Ibid., p. 106.

to act as a class' and could only produce 'sectarian movements' that formed around 'certain thinkers [who] criticise social antagonisms and suggest fantastic solutions [...] which the mass of workers is left to accept, preach, and put into practice'.[25] By contrast, Marx argues, the 'real organisation of the working class for struggle', represented by the First International — especially in its role as public defender of the Paris Commune at 'a time when the old world is seeking a way of crushing it' — stands 'in inverse ratio' to the 'socialist sectarianism' of its early days.[26] The communism of the anarchists is 'writerly', on Marx's account, because it takes 'what all socialists understand... anarchy' to mean — that 'the aim of the proletarian movement, the abolision of classes, ha[ving] been attained, the power of the State, which serves to keep the great majority of producers under the yoke of a numerically small exploiting minority, dissappears' (*Fictitious Splits* 121) — and inverts its meaning into a 'children's primer' about the 'equality of classes' (Marx to Bolte 252) that would dissolve the International into 'small *"groupes"* or *"communes"*, which [...] are to form an "association", but not a state'.[27] Because the anarchists reverse the meaning of communism from being 'the aim of the proletarian movement' arising out of its class antagonism with capital, into an ideological commitment to an ideal of 'equality' as 'the most infallible means' of smashing the power of capital, it is 'abstentionist by [its] very nature', according to Marx, and thus eschews 'all real action, politics, strikes, coalitions, or, in a word [...] any unified movement'.[28] In short, the anarchists put forward a writerly reinterpretation of communism as a sectarian belief in equality as an abstract ideal against Marx's speecherly understanding of communism as arising out of the concrete needs of the proletariat in active struggle 'to set free the elements of the new society with which the old collapsing

---

25 Karl Marx and Frederick Engels, 'Fictitious Splits in the International', Private Circular from the General Council of the International Working Men's Association, January-March 1872, *Karl Marx/Frederick Engels: Collected Works*, 50 vols (Moscow: Progress Publishers, 1988), 23, pp. 79–123 (pp. 106–7).

26 Ibid., pp. 121–22; Karl Marx, 'Marx to Friedrich Bolte in New York', 23 November 1871, *Karl Marx/Frederick Engels: Collected Works*, 50 vols (Moscow: Progress Publishers, 1989), 44, pp. 251–59 (p. 252).

27 'Fictitious Splits', p. 121; 'Marx to Bolte', p. 252; 'Marx to Engels in Manchester', 20 June 1866, *Karl Marx/Frederick Engels: Collected Works*, 50 vols (Moscow: Progress Publishers, 1987), 42, pp. 286–87 (p. 287).

28 'Fictitious Splits', p. 106.

bourgeois society itself is pregnant'.[29] Class is what explains this infantile regression to the pre-scientific sectarian socialism, according to Marx.

In order to contrast Marx's speecherly communism as 'the *real* movement which abolishes the present state of things' with the writerly communism of the anarchists for whom communism is an egalitarian '*ideal* to which reality will have to adjust itself', it is necessary to clarify that the '*continual struggle*' of scientific socialism against the 'socialist sectarianism' within the International undertaken by Marx and Engels — both 'at the *Congresses*, but far more in the private dealings of the General Council with the individual sections' — is a class struggle.[30] In class terms, the struggle reflected the fact that the International admitted 'people of all sorts [...] communists, Proudhonists, unionists, commercial unionists, co-operators, Bakuninists, etc.', men and women of 'wildly differing opinions' who all aim 'for the complete emancipation of the working classes'.[31] It was precisely because the International represented a common, a trans-class plurality, that the 'lawyers, journalists, and other bourgeois doctrinaires' were able to use it 'to organize not in accordance with the requirements of the struggle it [the proletariat] is daily and hourly compelled to wage, but according to the vague notions of a future society entertained by some dreamers'.[32] Marx's speeches on the Paris Commune reveal this continual class struggle carried out by the General Council of the International 'against sects [...] which sought to assert themselves within the International against the real movement of the working class' by preaching such 'childish' nonsense as 'abstention from politics' and the '*equality of classes*'.[33] In a speech at a conference in London in September 1871, Engels argued that the 'abstention from politics' put forward by the 'professional sectarians' in

---

29 Karl Marx, 'Civil War in France', Address of the General Council of the International Workingmen's Association, 30 May 1871, *Karl Marx/Frederick Engels: Collected Works*, 50 vols (Moscow: Progress Publishers, 1986), 22, pp. 307–59 (p. 335).

30 'German Ideology', p. 49; 'Marx to Bolte', p. 252.

31 'Engels to Carlo Cafiero in Barletta', 1–3 July 1871, *Karl Marx/Frederick Engels: Collected Works*, 50 vols (Moscow: Progress Publishers, 1989), 44, pp. 161–65 (pp. 162–63).

32 'Marx to Paul Lafargue in Madrid', 21 March 1872, *Karl Marx/Frederick Engels: Collected Works*, 50 vols (Moscow: Progress Publishers, 1989), 44, pp. 346–52 (p. 347); Frederick Engels, 'The Congress of Sonvillier and the International', January 1872, *Karl Marx/Frederick Engels: Collected Works*, 50 vols (Moscow: Progress Publishers, 1988), 23, pp. 64–70 (p. 66).

33 'Marx to Bolte', p. 255.

the International would put the party in an 'impossible' position given the 'real life, political oppression [...] imposed on [the workers] by the existing governments... particularly after the Paris Commune' when 'all the European governments [were] united against it'.[34] Abstention from politics in the context of an ongoing class struggle, in short, amounted to 'bourgeois politics'.[35] In other words, the anarchist tendency organized by Bakunin within the International represented the bourgeois influence within the vanguard party of the workers, doing the work of the police by destroying what makes the workers' party a threat to the bourgeois State in the first place — its organization of the international proletariat from a 'class-in-itself' into a 'class-for-itself' conscious of the revolutionary necessity of taking power and using it to emancipate society from the rule of capital so as to establish a classless society.[36]

The 'speecherly' Marx is the Marx who directly addresses the concrete needs of workers in their daily struggles and connects the issues of the day with the historic revolutionary tasks of the class as a whole to abolish the economic exploitation of wage-labor/capital

---

34　'Congress of Sonvillier', p. 68; Frederick Engels, 'On the Political Action of the Working Class', Handwritten Text of the Speech Delivered at the Conference Session on 21 September 1871, *Karl Marx/Frederick Engels: Collected Works*, 50 vols (Moscow: Progress Publishers, 1986), 22, pp. 417–18 (p. 417).

35　Ibid., p. 417.

36　Not only did the anti-authoritarianism of the anarchist opposition within the International advance the 'class terrorism' (Marx, 'Civil War', p. 329) of the bourgeoisie against the workers' vanguard from within, it also destroyed the Commune itself because, 'if there *had been* a little more authority and centralization in the Paris Commune, it would have triumphed over the bourgeois' ('Engels to C. Terzaghi', p. 293). As Engels explains, the anarchist opposition to 'authority and centralization' as 'two things to be condemned outright' shows 'a superstitious reverence for the state' ('Introduction to *Civil War in France*', p. 190) by people who 'think they have taken quite an extraordinary bold step forward when they have rid themselves of belief' (p. 190) in it. 'Those who say this either do not know what a revolution is, or are revolutionaries in name only', he concludes ('Engels to C. Terzaghi', p. 293). It is this that explains for Engels that which is 'the hardest thing to understand' about the Commune — 'the holy awe' with which the revolutionaries 'remained standing respectfully outside the gates of the Bank of France', which would have 'been worth more than ten thousand hostages' in pressuring the Versailles government in favor of peace with the Commune' (Introduction, p. 187; see also, 'Marx to Domela-Nieuwenhuis'). For Marx, what defeated the Commune was the anarchist dogma of the 'equality of classes' that enticed the Central Committee of the National Guard, dominated by Blanquists and Proudhonists, to forego such measures they feared would '*start a civil war*' and caused them to 'surrender[ ] power too soon, to make way for the Commune' ('Marx to Kugelmann' p. 132).

relations and advance the communist revolution in which the 'the free development of each is the condition for the free development of all'.[37] As Lukács argues in his study of Lenin's thought, Marx's speecherly interventions also demonstrate the 'actuality of the revolution' and how 'the development of capitalism turned proletarian revolution into an everyday issue'.[38] It is in the speecherly mode of address that Marx, to put it another way, demonstrates the unity of theory and practice, specifically the unity of his materialist theory of the self-negation of capitalism through the working out of its own law of value and the dialectic of the workers' movement that forms and is shaped by the inevitable systemic crises. I focus on Marx's speecherly interventions within the contestations of the International following the defeat of the Paris Commune of 1871 — the first successful revolutionary seizure of power by the modern proletariat to build a classless society — because I believe that these texts provide us with necessary lessons capable of guiding the new working class struggles of the twenty-first century from their currently reactive, defensive, and reformist orientation onto the revolutionary path of building international communism. Marx's speeches on the Commune and their speecherly mode of address are especially important today as workers are once again in a militant state to challenge capitalism while lacking a revolutionary class theory to do so because of the dominance of the 'writerly' view of class. As the popular anti-austerity movements around the world show — from Occupy to Bernie Sanders' 'political revolution' in the US, from Syriza in Greece and the Indignados in Spain, from Nuit Debout in France to Die Linke in Germany — workers are in a militant state to challenge capitalism at a time when 'all the *material* necessary for the social revolution' is available, while what is lacking is the '*spirit of generalization and revolutionary ardour*' to overthrow it.[39] These movements are guided by a 'readerly' view of class as 'inequality' that merely (re)describes what is already well known, joined to a 'writerly' theory of how to change it — a 'horizontalism', or, 'commons-ism', that suppresses class

---

37 'Manifesto', p. 506.
38 Georg Lukács, *Lenin: A Study on the Unity of his Thought* (New York: New Left Books, 1970), p. 13.
39 Karl Marx, 'Confidential Communication', *Karl Marx/Frederick Engels: Collected Works*, 50 vols (Moscow: Progress Publishers, 1985), 21, pp. 112–24 (p. 118).

consciousness in order to build coalitions around popular demands for reform that maintain the global system of wage slavery at a time of crisis. The resurgence of Left populism today has already proven itself to be unequal to the tasks of revolutionary working class politics, not only in places like Venezuela, Brazil, and Argentina, but also in Greece, Spain, and France. In all these countries the Left was brought to power by a popular wave of struggles against capitalist austerity only to be co-opted by the bourgeois state to divert the insurgent workers to the path of peaceful reform and acceptance of ever more austerity. These failures have now strengthened the rise of the reactionary Right, a 'global Trumpism', that in an economic populist rhetoric that (re) writes class as cultural pride seeks to scapegoat the cultural 'other' as responsible for the crisis.[40] It is in Marx's speeches to the International that we can find an answer to this contradiction as to why the working class fails to make the revolution despite the widespread popularity of anti-capitalist and pro-socialist sentiment due to the dominance of bourgeois ideology in the workers' movement. Against the readerly/writerly view of class dominant today, I argue that it is necessary to turn to Marx's speecherly one to advance global social(ist) struggle. By focusing mostly on Badiou, I will contrast Marx's speecherly approach to communism with the writerly theory of the anarchists, which is once again dominant today in the textwares of the 'new communists'. In the writerly new communism, class-consciousness is voided of the material antagonism inscribed in the productive base of society between capital and labor and class resignified as merely a discursive difference and lifestyle politics.

Badiou's Writerly Marx(ism)

Marx's speecherly engagement with the Paris Commune has once again become an important proof text for thinking about communism today. One reason for this is because of the way that Alain Badiou has made them exemplary for defending the 'Idea of Communism' against the 'dominant imperative in the world today' to 'live without

---

40   Mark Blyth, 'Global Trumpism', *Foreign Affairs*, 15 November 2016, https://www.foreignaffairs.com/articles/2016–11–15/global-trumpism.

an Idea' as a 'mere human animal' following the 'Statist constraints of mere survival'.[41] The idea of communism Badiou locates in Marx's speeches on the Commune is a matter of how, for him, they renounce the 'impure language of the State' by remaining true to the 'fundamental randomness' of the 'evental origins' of the communist Idea.[42] According to Badiou, Marx's speeches 'admit' as their own real this 'aleatory, elusive, slippery, evanescent dimension' and 'invent a new political subject' that by implication 'ruptures' Marx's materialist theory of history found in such texts as *Capital* and *The Manifesto of the Communist Party*.[43] As in Benjamin's writings on Marxism that seek to bring dialectics to a 'standstill', Badiou's reading too seeks to 'blast a specific era out of the homogenous course of history' so as to make communism into a cause-less event, 'a messianic cessation of happening'.[44] On this messianic logic, Badiou strikes from the annals of communism the founding texts of Marxist theory that have guided the speecherly praxis of communist militancy in the daily struggles against the dominance of bourgeois ideology in the workers' movement on the grounds that by using language in an explanatory way, they identify the Real (the logic of History) and the Idea (Communism) and thus deny the need for Symbolic 'subjectivation'.[45] What Badiou is alluding to as Marx's 'impure' language is the way that the *Manifesto* argues that because 'the development of Modern Industry [...] cuts from under its feet the very foundation on which the bourgeoisie produces and appropriates products [...] its fall and the victory of the proletariat are equally inevitable', or, in the words of *Capital*, the 'expropriators are expropriated [...] by the action of the immanent laws of capitalistic

---

41 Alain Badiou, *The Communist Hypothesis* (New York: Verso Books, 2010), pp. 231, 233, 252. Badiou's defense of the 'Idea' of communism is part of his broader philosophical project to rethink dialectical materialism as 'materialist dialectic' that figures the real as a set of 'generic multiplicities' that 'no linguistic predicate allows [...] to be discerned' and 'no proposition can explicitly designate' that therefore 'exist as exceptions to what there is' (*Logic of Worlds*, pp. 4, 6).

42 *Communist Hypothesis*, pp. 244, 255.

43 Ibid., p. 247; Alain Badiou and Peter Engleman, *Philosophy and the Idea of Communism*, trans. by Susan Spitzer (Boston and New York: Polity Press, 2015), p. 32.

44 Walter Benjamin, *The Arcades Project*, trans. by Howard Eland and Kevin McLaughlin (Cambridge: Belknap Press, 1999), p. 865; Walter Benjamin, 'Theses on the Philosophy of History', in *Illuminations* (New York: Schocken, 1977), p. 263.

45 *Communist Hypothesis*, p. 239.

production itself'.[46] According to Badiou, Marx's historical materialist theory of communism as arising from the self-negation of capitalism through its own laws of motion represents the imposition of an authoritarian 'State-fiction' that attempts to 'maintain the theory of the structure under the rupture of the revolutionary event' that, conversely, Marx remains true to in his speeches on the Commune.[47] For Badiou, the State as a material force doesn't actually exist: it is a 'fictional structure' or 'symbolic narrative' with the function of containing awareness of the 'political real' whose 'fundamental randomness' represents for him the 'evental origins' of what is taken to be true.[48] By making the idea that a classless society is a necessary consequence of class society, Badiou argues that Marx in his historical and theoretical writings constructs a 'State fiction' that identifies the Real and Idea and, by implication, reveals the 'unsuitability' of the 'Party-form' and the 'Socialist State' for the communist cause.[49]

Badiou, in other words, constructs a binary according to which Marx's speeches of the Commune are to be celebrated for their embrace of the aleatory event, while his theoretical writings are read as rigid impositions on the real. Marx's speeches are thus made the space of 'openness', the 'image of a triumphant plural' that is the writerly for Barthes, while his writings are the space of 'closure', the readerly 'constraint of representation (of imitation)'.[50] Such binaries and their associated values may seem at first glance to be a reversal of the Derridean framework in which speech is associated with metaphysical presence ('logocentrism') and writing is associated with the space of free play and plurality.[51] Badiou's binaries are, in actuality, a reiteration of the class logic of what Derrida calls 'writing' and what Barthes calls the 'writerly'. Badiou's treatment of Marx's speeches, I will demonstrate, updates the (ideo)logic by which what becomes privileged is that which exceeds the order of the conceptual. In short, behind what has become

---

46   'Manifesto', p. 496; Karl Marx, *Capital, A Critique of Political Economy*, vol. I, *Karl Marx/Frederick Engels: Collected Works*, 50 vols (Moscow: Progress Publishers, 1983), 35, p. 750.

47   *Communist Hypothesis*, p. 239; *Idea of Communism*, p. 35.

48   *Communist Hypothesis*, pp. 238–39, 244.

49   Ibid., p. 257.

50   *S/Z*, p. 5.

51   Jacques Derrida, *Of Grammatology* (Baltimore: Johns Hopkins University Press, 1998).

known as the 'new communism' is a theory of language that, like all forms of idealism, severs consciousness from material relations in order to make consciousness (the Communist Ideal) the basis of history, and to free up 'difference' (as in the neo-/liberal discourse of freedom from the State) from determination by class. The speaking subject, for Badiou, is a subject whose agency is equated with an act of pure inventiveness, a voluntarist act that breaks from the historical material series as in the bourgeois imaginary of the subject as existing above and beyond its material determinations. Such a notion of the subject is of course necessary to justify the coercion of wage-labor/capital relations under the guise of a voluntary exchange between equal persons so that the consequences of class society appear as merely personal successes and failures that cannot be systemically explained. Marx's speeches on the Commune offer not only an urgently needed intervention into the bourgeois re-writing of communism as a post-revolutionary movement in defense of difference, randomness and the event, but also develop a materialist theory of language and consciousness that explains the dialectic of agency from out of its material socioeconomic preconditions.

By emptying Marxism of its materialist theory of history, and re-writing it as a Statist constraint upon the Idea of Communism, Badiou seeks to defend it as an exception to what he calls the reigning 'democratic materialism' that reduces life to 'bodies and languages' without access to 'truth'.[52] What Badiou assumes, as do conservatives everywhere, is that capitalism is a cultural logic of homogenization which reduces the multiplicity of life to brute matter, thereby eliminating its value in-itself. In fact, it is this same reactionary logic which, as I have marked, leads Badiou to reject all past forms of communism as 'state fictions' because of what he deems their overly reductive theory of the social as divided by class. In contrast, he seeks to imbue matter with an immanent force of resistance to any and all 'reductive' theories of the social. In this sense, it becomes clear that what is meant by the 'material' in Badiou's 'materialist dialectic' has more in common with Barthes' idea of the 'writerly' text as 'the image of a triumphant plural' that militates against 'readerly' common sense than it does with Marx's theory of the material as class. Because of the way it voids materialism of its class base by equating

---

52 *Logic of Worlds*, pp. 3, 5.

the material with the uncontainable 'spacing' of language, Badiou's is a writerly idea of communism.

The way Badiou pluralizes Marx's writings into a multiplicity of voices in which the inventive literariness of Marx's speeches testifies to a desire to subtract the Commune from its class base follows Barthes' opposition of the 'writerly' to the 'readerly' code. The readerly code, according to Barthes, is that mode of intelligibility in which the text as a 'whole' possesses a value through a shared agreement between 'the producer of the text and its user, between its owner and its customer' as to its meaning.[53] The assumption here is that the 'literary institution' which circulates the text as a commodity requires that texts be thought to contain a singular meaning produced by the realist code of mimesis by representing a ready-made world with predetermined meanings that have already been produced.[54] Similarly, in Badiou's discourse, the 'readerly' Marx is a product of the 'contemporary consensus' brought about by the dominant 'democratic materialism' that reduces the 'plurality of languages' to a 'juridical equality' that 'aims to regulate all other languages and to govern all bodies' in a 'dictatorial and totalitarian' way.[55] In other words, what matters for Badiou is securing spaces of cultural playfulness and inventiveness of interpretation as acts of resistance within themselves. Badiou's opposing an 'inventive' or writerly Marx that uses language in a non-mimetic 'truth-full' way, as against a readerly Marx who explains the logic of capitalism by using language in an impurely mimetic and authoritarian way, relies on Barthes' ludic theory of signification in which the 'writerly' figures as an 'ideal text' that models a subjectivity freed of any regulative restraint on the pleasures of *'interpretation'*.[56] Rather than interpret the text in an Author-itarian way as 'a structure of signifieds' that 'imitates' an original, Barthes proposes that the writerly foregrounds the 'plurality' of meaning that constitutes the text as 'a galaxy of signifiers' that 'has no beginning' whose meaning is therefore 'reversible' and 'indeterminable' because 'nothing exists outside the text' on which to fix a 'principle of determination' as 'there is never a *whole* of the text' or a 'logic'

---

53 *S/Z*, pp. 4, 6.
54 Ibid., p. 4.
55 *Logic of Worlds*, p. 2.
56 *S/Z*, p. 5.

that 'can be authoritatively declared to be the main one'.[57] It is on the basis of this same writerly understanding of signification that allows Badiou to argue that Marx's speeches on the Commune make the Idea of Communism correlative with a non-totalizable 'multiplicity' that exceeds language and thus is engaged in the 'construction [...] of a new political subject' that would have 'universal value' for 'humanity as a whole', what he calls the 'generic [...] aim of a politics', whose presence and agency, because it is missing from Marx's scientific socialist theory, voids it of any positive knowledge of the real grounded in class such as is necessary to change it.[58] The voiding of Marx's scientific conception of communism as inscribed in the logic of class is thus made synonymous by Badiou with opposition to 'Statist constraints'.[59]

By saying Marx's theory is 'true' to the extent that it remains faithful to the *alea* of the real against which its explanatory grasp of history as class struggle is a 'State fiction', Badiou reveals his fidelity to the writerly Marxism that has become dominant since Derrida's *Specters of Marx*, which is predicated on pluralizing Marx into a multiplicity of 'voices' (following Blanchot in 'Marx's Three Voices') and dematerializing the social totality into a spectral 'hauntology' that mystifies class for the benefit of the owners.[60] Class, on this writerly logic, is made into a cultural difference of 'interpretations' over the real — of an 'event-al' discursive regime that is open to the other, versus a 'totalizing' one that reduces the other to the self-same — so that ending class is equated with the freedom of speech from any regulative restraint, rather than freedom from the exploitation of wage-labor by capital. Badiou's pluralization of Marx's speech into an 'impure fiction' on the one hand and 'purely inventive' on the other requires identifying the idea of communism with the language game of constructing a purified discourse subtracted of class, which actually explains language as 'an arena of class struggle'.[61] In its opposition to referentiality, Badiou's voiding communism of class

---

57   Ibid., pp. 5–6.
58   *Idea of Communism*, pp. 32, 45; *Metapolitics*, p. 81.
59   *Communist Hypothesis*, p. 252.
60   Jacques Derrida, *Specters of Marx: The State of the Debt, The Work of Mourning & the New International* (London and New York: Routledge, 1994); Maurice Blanchot, 'Marx's Three Voices', in *Friendship*, trans. by Elizabeth Rottenberg (Stanford: Stanford University Press, 1997), pp. 98–101.
61   V. N. Vološinov, *Marxism and the Philosophy of Language*, trans. by Ladislav Matejka and I. R. Titunik (Cambridge: Harvard University Press, 1993), p. 23.

echoes Paul de Man's linguistic objection to historical materialism as a
'poor read[ing] of Marx' that confuses the 'materiality of the signifier
with the materiality of what it signifies', or, in other words, 'linguistic
with natural reality [...] reference with phenomenalism'.[62] The point of
reading Marx on this writerly view is not to understand the world so as
to change it, but to interpret Marx's text as an 'allegory of reading' in
which the 'undecidability' of meaning is made synonymous with the
liberation of meaning beyond all Author-itarian codes.

The anti-dialectics of the writerly is indebted to Saussure's
synchronic theory of language as a self-enclosed system *'without positive
terms'* and the formal ahistorical opposition it maintains between
langue — language as a system of signs, the codes and conventions of a
culture — and *parole* — language as a speech-act.[63] Classical Aristotelian
poetics traditionally essentializes the speaking subject as the origin of
thought and reduces language to a kind of (passive) tool or medium
for the (active) communication of ideas. Derrida has foregrounded how
language is not a passive thing but the cultural condition of possibility
for all knowing and has argued that the experience of the speaking-
subject (parole) is on the one hand a category error — a signifier taken
to be a transcendental signified — and, on the other, the trace of a desire
that exceeds and haunts language as such (as the 'singular', 'unique',
or, a 'hope' to-come). However, the binary opposition of langue/
parole, regardless of which is taken to be the effect of the other, reifies
language from the labor process in which it is always a part — language
as 'practical consciousness', which is the forum where people become
aware of the class struggle and 'fight it out'.[64] Language is in actuality
a social medium that people use to reflect on the material outside of
language that exists independently of what they hope and desire it to be
so as to change it. And, because humans are divided into classes with
opposed interests we find that the way they use language to conceptualize
the real reflects their material conflicts of interest, either to mystify
the real so as to ideologically resecure the status quo, or, to critique

---

62   Paul de Man, *The Resistance to Theory* (Minneapolis: Minnesota University Press,
     1986), p. 11.
63   Ferdinand de Saussure, *Course in General Linguistics*, ed. by Charles Balley and
     Albert Sechehaye, trans. by Wade Baskin (New York: McGraw Hill, 1966), p. 120.
64   Marx and Engels, 'German Ideology', p. 44; Marx, 'Preface to *Contribution*', p. 263.

ideology and produce the knowledge necessary to make change. The recognition of language as praxical 'this-sided' relation to the world is what is speecherly in Marx, and it explains how 'speech' (the individual speaking body of *parole*) and culture (the forms of thought codified in *langue*) are produced by social labor. The speecherly, language as social praxis, is a transformative social process in which humans use sounds and images (signifiers) to conceptualize (signifieds) 'the ensemble of the social relations' so as to coordinate themselves to engage with and change their relation to the social totality.[65] As I will explain more fully below, in Marx's speeches on the Paris Commune, there is developed a dialectical theory of the material that layers the readerly/writerly with the speecherly dimension of language in such a way as to reveal how language is a revolutionary force capable of grasping the material outside of social praxis.

Against the ludic writerly Marx(ism) of Badiou I argue that Marx's speeches on the Paris Commune are neither readerly (mimetic) nor writerly (performative), but speecherly (explanatory) in how they use language to conceptualize the existing so as to practically explain how the workers alone are able to change it. It is the revolutionary value of the speecherly in Marx that I argue needs to be reactivated today against the return to Marx on the North Atlantic left as a messianic preacher for a merely heuristic idea of communism as an 'event-al' cause-less arrival in order to transform the emergent class struggles of the twenty-first century into revolutionary struggles for international communism.[66]

The Speecherly Marx(ism)

What I understand as Marx's 'speecherly' theory of communism requires analyzing how, specifically in his discussions on the Paris Commune, in the Addresses to the General Council of the International that were later published as *The Civil War in France*, he goes about addressing that 'sphinx'-like question that has proven 'so tantalizing to the bourgeois mind' — 'What is the Commune?'.[67] By engaging this

---

65 Marx, 'Theses', p. 4.
66 On messianic materialism see Chapter 7 and, for an example, see, Slavoj Žižek and Costas Douzinas, eds. *The Idea of Communism* (New York: Verso Books, 2010).
67 'Civil War', p. 328.

question, Marx is able to critique the 'multiplicity of interpretations' surrounding the Paris Commune so as to uncover its 'true secret' — that it was 'essentially a working class government' that set itself the task of 'work[ing] out the economic emancipation of labor'.[68] By posing the question 'What is the Commune?', Marx was opposing the dismissive 'readerly' account of the Commune that reduces it to the self-same as the terroristic other of civilization given by the monarchist Party of Order who could only see in its advent the end of 'family, religion, order and property'.[69] Marx's critique of the readerly, however, is not that it is insufficiently or disastrously mimetic, as Badiou would have it. To simply show how the reactionaries are wrong about the idea of communism would not amount to a critique, of course, and for Marx it is critique alone that 'represents [...] the proletariat' because 'it includes in its comprehension and affirmative recognition of the existing state of things, at the same time also, the recognition of the negation of that state' and thereby aligns itself with the only class 'whose vocation in history is the overthrow of the capitalist mode of production and the final abolition of all classes'.[70] What Marx therefore does in his speech on the Commune is to demonstrate how it represents a 'ruthless critique [*Kritik*] of all that exists' because of the way it laid bare 'the deeper under-currents of modern society' and exposed how the 'mulitplicity

---

68 Ibid., p. 334.
69 Ibid., p. 313.; The depiction of the communists as against family, religion, order, and property by the 'feudal, liberal, and police press' ('Fictitious Splits', p. 101) was the main way to culturally divide the workers to lower their wages and block their political organization as a class. Consider that the International Workingmen's Association, that under Marx's direction was most associated with the Commune in the public consciousness, was at that time in many ways the sole working class organization, functioning as a trade union in countries where they were illegal, as well as a mutual aid society (taking in refugees from the Paris Commune, e.g.) many years before social welfare services were adopted by bourgeois governments. It had also already proven its necessity to the workers' movement in practice by, for example, preventing foreign workers from being used as strike breakers in Britain, building support for national liberation in countries like Poland and Italy which had yet to emancipate the peasants from serfdom, as well as leading British textile workers (themselves dependent on the cotton trade) to oppose slavery during the American Civil War. By dividing the workers along cultural lines of religion and family values, the owners sought to destroy the global working class solidarity brought about by the First Communist International.
70 Karl Marx, 'Afterword to the Second German Edition of *Capital*', *Karl Marx/Frederick Engels: Collected Works*, 50 vols (Moscow: Progress Publishers, 1996), 35, pp. 2–20 (pp. 16, 20).

of interpretations [and] interests which construed it in their favour' failed to penetrate 'the surface of this tremendous historic event'.[71] Thus, against the terrified reaction to the Paris Commune by the Party of Order — 'But this is Communism, "impossible" Communism!' — Marx explains why, despite their being factually correct — 'Yes, gentlemen, the Commune intended to abolish that class-property, which makes the labour of the many the wealth of the few' — they are unable to grasp its historic material necessity.[72] Their failure to explain the Commune reflected their own class interest, as one of the effects of the Commune was indeed to expose the 'hideous face' of 'bourgeois civilization and justice' whose 'undisguised savagery and lawless revenge [...] comes out in its lurid light whenever the slaves and drudges of that order rise against their masters'.[73] But, Marx's critique does not stop there, as he encourages his working class audience to also consider the 'strange fact' that no sooner did the workers of Paris 'take the subject [of governance] into their own hands with a will' and at last concretely demonstrated how to go about 'uprooting the economical foundations upon which rests the existence of classes, and therefore, class rule', that all the 'tall talk and all the immense literature, for the last sixty years, about the Emancipation of Labour' of 'bourgeois-doctrinaires' arose in unison to mystify 'the deeper under-currents of modern society'.[74] These representatives of '"possible" Communism', he explains, speak for those 'members of the ruling classes who are intelligent enough to perceive the impossibility of continuing the present system' and have therefore 'become the obtrusive and full-mouthed apostles of co-operative production'.[75] If, on the one hand, Marx's critique of the fearful resistance to the speecherly as '"impossible" Communism' implicates the readerly mode of address in the class interests of the landlords, his critique of the '"possible" Communism' of the socialist literati, on the other, shows his opposition to the writerly attempt to contain the proletarian revolution to the maintenance of capitalism for the benefit of the bourgeoisie. Against their 'sectarian crotchets' to manage capitalism in crisis, Marx

71   'Marx to Ruge', p. 142; 'Civil War', p. 317, 334, 353.
72   Ibid., p. 335.
73   Ibid., pp. 348–49.
74   Ibid., pp. 317, 334, 336.
75   Ibid., p. 335.

put forward the revolutionary international interests of the proletariat
to abolish class society itself and argued that 'if co-operative production
is not to remain a sham and a snare' but a means 'to supersede the
Capitalist system' the co-operative societies must be united 'to regulate
national production upon a common plan' thus 'putting an end to the
constant anarchy and periodical convulsions which are the fatality of
Capitalist production'.[76] In a later circular from the General Council of
the International, Marx argued that while all socialists understand by
anarchy the 'disappearance' of 'the power of the State, which serves to
keep the great majority of producers under the yoke of a numerically
small exploiting minority', this required opposing Bakunin's messianic
idea of anarchism because of how it 'puts matters the other way around'
and turns communism into a 'fantastic phrase' in which the 'Abolition
of the State' requires maintaining 'anarchy in the proletarian ranks' by
dissolving the International 'into small *'groupes'* or *'communes'*, which in
turn are to form an 'association', but not a state' and limit themselves to
the local economic struggles with their employers (who were themselves
internationally coordinated).[77]

For Marx, the sphinx-like question 'What is the Commune?' does
not yield its 'true secret' to 'readerly' transparency, which can only see
in 'the surface of this tremendous historic event' an inverted reflection
of its own class prejudices, rather than how it has laid bare 'the deeper
under-currents of modern society'.[78] However, Marx also explains why
the Commune does not reveal itself to a 'writerly' approach either, as
he includes among the 'mulitplicity of interpretations [and] interests
which construed it in their favour' all the 'tall talk' of the socialist Left
who failed to grasp what is 'completely new' in the Commune because
of their fidelity to their own 'sectarian crotchets', such as the egalitarian
idea of communism put forward by the Proudhonian anarchists, echoed
today by Badiou, who only saw in the Commune a return to an 'older
[...] defunct form[ ] of life': the medieval Commune and its 'ancient
struggle against over-centralization'.[79] Marx's critique of the 'multiplicity
of interpretations' of the Commune is not done to 'void' it of all 'impure'

---

76   Ibid., pp. 335–6.
77   Ibid., p. 335; 'Fictitious Splits', p. 121; 'Marx to Engels', p. 287.
78   'Civil War', pp. 317, 334, 353.
79   Ibid., pp. 333–34, 336.

attempts to contain its 'evental truth', in the way Badiou claims he does, so as to 'invent' a new 'generic' communism. This is because, although Marx argues that the Commune was 'in no sense socialist', that the insurgent workers of Paris 'have no ideals to realize' — 'no ready-made utopias to introduce *par décret du peuple*' (by decree of the people) — their actions nevertheless 'set free the elements of the new society with which old collapsing bourgeois society itself is pregnant'.[80] The 'true secret' of the Commune for Marx is that it represented the 'dictatorship of the proletariat' — 'a working, not a parliamentary, body, executive and legislative at the same time' — made up of workers who had acquired 'full consciousness of their historic mission' to 'work out the economic emancipation of labor' for themselves.[81] By destroying the repressive State power 'which claimed to be the embodiment of [...] the nation itself' the Commune established the 'self-government of the producers' and had begun 'a series of historic processes' that would 'transform[ ] circumstances and men' thereby undermining the 'systematic and hierarchic division of labour' and thus ultimately 'class-rule itself'.[82] It was the 'expansive political form' of the Commune that created a 'completely new' form of 'working men's Government' — 'champion of the emancipation of labor' and 'emphatically international'— that led Marx to speak on behalf of the Parisian workers as the 'advanced guard of the modern proletariate' and to revise his own theory of revolution as well in its wake.[83]

---

80 Ibid., p. 335; Karl Marx, 'Marx to Ferdinand Domela-Nieuwenhuis in the Hague', 22 February 1881, *Karl Marx/Frederick Engels: Collected Works*, 50 vols (Moscow: Progress Publishers, 1987), 46, pp. 65–67 (p. 66);

81 Karl Marx, 'Marx to Joseph Weydemeyer in New York', 5 March 1852, *Karl Marx/Frederick Engels: Collected Works*, 50 vols (Moscow: Progress Publishers, 1983), 39, pp. 61–66 (p. 62); 'Civil War', pp. 331, 334, 336.

82 Ibid., pp. 328, 331–32, 335. The 'series of historic processes' that would undermine class rule included: 'the suppression of the standing army, and the substitution for it of the armed people'; 'universal suffrage'; 'public servants, magistrates and judges [...] to be elective, responsible, and revocable'; 'public service [...] at *workmen's wages*'; 'disestablishment and disendowment of all churches as proprietary bodies'; 'education [...] cleared of all interference of Church and State [and] freed from the fetters [of] class prejudice [...] made accessible to all'; 'abolition of the nightwork of journeymen bakers'; 'prohibition, under penalty, of the emploers' practice to reduce wages by levying upon their workpeople fines under manifold pretexts'; and 'surrender, to associations of workmen, under reserve of compensation [...] all closed workshops and factories' ('Civil War', pp. 331–32, 335, 339).

83 Ibid., pp. 333–34, 338, 354.

Marx's speeches on the Paris Commune are a marker for the revolutionary truth of Marxism that 'it is not the consciousness of men that determines their existence, but their social existence that determines their consciousness'.[84] It is on this principle that the speecherly for Marx is 'a historically dynamic, revolutionary force' that when applied to an assessment of the Paris Commune led him to conclude after close observation of its practices, and against the multiplicity of interpretations generated in its wake, that 'the class struggle necessarily leads to the *dictatorship of the proletariat*' and subsequently 'the transition to the *abolition of all classes* and to a *classless society*'.[85] By contrast, in the *The Manifesto of the Communist Party*, the transition from capitalism to socialism was initially conceived as 'winning the battle of democracy' by the proletariat using

> its political supremacy to wrest, by degree, all capital from the bourgeoisie, to centralise all instruments of production in the hands of the State, i.e., of the proletariat organised as the ruling class; and to increase the total productive forces as rapidly as possible

and so begin the process of abolishing class society.[86] What the Commune taught Marx was that the *Manifesto*'s conception that the working class could establish democracy by 'simply lay[ing] hold of the ready-made state machinery, and wield[ing] it for its own purposes' had become

---

84   'Preface to *Contribution*', p. 263.
85   Frederick Engels, 'Karl Marx's Funeral', *Karl Marx/Frederick Engels: Collected Works*, 50 vols (Moscow: Progress Publishers, 1989), 24, pp. 467–71 (p. 468); 'Marx to J. Weydemeyer', pp. 62, 65; In a speech at a public meeting in Amsterdam after the Hague Congress (September 1872), Marx gave his critical assessment of the Paris Commune, arguing that 'it fell because there did not simultaneously occur in all the capitals, in Berlin, in Madrid, and the rest, a great revolutionary movement linked with the mighty upheaval of the Parisian proletariat' (Stekloff, Chapter Fourteen). What 'we can learn [...] from the great example of the Commune of Paris', he concluded, was that '*The revolution must be the work of solidarised efforts*'. In a letter written contemporaneously with the events (April 1871) cited above, when Marx argued that it was the anarchist dogma of the 'equality of classes' that led the Central Committee of the National Guard, dominated by Blanquists and Proudhonists, to forego such measures they feared would '*start the civil war*' that caused them to 'surrender [ ] power too soon, to make way for the Commune' ('Marx to Kugelmann', p. 132), he echoes Engel's assessment that 'if there *had been* a little more authority and centralization in the Paris Commune, it would have triumphed over the bourgeois' ('Engels to C. Terzaghi', p. 293).
86   'Manifesto', p. 504.

outdated and had to be revised.[87] The brutal crushing of the Commune by the ruling classes showed that in order to realize democracy the workers needed to 'smash' (*zerbrechen*) the 'ready-made state machinery' and replace it with a workers' state guided by the principles of workers' self-governance to make the revolution 'permanent'.[88] It is precisely this materialist commitment to draw 'theoretical conclusions' that 'express, in general terms, actual relations springing from an existing class struggle, from a historical movement going on under our very eyes' that is speecherly in Marx and stands in stark contrast with the metaphysical idealism of the writerly approach of 'other working-class parties' whose 'ideas or principles [...] have been invented, or discovered, by this or that would-be universal reformer'.[89] It was because the International 'was established by the working men themselves and for themselves' rather than by 'radicals among the ruling classes' that Marx saw in it the opportunity to negate the negation of philosophy announced in Thesis Eleven decades prior — to 'change the world' rather than only 'interpreting' it — by 'entering into real struggles and identifying ourselves with them', by 'taking sides in politics', in other words, not with 'new doctrinaire principles' but by simply showing the world 'why it is struggling'.[90]

---

87 Karl Marx and Frederick Engels, 'Preface to the 1872 German Edition of the *Manifesto of the Communist Party*', *Karl Marx/Frederick Engels: Collected Works*, 50 vols (Moscow: Progress Publishers, 1986), 23, pp. 174–75 (p. 175).

88 'Marx to Kugelmann', p. 131; cf., V. I. Lenin, 'State and Revolution: The Marxist Theory of the State and the Tasks of the Proletariat in the Revolution', *V. I. Lenin Collected Works*, 45 vols (Moscow: Progress Publishers, 1968), 25, pp. 381–492 (pp. 411–22); Karl Marx and Frederick Engels, 'Address of the Central Authority to the League', March 1850, *Karl Marx/Frederick Engels: Collected Works*, 50 vols (Moscow: Progress Publishers, 1978), 10, pp. 277–87 (p. 281).

On 'permanent revolution' see Marx: 'While the democratic petty bourgeois wish to bring the revolution to a conclusion as quickly as possible, and with the achievement, at most, of the above demands, it is our interest and our task to make the revolution permanent, until all more or less possessing classes have been forced out of their position of dominance, the proletariat has conquered state power, and the association of proletarians, not only in one country but in all the dominant countries of the world, has advanced so far that competition among the proletarians in these countries has ceased and that at least the decisive productive forces are concentrated in the hands of the proletarians. For us the issue cannot be the alteration of private property but only its annihilation, not the smoothing over of class antagonisms but the abolition of classes, not the improvement of the existing society but the foundation of a new one' ('Address of the Central Authority', p. 281).

89 'Manifesto', p. 498.

90 Karl Marx, 'Record of Marx's Speech on the Seventh Anniversary of the

Marx's speecherly approach to the Commune is a matter of how a truly materialist theory of class, taken in the totality of its determinations, necessitates opposing all one-sided non-dialectical ideas about class as the 'event-al' rupture of dissonance from within homogenizing cultural formations. For example, Marx opposes both the descriptive readerly view of class, held by the anarchists, as 'autonomy' and 'freedom from below' on the one hand, and the performative writerly view of class, articulated by the Blanquists, as constituted 'from above', on the other.[91] Marx's speeches on the Commune thus represent a critique of all 'interpretations' put forward in the 'oracular tone of scientific infallibility' — not only such nostrums as the 'equalization of all classes' and workers' 'autonomy' from authority put forward by the Proudhonists, but also the messianic voluntarism of the Blanquists — for stifling working class political action which comes from the fact that the workers 'have no ready-made utopias to introduce' and because of this are able to learn in their daily struggles how to 'work out their own emancipation for themselves' by coming to 'full consciousness of their historic mission' to establish 'that higher form to which present society is irresistibly tending by its own economical agencies'.[92] It is Marx's dialectical opposition to both the common sense appeal of the readerly mode of address on the one hand, in which the Commune was transparently taken to be 'terroristic' and the end of 'civilization', and the 'oracular tone' of the writerly on the other, which saw in it a ready-made classless society, that makes Marx's addresses to the working class speecherly and therefore able to connect the local and immediate concerns of workers with the aim of the workers' movement as a whole to abolish class and establish communism.[93]

International', 15 October 1871, *Karl Marx/Frederick Engels: Collected Works*, 50 vols (Moscow: Progress Publishers, 1986), 22, pp. 633–34 (p. 634); 'Marx to Ruge', p. 144.

91   Frederick Engels, 'Introduction to Karl Marx's *Civil War in France*', *Karl Marx/ Frederick Engels: Collected Works*, 50 vols (Moscow: Progress Publishers, 1990), 27, pp. 179–91 (pp. 187–89).

92   'Civil War', p. 335.

93   The success of Marx's speecherly approach can be seen in the policies of the International which under Marx's leadership was able to end the importation of strike breakers in Europe, organize international opposition to slavery in the U.S., support Italian and Polish independence, as well as eject the anarchists from the International for advancing the 'class terrorism' of the bourgeoisie against the workers' vanguard party from within (Marx, 'Civil War', p. 329).

It is the same praxical use of speech in the workers' struggle that I argue divides the speecherly Marx from the writerly interpretation of Marx which is currently dominant in the texts of the 'new communists' who make communism the sign of an impossible otherness that subverts the 'Master-Signifier' in culture.[94] In the writerly new communism, class-consciousness is voided of the material antagonism inscribed in the productive base of society between capital and labor and class is resignified as merely a discursive difference and lifestyle politic. The consequence is to immunize capitalism from a root critique that alone can explain what is to be done to change it.

The 'New' Infantile Communism

In the writings of the 'new communists', Marx's speecherly theory of communism as 'the real movement that abolishes the present state of things' (the outside as produced from inside the logic of class) is co-opted to a writerly approach in which communism is 'an ideal to which reality will have to adjust itself' (the outside as unknowable and constitutive of the inside).[95] The truth of Marxism is writerly, on this view, as it is predicated on the question as to what extent Marx's idea of communism remains true to the 'fundamental randomness' of its 'evental origins', 'admits as its own real this aleatory, elusive, slippery, evanescent dimension' and renounces 'the impure language of the State' by acknowledging the 'unsuitability' of the 'Party-form' and the 'Socialist State' for the communist cause.[96] The result is that Badiou, in his defense of the Idea of Communism, returns communism to its infantile origins as merely an egalitarian norm of Western humanism 'since Plato' and turns it away from being 'the real movement that abolishes the present state of things' by the class-conscious vanguard of the global proletariat.[97]

According to Badiou the Idea of Communism is best conceived as a Platonic conception of equality because the role of language for him

---

94   Slavoj Žižek and Mao Zedong, 'Introduction,' *On Practice and Contradiction* (New York: Verso Books, 2007), p. 94.
95   Marx and Engels, 'German Ideology', p. 49.
96   Badiou, *Communist Hypothesis*, pp. 244, 247, 254, 257.
97   Ibid., p. 254.

consists 'in giving a general or generic meaning to, the ultimate aim of a politics'.[98] On this logic, communism and democracy are synonyms for the same idea of 'equality'.[99] However, because 'democracy' is also a 'form of the State', this raises the question of the relation of politics (the aim of which is 'generic communism') to the State (the form of which is inegalitarian). The 'democratic' State form is inegalitarian because it 'authorizes a placement of the particular under the law of the universality of the political will'.[100] On these terms, communism cannot be 'spoken in the impure language of the State' because the State must subsume the general, or what Badiou calls 'the truth of the collective', under the particular and pragmatic — using some 'identitarian assignation' of a 'racial or sexual [...] or [...] social status' nomination — thereby dividing the social whose 'generic' aims it professes to express.[101]

The State thus always assumes a fictional 'communitarian' form such that while it symbolically legitimates itself in terms of 'mass sovereignty', it also necessarily embodies a performative contradiction as it cannot realize the egalitarian aim of 'generic communism'.[102] Because the State form is doomed to divide the social — as it 'authorizes a placement of the particular under the law of the universality of the political will' of some 'identitarian assignation' of a 'racial or sexual [or] social status' nomination — it is imperative, according to Badiou, to 'retrieve[ ] democracy as a philosophical category' but in a form that is both 'freed from its subordination to the State' while yet being politically 'effective'.[103] Badiou's final word on this political designation is 'justice'.[104] Communism, however, is not synonymous with justice, democracy, or equality as these forms presuppose the continued existence of the very class inequality they purport to ameliorate politically. On the contrary, communism, as Marx explains, refers to a classless society that has abolished the need for the 'government of persons' because it has established the principle of 'from each according to his abilities, to

---

98 *Metapolitics*, p. 81.
99 Ibid., p. 93.
100 Ibid., p. 92.
101 *Communist Hypothesis*, p. 254; *Metapolitics*, pp. 81, 93–94.
102 Ibid., pp. 88, 93.
103 Ibid., pp. 92–94.
104 Ibid., p. 94.

each according to his needs'.[105] Badiou's defense of communism as an egalitarian idea relies on the common sense of bourgeois ideology that class society cannot be materially superseded.

Badiou's discussion of the State is fundamentally writerly. Rather than consider the material State as an inventory of the historical ways in which the ruling class in society organizes the relations of production they require and control at a given stage of development, he reduces the State to an 'impure' language that normalizes a 'knowledge' of being (code words for materialism) and thus mars the immaterial void of the Platonic idea of egalitarianism (e.g., what he calls 'being *qua* being'). Because politics on his theory is synonymous with the activity of thought — which consists of de-materializing communism by giving it 'a general or generic meaning' such as 'equality' or 'justice' devoid of class — it is necessary to have some concept of effectivity, but because effectivity requires that transformations of the material world be translated into positive 'knowledge' (an 'impure' form of thought) it then becomes necessary to make effectivity synonymous with the 'impossible' to save the Communist Idea from 'subordination to the State'.[106] Thus, on the one hand, there is 'the impossibility, in the situation, of every non-egalitarian statement concerning this situation' because of how the hegemonic State language cannot actually capture the Multiple and make 'two into one' and, on the other, the impossibility of the communist idea becoming an actuality because of the ethical imperative that communism not be articulated 'in the impure language of the State'.[107] The 'impossible' is thus raised to the status of the 'Real' and it seems impossible that any politics could possibly advance on a materialist basis because, as Badiou must ultimately conclude, is not any political 'designation' a form of inequality and thus self-defeating?[108] Because on this logic all politics is 'impossible' as it can only be put forward under 'generic' terms that cannot actually explain inequality thus leaving it intact, no actual movement can take place as that would

---

105 Karl Marx, 'Critique of the Gotha Programme', *Karl Marx/Frederick Engels: Collected Works*, 50 vols (Moscow: Progress Publishers, 1984), 24, pp. 75–99 (p. 87).

106 *Metapolitics*, p. 92.

107 Ibid., p. 93; Alain Badiou, 'One Divides Itself into Two', in *Lenin Reloaded: Toward a Politics of Truth*, Sebastian Budgen, Stithies Kouvelakis, and Slavoj Žižek (eds) (Durham: Duke University Press, 2007), 7–17.

108 *Metapolitics*, p. 93.

require that the social be conceptually and practically divided in relation to class 'assignations'. This cessation of movement is what is truly desired — the proclamation of a stalemate between capital and labor, i.e., a merely formal 'equalization' of the classes. In this way abstention from class politics is made the height of politics and synonymous with communism in Badiou's discourse.

In *The Manifesto of Communist Party*, Marx and Engels argue that the 'first step in the revolution' is 'to win the battle of democracy' by 'rais[ing] the proletariat to the position of ruling class' and they defend the Paris Commune as the concrete example of workers' self-governance. The question is — *Why?* Why do communists who argue that society has reached the stage of development which affords it the ability to abolish classes, and therefore the need of the State (which arises out of class relations), advocate for the working class to become the ruling class in the State, and call the proletarian state dictatorship 'democracy'? Is this fundamentally contradictory in the way Badiou argues because it contradicts the communist principle of egalitarianism? Does it reduce communism to a populist 'communitarianism' that subjugates others (along ethnic and gender lines)? Along the same lines, is rejection of the claim that the 'fall' of communism is 'inscribed in the very origins' of Marxism but rather due to 'outside' (material) forces necessarily 'anti-Semitic', as Žižek claims?[109] Is there really no difference between the dictatorship of capital, fascist dictatorship, and communist dictatorship then?

On Marx's terms what makes a workers' state *democratic* is that it advances the interests of the majority of society, the working class. What makes it a *dictatorship* is that it must do so by subordinating the interests of other classes to its goal of abolishing exploitation in production as a means to abolish the existence of classes as such.[110] It is this

---

109 'Introduction', *On Practice*, p. 1.

110 Although the Commune was a working class government that did not include the 'rural proletariate', 'the large mass of producers not directly involved in the struggle of capital and labor', it nevertheless represented 'the direct antithesis to the Empire' in terms of its agrarian policy. Thus, while the populist government of Louis-Napoléon Bonaparte which 'professed to rest upon the peasantry' was all the while increasing 'the debt, lying like an incubus upon [...] the rural proletariate', so as to expropriate them from the land and 'enforce at at a more and more rapid rate' the 'development of modern agriculture and the competition of capitalist farming' in the countryside, it was the Commune alone, however, that 'was able, and at the

'identification' of the rule of the working class with the interests of the whole of society (and against the narrow self-interest of other classes) that Badiou argues is ineffective politically because it does not appear to be a change at all to the normal state of affairs (the 'communitarian' form of the State). The difference, however, cannot be grasped at the formal level of appearances where Badiou contains the discussion of the State, but must move 'outside' philosophy to include an awareness of the class struggle, of how the State is used in accordance with the interests and aims of different classes: the exploiters or the exploited.[111]

On Marx's understanding the proletariat as a class has an interest in abolishing classes because of its shared conditions of life in capitalist society: besides sharing an antagonistic relation to their exploiters, they also set in motion the means of production and share a condition of life in which class distinctions are counter-productive and self-defeating. This is what Marx argues makes the proletariat a truly revolutionary class uniquely positioned to use democratic means to realize freedom from necessity for all. It is only when and to the extent that the proletariat organized as the ruling class can abolish class in material practice (by raising the level of productive forces to meet the needs of all, excluding the needs that contradict the goal of communism), will the need for the coercive power of the socially democratic State 'wither away' and society move beyond 'socialism' (workers' state) to communism (classless, and so, stateless, society).[112]

On Badiou's theory the workers' state should be opposed, however, because its 'communitarian' or 'identitarian' populism promotes the State fiction that 'two becomes one' that masks how its 'pragmatic' use of force militantly divides the social in two and actually undermines 'democracy' (the generic ideal of equality). However, democracy is always class divided, not because social equality is impossible in reality and is always doomed to be a communitarian populism excluding difference and producing an other, but because democracy reflects its origins in class division which alone gives it its reason for being. Badiou's opposition of the Idea of Communism to communitarian populism fails

---

same time compelled, to solve [the debt problem] in favor of the peasant' ('Civil War', pp. 330, 338).

111 See, 'One Divides Itself into Two'.

112 See, Marx, *Critique of the Gotha Programme*.

to grasp the material interests at work behind the democratic form of the State, which are not simply the dominance of one or another 'identity' assignation, but classes. Is it a bourgeois populism that is disguising the bourgeois interest to exploit the labor of the many as in the interest of all, or is it a proletarian form of governance that actually works in the interests of the majority to abolish their own exploitation and end class society? Badiou's opposition to 'populism' as such and retreat to Platonic idealism and infantile Leftism expresses a petty bourgeois reaction to the 'battle of democracy' going on between capital and labor 'right before our eyes' that fears the struggle will disrupt its normal privileges in class society. His writerly defense of the 'fundamental randomness' of the 'evental origins' of the generic idea of communism, is, in other words, a contemporary example of the kind of '"left-wing" communism' that Lenin, following Marx's critique of anarchism, calls the 'infantile disorder' of the petty bourgeoisie who, 'driven to frenzy by the horrors of capitalism' and an 'acute and rapid deterioration in his conditions of life [...] easily goes to revolutionary extremes, but is incapable of perseverance, organisation, discipline and steadfastness'.[113] In fact, this social layer (a part of the working class that misrecognizes its relation to capital), gravitates to bourgeois populism because it will not fundamentally change the existing social arrangements in which it has found a niche for the time being (through credit and debt financing). This explains the popularity of Trumpism to this class fraction — Trump is writerly: he makes class into a 'generic' classification without class content which appears radically egalitarian all the while undermining class-conscious solutions to the crisis of capitalism. Marx's speecherly communism is the antidote to the sectarian disorder of infantile communism that emerges at times of crisis because it not only explains why capitalism is unsustainable for systemic structural reasons, but also why, for the same reasons, the proletariat alone is a truly revolutionary class as it concretely possesses both the material interest as well as the practical means to build a classless society.

The ethics of egalitarianism Badiou substitutes for Marx's idea of communism is ideologically the same as Rancière's, another of the leading post-1968 'new communist' re-writers of Marx, despite

---

113 V. I. Lenin, '"Left-Wing" Communism – An Infantile Disorder', *V. I. Lenin Collected Works*, 45 vols (Moscow: Progress Publishers, 1966), 31, pp. 17–118 (p. 32).

whatever surface differences there are between them (e.g., Rancière preferring 'democracy' to 'communism'). Rancière also assumes that politics is basically a cultural matter (writerly). Politics, he writes, is not a matter of 'state institutions' that establish some 'basic wrong' in terms of 'the distribution of jobs, roles, and places', nor is it 'the organization of powers [...] and the systems for legitimizing this distribution', but, rather, it is in itself an empty form that stages a discursive conflict of values between, on the one hand, the organization of bodies by the 'police', and, on the other, the 'dissensus' that results when the bodies move out of their assigned places.[114] Marx, on this reading, is said to be 'policing' the proletariat in his speeches on the Paris Commune by 'assigning' the workers the task of establishing a dictatorial State socialism. As in Badiou's discourse, by using 'the impure language of the State' (in which the Multiple counts as One), Marx violates the truly radical egalitarian idea of communism (that divides One into Two so as to clear the void of the Real for transvaluation). Democracy, on Rancière's reading, is the 'dissensus' of communism (the multiple) within Marx's police-State language that wants to dominate the world. The writerly Marx(ism) which passes as a more subtle and radical interpretation of Marx for a 'new communism' today is on closer inspection indistinguishable from the normal crude anti-communism of regular Right-wingers.

What is considered revolutionary on the North Atlantic left today is the hollowing out of Marxism of what makes it Marxism — Marx's theory of class as a matter of grasping '*what the proletariat is*, and what, in accordance with this *being*, it will historically be compelled to do' — so as to construct a 'marxism beyond marxism' as an egalitarian commons-ism without class.[115] However, the proletariat is the class of propertyless wage-laborers who have nothing but their labor power to exchange for their means of subsistence and whose unpaid surplus labor is accumulated as profit by the owners. What this condition compels them to do is unite and struggle to emancipate themselves from the dictatorship of capital. Marx's speecherly relation to class is a critique of the readerly common sense of class as 'inequality' and the writerly

---

114 Jacques Rancière, *Disagreement* (Minneapolis: Minnesota University Press, 1999), pp. 28, 33, 35.

115 'Holy Family', p. 37; Antonio Negri, *Marx Beyond Marx: Lessons on the Grundrisse* (Brooklyn: Autnomedia/Pluto Press, 1991).

view of class as cultural 'difference' which fail to see beyond the surface
effect of the exploitation of wage-labor by capital as merely different
'life chances on the market'.[116] Marx's theory of class is speecherly
because it goes beyond the merely descriptive and interpretative
modes of making sense of class that underwrite the dominant market
logic by explaining its roots in the capitalist relations of production.
Marx's explanation of class is necessary for changing it. Without Marx's
materialist theory of class, there can be no revolutionary movement to
end class, which is why the ideology of class as cultural differences is
so popular and the voiding of Marx's theory of class so lucrative in the
academic theory market. Marx's speecherly mode of addressing class
goes beyond the mystifications of class of the readerly/writerly mode
that form the dominant common sense of class and, in doing so, is able
to address the needs of workers with a transformative way of making
sense of their lives — a method that is able to explain why, for example,
despite working long hours in alienating jobs they find themselves
unable to meet their basic needs for nutritious food, safe and healthy
environments, accessible quality education, fulfilling and meaningful
relationships, stimulating recreational activities,... while the wealth of
their labor is accumulated to benefit a tiny minority — and speak for
them in the *agora*, as Marx so forcefully does in his speeches on the Paris
Commune.

Badiou's focus on Marx's idea of communism in his speeches on
the Paris Commune represents a tutor-text of the 'new communism'
which is attempting to turn the popular movements that have emerged
around the world to contest the austerity culture of capitalism in decline
away from the path of socialist revolution toward 'saving capitalism'.
Consider, for instance, how Michael Hardt, who along with Antonio
Negri has turned class into a mystical idea of the 'autonomy of the
Multitude', argues that Marx's theory of class must be rejected because
of its 'negative' stance toward the 'positive project to generate an
ontology of ourselves and create a new social world' in common.[117] On

---

116 Max Weber, 'Class, Status, Party', *The Inequality Reader: Contemporary and Foundational Readings in Race, Class, and Gender*, ed. by David B. Grusky and Szonja Szelényi (London and New York: Routledge 2011), pp. 64–74.

117 Michael Hardt, 'The Militancy of Theory', *The South Atlantic Quarterly*, 110:1, Winter (2011), pp. 19–35 (p. 26).

this account, Marx's speaking of class as the irreconcilable antagonism between capital and labor inscribed in the economic base is to be rejected for an empty populist phrase of class as the common. For Marx, class is the relation of exploitation of labor by capital that explains why there can be no common while classes exist. The problem with Marx's critique of the post-class 'commons'-ist theory of the social, according to Hardt, is that it produces an authoritative knowledge of class that denies the 'autonomy of those it is aimed to help', and thus has no place in the process of social change.[118] Against the *radical* negation of the existing that comes with 'grasping things by the root' in exploited labor, as Marx argues, cultural theory should instead become more affirmative, according to Hardt, by having 'the courage not only to speak the truth to and about ourselves but also to live in a way harmonious with that truth'.[119] The harmonious 'truth' of the autonomous subject is 'beyond critique' according to Hardt, because it 'seeks to change social life while being a part of it', rather than 'stand above the lives of others [...] as a vanguard'.[120] Thus, the problem with Marx's speeches, in this framing, and precisely because of their speecherly insistence on producing class-consciousness of the objective material 'outside' of ideology lying in the extraction of the surplus-value of wage-labor by capital, is its ethical blindness to the desire of the other, those whom Hardt embraces because they are in 'voluntary insubordination' of global knowing.[121] In place of Marx's speecherly critique of class, which negates the ideological 'inside' by bringing to bear upon it the 'outside' of class that explains why the critique of the false-consciousness of class in culture is necessary to change it, Hardt puts forward what he takes to be the more 'positive' idea that a 'new mode of life' comes from within, by a change in 'moral attitude' by anyone who so desires it.[122] The appeal here of course is to the market subject who experiences their desire as free of need, as in the libertarianism of consumerist ideology. Rather than speak to the need of workers for their emancipation from capital, Hardt instead speaks on behalf of bourgeois interests by mystifying the social in terms of desire.

---

118 Ibid., p. 26.
119 Ibid., p. 30.
120 Ibid., pp. 29, 33.
121 Ibid., p. 22.
122 Ibid., p. 31.

The evacuating of Marx's speecherly relation to class is done so as to make Marx more writerly and construct a pluralized Marxism that deploys communism as an empty signifier of 'equality' to contain awareness of the failure of capitalism and what is to be done to change it. This hollowing out of Marxism of its commitment to speaking for the workers — that has become popular through the writings of Badiou, Negri, Rancière, and Žižek — has of course most famously replaced Marx's explanation for why the working class alone is a revolutionary class with its own 'post-class' theory: what Badiou calls the 'new political subject' is what Rancière calls 'the part of no part', Negri, the 'multitude', and Žižek, 'slum dwellers'. The multitude are of course those who work within the circuits of immaterial labor who desire to 'invent' a common, while Badiou's 'new political subject' refers to those who have 'absolute conviction' in 'event-al' ruptures with the historical material series who form group adherence to this messianic idea, while Žižek's 'slum-dwellers' are those he considers 'free' to so identify because, like those Rancière say play 'the part of no part', they lack any 'social substance' due to their 'exclusion' from the neoliberal economic order.[123] What the 'new communist' writings show in their writerly transvaluation of class from its speecherly roots in the division of labor is abstention from class politics (speaking for what is to be done to end class) and its replacement with the cultural politics of the sign (learning to live with class by resignifying it). In Marx's speeches on the Paris Commune, the communism of which he spoke stands for the interests of the global working class and in intransigent opposition to this petty-bourgeois tendency to conflate revolution with a doctrine that appeals to a socially marginalized group with a messianic message that absolutizes their local agency in the voluntarist terms of bourgeois ideology.

123	Antonio Negri and Michael Hardt, *Multitude: War and Democracy in the Age of Empire* (London: Penguin Books, 2004); Badiou, *Communist Hypothesis* and *Philosophy of Communism*; Slavoj Žižek, 'Learn to Live Without Masters', *Naked Punch*, 3 October 2009, http://www.nakedpunch.com/articles/34.

Readerly/Writerly, or Speecherly?

In order to clarify why Marx's speeches reveal a speecherly use of language that argues against the writerly Marx(ism) put forward in the writings of the 'new communists' today, it will be useful to consider Barthes' theorization of the difference between the readerly and writerly in more detail. In the following I will first outline how the 'writerly' acquires its value against the 'readerly' in Barthes' theorization of the literary text and then show how Lukács develops a concept of the speecherly to explain the readerly and writerly (what he calls 'narration' and 'description') in terms of the development of capitalism and the conflict between opposed class methods of revolt against it, before relating these terms again to Marx's speeches on the Paris Commune.

The readerly text, according to Barthes, is that mode of intelligibility authorized by the 'literary institution' which circulates the text as a commodity (hence, 'we call any readerly text a classic text', i.e., timeless) through a shared agreement between 'the producer of the text and its user, between its owner and its customer' as to its value.[124] In the logic of the market, the text as a *'whole'* possesses a value (meaning) that has been instilled in it by its owner-producer such that the act of reading is thought of as an act of exchange in which ownership of the meaning is transferred to the reader-consumer.[125] The act of market exchange requires agreement between the owner-producer and reader-customer that the text has a meaning or value, moreover, it requires the reader to believe that 'reading is nothing more than a *referendum*' in which the reader is free to choose to 'accept or reject the text', as if its meaning could be decided and further interpretation closed.[126] Such a reader is 'idle' or passive in relation to meaning, on the assumption that meaning is 'found' in the text rather than 'produced'. They are also 'serious' and 'intransitive', and, therefore, 'impoverished', because they are barred from enjoying the 'pleasure of writing' which comes with 'appreciation' of the playfulness of the signifier.[127] In short, the 'readerly' mode of making sense of the literary devalues the text and reader both. Barthes'

---

124 *S/Z*, p. 4.
125 Ibid., p. 6.
126 Ibid., p. 4.
127 Ibid., pp. 4–5.

theorization of the literary text is concerned with how 'to make the reader no longer a consumer, but a producer of the text' and thereby move them from their 'impoverished' state to one where they 'gain[ ] access to the magic of the signifier'.[128] This magical epiphany, by abandoning the 'readerly' and coming to an 'appreciation' of the 'writerly' dimension of literature, represents for Barthes an 'escape' from the authoritarian logic of the market.[129]

What makes the passive-reader become an active-writer/producer of meaning is an act of *'interpretation'* that is no longer bound to 'any constraint of representation (of imitation)'.[130] The assumption here is that the logic of the market that reduces the literary to a commodity requires that texts be thought to have a singular meaning produced by the realist code (mimesis) by representing a ready-made world with predetermined meanings that have already been produced. Rather than interpret the text as 'a structure of signifieds' that 'imitates' an original, the writerly foregrounds the 'plurality' of meaning that constitutes the text as 'a galaxy of signifiers' that 'has no beginning'.[131] The meaning of the writerly text is thus 'reversible' and 'indeterminable' because 'nothing exists outside the text' on which to fix a 'principle of determination', and 'there is never a *whole* of the text' or a 'logic' that 'can be authoritatively declared to be the main one'.[132] The writerly text is an 'ideal text' — 'the image of a triumphant plural' — that models a subjectivity that is freed of any regulative restraint on the pleasures of interpretation.[133] Free of any reality principle, the reader 'gain[s] access to the magic of the signifier, to the pleasure of writing'.[134] Against the 'impoverished' reader who reads 'seriously' in order to extract a decided meaning about the world, Barthes places the mystical interpreter who luxuriates in the plurality of meanings and thus appreciates the true pleasures of writing.[135]

Barthes' literary theory traces itself in the writerly Marx(ism)

---

128 Ibid., p. 4.
129 Ibid., p. 5.
130 Ibid.
131 Ibid.
132 Ibid., pp. 5–6.
133 Ibid., p. 5.
134 Ibid., p. 4.
135 Ibid.

dominant today. Take Rancière, for instance.[136] What makes Marx's speeches on the Commune revolutionary for Rancière is a matter of how the question of the subject emerges unexpectedly in them where it was thought not to exist before, in 'the part which is not a part' of society — the proletariat. By giving the workers human status at a time when they were taken to be non-human tools or beasts of burden, Marx's speech makes them into a political subject that are due all the rights and privileges of human beings while at the same time assigning them a place in the social order as the source of value and subject of history. Marx is said to be applying the principle of 'equality' to 'knowledge' — as he assumes that the workers have 'spoken' and established a name for themselves as 'communists' in the Paris Commune — even as he attributes the reason for the failure of the Commune to their 'ignorance' of scientific socialism. For Rancière, Marx's speech is 'writerly' as he reconfigures the idea of the proletariat and thereby constructs his own 'part that is not a part' of it, the part that remains 'invisible' and 'ignorant' that Marx calls 'anarchist' or 'peasant'. But, against this writerly Marx whose speech constitutes the proletariat as an 'outside' that 'exceeds' the logic of the 'inside' to which the discourse of scientific socialism of Orthodox Marxism seeks to contain it, there is the speecherly Marx who speaks for the vanguard of the workers by producing the concepts necessary for their grasping and changing the world.

In Barthes' account of the writerly, the agency of the signifier is alienated from itself in the code of the readerly when it is taken to have a singular meaning — the text 'as a whole' that 'reflects' a prior reality unmediated by language. The mechanism of this alienation is the literary institution that produces the text as a commodity to which it attributes a mimetic (readerly) value. The result of the reification of meaning is the alienation of the reader who encounters the text as a passive consumer rather than active producer of meanings. Rather than an escape from this condition, as Barthes supposes, the equation of agency with the 'appreciation' of the 'plurality' of possible 'interpretations' of the text only deepens the alienation of the text with itself as well as of the reader. Leaving aside for now the equation of agency with the production of meaning and how this reinforces through a textual relay the social

---

136 *Disagreement*, pp. 28–35.

alienation of the worker from the material conditions of production, to equate the production of meaning to the 'appreciation' of the writerly is simply a Nietzschean revaluation of the alienation of the reader, not its abolition in practice — the text remains objectified as 'the image of a triumphant plural'.[137] The reader is still related to their own labor (of interpretation) as an alien object (writerly) to which, Barthes insists, they must subordinate themselves (appreciation). Furthermore, such an act of interpretation simply leaves the literary institution intact which has reified the writerly as the readerly in the first place. Barthes' identification of a consumer who lacks access to and appreciation of the 'pleasure of the text' is, despite its rejection of mimesis, a repetition of the same market logic of the readerly it opposes. In other words, it represents a 'mirror that does not reflect things', that therefore redoubles the realm of necessity by failing to engage the speecherly dimension of language to produce the concepts necessary to change it.[138] It is the common sense of advertising that it does not sell the practical virtues of the product but the 'better' in some way person the buyer will become by consuming it. The logic of the market is desire-al, writerly rather than readerly, and thus the equation of language with the writerly against the speecherly represents the hegemony of ruling class ideology in Barthes' writerly theory. Barthes' theory is really an affective rather than conceptual one that localizes the production of meaning to readers' 'interpretations' of the textual rather than a rigorous interrogation of the place of the literary in the social. As it assumes that the value of language is due to the disposition of the subject who is either 'impoverished' or 'appreciative' of the mystical properties of the writerly, it functions as a class allegory on behalf of the ruling class. It is precisely at the point where Barthes assumes the freedom of speech (interpretation) in the writerly as against the 'logic' of capitalism when he speaks most forcefully on behalf of capital. It is this speaking for the logic of capital in the code of the free agency of the writerly that Barthes' text surfaces the speecherly dimension of language in its relation to class that is suppressed in his theorization under the rejection of the readerly.

Although at a surface level Barthes opposes the writerly to the readerly,

---

137 *S/Z*, p. 5.
138 V. I. Lenin, 'Leo Tolstoy as the Mirror of the Russian Revolution', *V. I. Lenin Collected Works*, 45 vols (Moscow: Progress Publishers, 1977), 15, pp. 202–09 (p. 202).

under Lukács' theorization the speecherly dimension underlying them becomes apparent as they are understood to be modes of side-taking under capitalism. On Lukács' terms, the readerly/writerly — what he variously calls narration/description or realism/naturalism — are not just 'two basically divergent styles' or 'artistic methods of handling content', but 'two basically divergent approaches to reality' that reveal the 'need to adapt fiction to provide an adequate representation of new social phenomena' appropriate to 'two different periods of capitalism'.[139] Because 'style is socially and historically determined and is the product of a social development', it is necessary to grasp the 'readerly', as in the narrative realism of Balzac, Scott, Stendhal, Dickens, and Tolstoy, as a depiction of 'bourgeois society consolidating itself after severe crisis, the complicated laws of development operating in its formation, and the tortuous transitions from the old society in decay to the new society in birth'.[140] Because these writers 'were not 'specialists' in the sense of the capitalist division of labor' they did not 'stand aloof as observers and critics of capitalist society' but 'participated variously and actively in the great social struggles of their times' by dramatizing them.[141] Conversely, the 'writerly' modernism of 'western avant-garde movements' represents a more 'perfected' consolidation of capitalism in which 'the book ha[s] become merchandise, the writer, a salesman of this merchandise' and a 'specialist[ ] in the craft of writing'.[142] Under conditions in which the arts become 'absolutely dependent [...] upon capital' (113) those like Flaubert and Zola who yet express their 'contempt for the political and social order of their time' (119) and resist being turned into 'lying apologists for capitalism' (119) do so by staging a 'subjective protest' against the 'emptiness of capitalistic life' (147) as 'observers and critics' (119).[143] Their protest takes the form of representing events through a hypertrophy of descriptive details whose significance 'does not arise out of the subjective importance of the events, which is scarcely related, but from the artifice in the formal stylization' (115).[144] Barthes' self-reflexive textuality (the writerly), despite its opposition to the mimetic (as readerly),

---

139 Georg Lukács, 'Narrate or Describe?', *Writer & Critic and Other Essays* (The Universal Library, 1971), pp. 110–48 (pp. 116, 119–20).
140 Ibid., pp. 118–19.
141 Ibid.
142 Ibid., pp. 9, 119, 145.
143 Ibid., pp. 113, 119, 147.
144 Ibid. p. 115.

represents a further hypertrophy of the descriptive turned in upon itself. Separated even more from the narrational, it reflects the greater alienation of the writer dependent on capital in the post-war period, a time when (post)structuralist theory was subsidized by the United States while the CIA was weaponizing it, as it did with modern art, against the Soviet Union in the Cold War.[145] The principle effect of modernist literature in which description is no longer 'a base for the [...] dramatic' representation of events as it is under realism and instead becomes 'the principle mode', as in French naturalism after 1848, is one of ironic detachment that 'debases characters to the level of inanimate objects'.[146] They become 'abstract' like 'dabs of color in a painting' that presents a 'tableau' to the spectator in a way that reflects, but does not explain, how 'the individual [...] is transformed into a soulless appurtenance of the capitalist system'.[147] In the descriptive method we see 'the result but not the struggle of opposing forces' in capitalism.[148] We do not, in other words, watch someone 'whom we have come to know and love being spiritually murdered by capitalism in the course of the novel, but follow a corpse in passage through still lives becoming increasingly aware of being dead'.[149] Thus, although 'modern bourgeois literature bears witness against bourgeois society' by reflecting its dehumanization and decline into 'fascist bestiality' in the posthuman alienation of the signifier from the signified, it does so from the vantage point of the 'proprietary class' who 'feels at ease and justified in this alienation, recognizing in it a source of power' to derive ironic pleasure from taking an artistic stand, rather than from the standpoint of the proletariat who 'feels destroyed in this alienation, recognizing in it its helplessness and the inhumanity of its existence' (Marx, qtd. in Lukács) and requires revolutionary politics (freedom from necessity) not just more cultural politics (freedom of speech).[150]

---

145 Frances Stoner Saunders, *The Cultural Cold War: The CIA and the World of Arts and Letters* (New York: The New Press, 2001); Gabriel Rockhill, 'The CIA Reads French Theory: On the Intellectual Labor of Dismantling the Cultural Left', The Philosophical Salon: A *Los Angeles Review of Books* Channel, 28 February 2017, https://thephilosophicalsalon.com/the-cia-reads-french-theory-on-the-intellectual-labor-of-dismantling-the-cultural-left.

146 Lukács, 'Narrate or Describe?', pp. 115, 117–18, 133, 147.

147 Ibid., pp. 112–15, 146.

148 Ibid., p. 146.

149 Ibid.

150 Ibid., pp. 145, 147.

When Marx is summarizing the experience of the Commune in his address to the International, given two days after the last barricade had fallen in Paris, he formulates the doctrine of the dictatorship of the proletariat. In doing so, he demonstrates how the speecherly goes beyond both the readerly (mimesis) and writerly (poesis) in the way he very much earlier in the *Eighteenth Brumaire* (1852) theorized how the proletarian revolution of the nineteenth century could not 'present the new scene of world history' in a 'borrowed language' whose words exceed their class content, but, rather, would require a 'new language', a 'poetry of the future' whose social and historical 'content goes beyond [...] words'.[151] There he argues that because the bourgeois revolutions of the English, the Germans and the French, were 'dramatic' and 'storm swiftly from success to success' they could only 'soberly [...] assimilate the results' after their 'storm-and-stress period', and were therefore prone to 'magnifying the given task in imagination' by 'glorifying the new struggles' in a borrowed 'time-honoured disguise'.[152] Hence, 'Cromwell and the English people had borrowed speech, passions and illusions from the Old Testament for their bourgeois revolution', 'Luther donned the mask of the Apostle Paul', and the 'French Revolution performed the task of their time in Roman costume and with Roman phrases'.[153] For them the 'resurrection of the dead' served to 'dull themselves to their own [class] content'.[154] The proletarian revolution, on the other hand, 'cannot begin with itself before it has stripped off all superstition about the past' and in order to succeed must first soberly assess the relation of class forces through 'constant critique' so that in the meantime their class 'adversary [...] may draw new strength [...] and rise again, more gigantic, before them' until a 'situation has been created which makes all turning back impossible, and the conditions themselves cry out'.[155] On Marx's account, while bourgeois revolution necessarily falls short of its democratic promise, proletarian revolution always goes beyond what is imagined because what is imagined is always written in the borrowed language of its bourgeois antagonist. Hence Marx on how 'im-/possible

---

151 'Eighteenth Brumaire', pp. 104, 106.
152 Ibid., pp. 104–06.
153 Ibid., pp. 104–05.
154 Ibid., p. 106.
155 Ibid., pp. 106–07.

communism' is precisely the bourgeois response to communism.[156] On this view, because the 'true secret' of the Paris Commune was according to Marx historically unprecedented — 'essentially a working-class government [...] for uprooting the economical foundations upon which rests the existence of classes' — it necessarily generated a writerly 'multiplicity of interpretations' through which a 'multiplicity of interests [...] construed it in their favour'.[157] What proved 'so tantalizing to the bourgeois mind' about it was on the one hand its raw entertainment value as a spectacle of the 'vile multitude' run amok and, on the other, a reflection of its own self-image because of how it 'made that catchword of bourgeois revolutions, cheap government, a reality'.[158] In Marx's speecherly representation of the Commune he critiques the bourgeois mind for failing to grasp the 'new language' of proletarian revolution because of its dependence on a 'borrowed language', not that of the heroic revolutionary struggles of the past, but of the Theatre de la Porte-Saint-Martin. Thus, on the 'Paris of the Boulevards'

> male and female — the rich, the capitalist, the gilded, the idle Paris, now thronging with its lackeys, its blacklegs, its literary *bohème*, and its *cocottes* [...] considering the civil war but an agreeable diversion, eyeing the battle going on through telescopes, counting the rounds of cannon, and swearing by their own honour and that of their prostitutes, that the performance was far better got up than it used to be at the Porte St. Martin. The men who fell were really dead; the cries of the wounded were cries in good earnest; and, besides, the whole thing was so intensely historical.[159]

For Marx, on the contrary, the story of the Commune is a civil war epic told in the language of the Grand Guignol, in which 'the real Paris' of 'heroic, noble, and devoted [...] women', those once vilified as the 'vile multitude' who are now like rebel angels 'storming heaven', is faced with 'a phantom Paris' of 'ghouls', 'cannibals', 'blood suckers', and 'vampires', the 'absconding men of family, religion, and above all property'.[160] Certainly, Marx too, of necessity, here 'borrows language', but the

---

156 'Civil War', p. 335.
157 Ibid., p. 334.
158 Ibid., pp. 328–29, 334, 342.
159 Ibid., pp. 342–43.
160 Ibid., pp. 329, 337, 341–42; 'Marx to Kugelmann', p. 132.

language is used in a speecherly way to reveal the class structure, the 'hideous face' of 'bourgeois civilization and justice' whose 'undisguised savagery and lawless revenge [...] comes out in its lurid light whenever the slaves and drudges of that order rise against their masters'.[161] The Commune thus speaks the truth about bourgeois democracy as 'class terrorism'.[162] Marx, speaking for the Commune as 'the intellectual child of the International', cuts through the multiplicity of interpretations which seek to contain the 'new language' of the Commune to the terms of the old by showing how '"impossible" Communism' is only really *possible* when the workers 'have no ideals to realize' — 'no ready-made utopias to introduce', nor, 'miracles' to hope for — and come to 'know that in order to work out their own emancipation [...] they have [...] but to set free the elements of the new society with which the old collapsing bourgeois society itself is pregnant'.[163] Despite its being 'in no sense socialist', the true secret of the Commune that goes beyond the words borrowed to describe it is that it represents 'that higher form to which present society is irresistibly tending by its own economical agencies'.[164]

Today the speecherly is not, nor can it be, a return to readerly realism, and neither can it be more writerly anti-capitalism because of the subsumption and commodification by capital of culture as a whole. The speecherly must therefore go beyond the 'dramatization' of 'humanist revolt' of narrative realism as well as the 'ironic' reification of the social in a way already foreseen by Lukács when he argues how it will need to give a much more 'revolting and shocking' depiction of the 'daily and hourly unremitting transformation of thousands of human beings with infinite capacities into "living corpses"' than the merely ironic mode of the writerly work of art.[165] To do so requires recognizing why 'critique represents a class', why the 'living dead', in other words, are class-conscious appendages of a system in the process of self-destruction that strips 'civilization' of its venerable aura of 'justice'.[166]

---

161 Ibid., pp. 348–49.

162 Ibid., p. 329.

163 Frederick Engels, 'Engels to Friedrich Adolf Sorge in Hoboken' (12 [-17]. September 1874), *Karl Marx/Frederick Engels: Collected Works*, 50 vols (Moscow: Progress Publishers, 1991), 45, pp. 40–45 (p. 41); Marx, 'Civil War', p. 335.

164 Ibid., p. 335; 'Marx to Domela-Nieuwenhuis', p. 66.

165 Lukács, 'Narrate or Describe?', pp. 146–47.

166 Karl Marx, 'Afterword to the Second German Edition of *Capital*', *Karl Marx/Frederick Engels: Collected Works*, 50 vols (Moscow: Progress Publishers, 1996), 35, pp. 2–20

The writerly for Barthes, despite its opposition to the readerly (mimesis), represents in its purely formal understanding of the text as a collection of signifiers, a hypertrophy of the descriptive that reflects a 'higher level[ ] of "perfected" inhumanity'.[167] Its protest against the market logic that has turned literary art into a commodity is a purely subjective one that can only see in a speecherly approach to language as an arena of class struggle a boring and naive conformism in which the value of literature is determined by the State ('referendum') rather than being a pure 'disinterested' invention. Far from being an avant-garde practice to *épater la bourgeoisie*, writerly radicalism rehearses the common sense of bourgeois ideology. Class is the real that explains the appearance of the readerly/writerly as a local reification of the class relations of production that only benefits the ruling class. The readerly/writerly is always a product of the speecherly. The speecherly in Marx, however, functions as a critique of the appearance of difference between readerly/writerly by surfacing the totality of class relations and taking the side of the proletariat. The speecherly is not a matter of the location of the text in relation to its readers, or, an idealization of its potential meanings as a zone of pure pleasure in endless interpretation, as the writerly imagines. These are simply descriptive understandings that fail to explain the place of *langue/parole* in the totality. By surfacing the social totality, the speecherly relates language to its 'outside', which is not a pre-made world of fixed meaning nor an ideal pluralism, but the world as it is, the world made by exploited and alienated labor and the ongoing class struggle over the social real.

The point of surfacing the speecherly is not to democratize meaning by distributing it among a rich plurality of potential readings. Such a ludic operation simply transfers the alienated (from labor) agency of the writerly to the readerly and has become a popular way to further naturalize reading/writing in the affective and reject the implication of both in the speecherly, the ongoingness of side-taking in the agora.[168] But, it is only by grasping the speecherly dimension of language as

---

(p. 16); 'Civil War', pp. 328–43. For more on the tropics of 'horror', the 'power of abstraction', and the emergence of the new, see, *Weird/Dark/Gothic: Capitalism and the Literary Fantastic* (Tumino, forthcoming).

167 Lukács, 'Narrate or Describe?', p. 146.

168 On the affective as postcritique-al reading see, Rita Felski, *The Limits of Critique* (Chicago: Chicago University Press, 2015).

'practical consciousness' that it will cease being a tool of class oppression underwriting the alienation of wage-labor that commodifies the world on behalf of capital and become instead part of the struggle of human freedom. For this it is necessary to focus on the speecherly dimension of Marx(ism) against his writerly readers who want to pluralize Marx(ism) so as to empty it of its critique-al opposition to class ideology.

The speecherly represents the negation of the one-sided writerly negation of bourgeois society by producing awareness of its systemic cause in the class organization of society. It represents that mode of reading/writing/thinking that 'break[s] with descriptive mannerism' that believes '"artistry" can exist independently of and in isolation from social, historical, and subjective conditions' by committing itself to producing 'a rich, comprehensive, many-sided and dynamic artistic reflection of objective reality'.[169] The result is that the speecherly is able to 'demonstrate the significance of the revolt of the proletariat' and its 'struggles to restore meaning to life' at a time when capitalism has failed the masses of people and lost all legitimacy.[170]

---

169 Lukács, 'Narrate or Describe?', p. 121.
170 Ibid., pp. 145, 147.

Bibliography

Abbasi, Kamran, 'Covid-19: Social murder, they wrote—elected, unaccountable, and unrepentant', *BMJ*, 372:n314, 4 February 2021, https://doi.org/10.1136/bmj.n314

Acampora, Ralph R., *Corporal Compassion: Animal Ethics and Philosophy of Body* (Pittsburgh: University of Pittsburgh Press, 2006), https://doi.org/10.2307/j.ctvs89dhj

Agamben, Giorgio, *The Coming Community*, trans. by Michael Hardt (Minneapolis: University of Minnesota Press, 1993).

— *Homo Sacer: Sovereign Power and Bare Life*, trans. by Daniel Heller-Roazen (Stanford: Stanford: Stanford University Press, 1998), https://doi.org/10.1515/9780804764025

— *Infancy and History: On the Destruction of Experience*, trans. by Liz Heron (New York: Verso Books, 2007).

— *The Time That Remains: A Commentary on the Letter to the Romans* (Stanford: Stanford University Press, 2005), https://doi.org/10.1515/9781503619869

Alexander, Michelle, *The New Jim Crow: Mass Incarceration in the Age of Colorblindness* (New York: The New Press, 2012).

Althusser, Louis, *Lenin and Philosophy* (New York: Monthly Review Press, 1971).

'Arizona limits ethnic studies in public schools', *CNN*, 13 May 2010, https://www.cnn.com/2010/POLITICS/05/12/arizona.ethnic.studies/index.html

Badiou, Alain, *The Century* (Boston and New York: Polity Press, 2007).

— *The Communist Hypothesis* (New York: Verso Books, 2010).

— *Logic of Worlds: Being and Event II* (London and New York: Continuum, 2007).

— *Metapolitics*, trans. by Jason Barker (New York: Verso Books, 2005).

— 'One Divides Itself into Two', in *Lenin Reloaded: Toward a Politics of Truth*, ed. by Sebastian Budgen, Stithies Kouvelakis, and Slavoj Žižek (Durham: Duke University Press, 2007), 7–17, https://doi.org/10.1215/9780822389552–002

— 'On the Epidemic Situation', *Verso Blog*, 23 March 2020, https://www.versobooks.com/blogs/4608-on-the-epidemic-situation

— *Saint Paul: The Foundation of Universalism*, trans. by Ray Brassier (Stanford: Stanford University Press, 2003).

— , and Peter Engleman, *Philosophy and the Idea of Communism*, trans. by Susan

Spitzer (Boston and New York: Polity Press, 2015).

Ballhaus, Rebecca, Alexandra Berzon, and Shalini Ramachandran, 'Jan 6 Rally Funded by Top Trump Donor, Helped by Alex Jones, Organizers Say', *The Wall Street Journal*, 1 February 2021, https://www.wsj.com/articles/jan-6-rally-funded-by-top-trump-donor-helped-by-alex-jones-organizers-say-11612012063

Baran, Paul A., and Paul Sweezy, *Monopoly Capital: An Essay on the American Economic and Social Order* (Monthly Review Press, 1966).

Barker, Jason, 'Happy Birthday, Karl Marx. You Were Right!', *The New York Times*, 30 April 2018, https://www.nytimes.com/2018/04/30/opinion/karl-marx-at-200-influence.html

Barthes, Roland, 'The Death of the Author', *Image, Music, Text*, trans. by Stephen Heath (New York: Hill and Wang, 1977), pp. 142–48.

— *S/Z*, trans. by Richard Miller (Oxford: Blackwell Publishing Ltd., 1974).

'Glenn Beck: Occupy is SEIU world Marxist movement', YouTube, 14 October 2011 https://www.youtube.com/watch?v=_Dsdofs4lNE&ab_channel=ToddWTIC [accessed 8 June 2024].

Beck, Ulrich, *Risk Society: Towards a New Modernity* (Los Angeles: Sage Publications, 1992).

Benhabib, Seyla, *Critique, Norm and Utopia. A Study in the Foundations of Critical Theory* (New York: Columbia University Press, 1986).

Benjamin, Walter, *The Arcades Project*, trans. by Howard Eland and Kevin McLaughlin (Cambridge: Belknap Press, 1999).

— 'Theses on the Philosophy of History', in *Illuminations* (New York: Schocken, 1977).

Berardi, Franco 'Bifo', 'Sabotage and Self-Organization', *Ill Will*, 6 May 2024, https://illwill.com/sabotage-and-self-organization

Berman, Sarah, 'The Year in Film', *Adbusters*, January/February (2010), p. 87.

Berrett, Dan, 'Intellectual Roots of Wall St. Protest Lie in Academe', *The Chronicle of Higher Education*, 16 October 2011, https://www.chronicle.com/article/intellectual-roots-of-wall-st-protest-lie-in-academe

Beyoncé, 'Formation', *Lemonade* (Colombia, 2016).

Blanchot, Maurice, 'Marx's Three Voices', in *Friendship*, trans. by Elizabeth Rottenberg (Stanford: Stanford University Press, 1997), pp. 98–101.

Blyth, Mark, 'Global Trumpism', *Foreign Affairs*, 15 November 2016, https://www.foreignaffairs.com/articles/2016–11–15/global-trumpism

Bourdieu, Pierre, *Acts of Resistance: Against the Tyranny of the Market*, trans. by Richard Nice (New York: The New Press, 1998).

— 'A Reasoned Utopia and Economic Fatalism', *New Left Review*, I/227, Jan/Feb 1998, pp. 126–54.

— 'Doxa and Common Life. In Conversation: Pierre Bourdieu and Terry Eagleton', *New Left Review*, January/February 1992, pp. 111–21.

— *In Other Words: Essays Toward A Reflexive Sociology*, trans. by Matthew Adamson (Stanford: Stanford University Press, 1990), https://doi.org/10.1515/9781503621558

— *Practical Reason: On the Theory of Action* (Stanford: Stanford University Press, 1998).

— *The Logic Of Practice*, trans. by Richard Nice (Stanford: Stanford University Press, 1990).

Brenner Robert, 'From Capitalism to Feudalism? Predation, Decline and the Transformation of US Politics', University of Massachusetts Amherst Political Economy Workshop, 27 April 2021, YouTube, https://www.youtube.com/watch?v=XZJ-Bz4U4As&t=1s&ab_channel=UMassAmherstPoliticalEconomyWorkshop [accessed 8 June 2024].

Brettler, Marc Zvi, Carol A. Newsom, and Pheme Perkins, eds, *The New Oxford Annotated Bible with Apocrypha: New Revised Standard Version*, 5th edn (New York: Oxford University Press, 2018).

Brooks, Peter, 'The Humanities as an Export Commodity', *Profession 2008*, pp. 33–39, https://doi.org/10.1632/prof.2008.2008.1.33

Butler, Judith, 'Capitalism Has its Limits', *Verso Blog*, 30 March 2020, https://www.versobooks.com/blogs/4603-capitalism-has-its-limits

— 'The Compass of Mourning', *London Review of Books*, 45.20, 19 Oct. 2023, https://www.lrb.co.uk/the-paper/v45/n20/judith-butler/the-compass-of-mourning

— 'The Inorganic Body in the Early Marx: A Limit-Concept of Anthropocentrism', *Radical Philosophy*, 2.06, Winter (2019), pp. 3–17, https://www.radicalphilosophy.com/article/the-inorganic-body-in-the-early-marx

— 'Left Conservatism II', *Theory & Event*, 2:2 (1998).

— 'Merely Cultural', *New Left Review*, I/227, January-February (1998), pp. 33–44.

— 'Merely Cultural', *Social Text*, 52/53, 15.3/4, Fall/Winter (1997), pp. 265–77.

— *Precarious Life: The Powers of Mourning and Violence* (New York: Verso, 2020).

— 'Why Donald Trump will never admit defeat', *The Guardian*, 20 January 2021, https://www.theguardian.com/commentisfree/2021/jan/20/donald-trump-election-defeat-covid-19-deaths

Cassidy, John, 'Trump's Fascistic Rhetoric Only Emphasizes the Stakes in 2024', *The New Yorker*, 14 November 2023, https://www.newyorker.com/news/our-columnists/trumps-fascistic-rhetoric-only-emphasizes-the-stakes-in-2024

Clewell, Tammy, 'Mourning Beyond Melancholia: Freud's Psychoanalysis of Loss', *Journal of the American Psychoanalytic Association*, 52.1 (2004), pp. 43–67, https://doi.org/10.1177/00030651040520010601

Clough, Patricia Ticineto and Jean Halley (eds), *The Affective Turn: Theorizing the Social* (Durham: Duke University Press, 2007).

Cohen, Jon, 'Wuhan seafood market may not be source of novel virus spreading globally', *Science*, 26 January 2020, https://www.science.org/content/article/wuhan-seafood-market-may-not-be-source-of-novel-virus-spreading-globally

'The Day Beyoncé Turned Black', dir. Don Roy King (NBC, 2016), https://www.youtube.com/watch?v=ociMBfkDG1w&ab_channel=SaturdayNightLive

Dean, Jodi, 'Neofeudalism: The End of Capitalism?', *Los Angeles Review of Books*, 12 May 2020, https://lareviewofbooks.org/article/neofeudalism-the-end-of-capitalism/

DeFazio, Kimberly, 'Designing Class: Ikea and Democracy as Furniture', *The Red Critique*, No. 7, November/December 2002, http://redcritique.org/NovDec02/designingclass.htm

'Defending Our Right to Learn', ACLU/American Civil Liberties Union, 10 March 2022, https://www.aclu.org/news/free-speech/defending-our-right-to-learn

Deleuze, Gilles, and Félix Guattari, *Anti-Oedipus: Capitalism and Schizophrenia* (Minneapolis: University of Minnesota Press, 1983).

de Man, Paul, *The Resistance to Theory* (Minneapolis: Minnesota University Press, 1986).

Denning, Michael. 'Wageless Life', *New Left Review*, 66.6 (2010), pp. 79–97.

Derrida, Jacques, *The Animal That Therefore I Am* (Bronx: Fordham University Press, 2008).

— 'The Crisis in the Teaching of Philosophy: Right to Philosophy 1', *Who's Afraid of Philosophy?* (Stanford: Stanford University Press, 2002), pp. 99–116.

— *Dissemination* (Chicago: Chicago University Press, 1983).

— 'The Ends of Man', *Margins of Philosophy*, trans. by Alan Bass (Chicago: Chicago University Press, 1972), pp. 111–36.

— 'Force of Law: The "Mystical Foundation of Authority"', in *Acts of Religion*, trans. and intro. by Gil Anidjar (London and New York: Routledge, 2002), pp. 228–98, https://doi.org/10.4324/9780203724309-9

— *Margins of Philosophy* (Chicago: University of Chicago Press, 1986).

— *Of Grammatology* (Baltimore: Johns Hopkins University Press, 1998).

— *Positions* (Chicago: Chicago University Press, 1981).

— *Specters of Marx: The State of the Debt, The Work of Mourning & the New*

International (London and New York: Routledge, 1994), https://doi.org/10.4324/9780203821619

— 'Typewriter Ribbon: Limited Ink (2) ("within such limits")', *Material Events: Paul de Man and the Afterlife of Theory*, ed. by Tom Cohen (Minneapolis: University of Minnesota Press), pp. 277–360.

— *Writing and Difference*, trans. by Alan Bass (Chicago: University of Chicago Press, 2017).

—, and Bernard Stiegler, *Echographies of Television: Filmed Interviews* (Boston and New York: Polity Press/Blackwell Publishers, 2002).

—, and Maurizio Ferraris, *A Taste for the Secret* (London: Polity, 2001).

Dyer-Witherford, Nick, *Cyber-Marx: Cycles and Circuits of Struggle in High-Technology Capitalism* (Urbana-Champaign: Illinois University Press, 1999).

Eagleton, Terry, *After Theory* (New York: Basic Books, 2003).

Ebert, Teresa, *Ludic Feminism and After: Postmodernism, Desire, and Labor in Late Capitalism* (Ann Arbor: University of Michigan Press, 1996).

— *The Task of Cultural Critique* (University of Illinois Press, 2009).

— and Mas'ud Zavarzadeh. *Class in Culture* (London and New York: Routledge, 2016).

Emery, Kim, 'Outcomes assessment and standardization: A queer critique', *Profession 2008*, pp. 255–9, https://doi.org/10.1632/prof.2008.2008.1.255

Engels, Frederick, 'Anti-Dühring', *Karl Marx/Frederick Engels: Collected Works*, 50 vols (Moscow: Progress Publishers, 1987), 25, pp. 5–312.

— 'The Congress of Sonvillier and the International', January 1872, *Karl Marx/Frederick Engels: Collected Works*, 50 vols (Moscow: Progress Publishers, 1988), 23, pp. 64–70.

— 'Dialectics of Nature', *Karl Marx/Frederick Engels: Collected Works*, 50 vols (Moscow: Moscow: Progress Publishers, 1987), 25, pp. 452–65.

— 'Engels to Carlo Cafiero in Barletta', 1–3 July 1871, *Karl Marx/Frederick Engels: Collected Works*, 50 vols (Moscow: Progress Publishers, 1989), 44, pp. 161–65.

— 'Engels to Carlo Terzaghi in Turin', 6 January 1872, *Karl Marx/Frederick Engels: Collected Works*, 50 vols (Moscow: Progress Publishers, 1989), 44, pp. 291–93.

— 'Engels to Friedrich Adolf Sorge in Hoboken', 12 [-17] September 1874, *Karl Marx/Frederick Engels: Collected Works*, 50 vols (Moscow: Progress Publishers, 1991), 45, pp. 40–45.

— 'Introduction to Karl Marx's *Civil War in France*', *Karl Marx/Frederick Engels: Collected Works*, 50 vols (Moscow: Progress Publishers, 1990), 27, pp. 179–91.

— 'Karl Marx's Funeral', *Karl Marx/Frederick Engels: Collected Works*, 50 vols (Moscow: Progress Publishers, 1989), 24, pp. 467–71.

— 'Letters on Historical Materialism', *The Marx-Engels Reader*, ed. by Robert C. Tucker (New York: Norton, 1978), pp. 760–68.

— 'On the Political Action of the Working Class', Handwritten Text of the Speech Delivered at the Conference Session on 21 September 1871, *Karl Marx/Frederick Engels: Collected Works*, 50 vols (Moscow: Progress Publishers, 1986), 22, pp. 417–18.

— 'Outlines of a Critique of Political Economy', *Karl Marx/Frederick Engels: Collected Works*, 50 vols (Moscow: Progress Publishers, 1975), 3, pp. 418–43.

— 'To C. Schmidt', 12 March 1895. Letter 240 of *Marx and Engels: Selected Correspondence* (Foreign Languages Publishing House, n.d.), pp. 562–66.

Feeley, Lynne, 'How Eco-Fiction Became Realer Than Realism', *The Nation*, 18 August 2022, https://www.thenation.com/article/culture/elvia-wilk-death-landscape

Felski, Rita, 'From Literary Theory to Critical Method', *Profession 2008*, 108–16, https://doi.org/10.1632/prof.2008.2008.1.108

— *The Limits of Critique* (Chicago: The University of Chicago Press, 2015).

—, and Elizabeth S. Anker, eds., *Critique and Postcritique* (Durham: Duke University Press, 2017).

Fernández-Armesto, Felipe, 'A dog's dinner of an idea', *Times Higher Education*, 18 February 2010, https://www.timeshighereducation.com/comment/columnists/a-dogs-dinner-of-an-idea/410391.article

Fish, Stanley, *Save the World On Your Own Time* (Oxford: Oxford University Press, 2012), https://doi.org/10.1093/oso/9780195369021.001.0001

Fisher, Mark, *Capitalist Realism: Is There No Alternative?* (London: Zero Books, 2022).

Food, Inc., dir. Robert Kenner (Magnolia Pictures, 2008).

Foucault, Michel, *Discipline and Punish: The Birth of the Prison*, trans. by Alan Sheridan (New York: Vintage, 1995).

— *The History of Sexuality: An Introduction* (New York: Vintage, 1990).

— 'Intellectuals and Power: A Conversation Between Michel Foucault and Gilles Deleuze', *Language, Counter-Memory, Practice* (Ithaca: Cornell University Press, 1977), pp. 205–17, https://doi.org/10.1515/9781501741913-011

— 'Nietzsche, Genealogy, History', *Language, Counter-Memory, Practice*, ed. by Donald F. Bouchard, trans. by Donald F. Bouchard and Sherry Simon (Ithaca: Cornell University Press, 1977), pp. 139–64, https://doi.org/10.1515/9781501741913-008

— *The Order of Things: An Archaeology of the Human Sciences* (New York: Vintage, 1973).

— 'Theatrum Philosophicum', in *Language, Counter-Memory, Practice*, ed. with an intro. by Donald F. Bouchard, trans. by Donald F. Bouchard and Sherry Simon (Ithaca: Cornell University Press, 1977), pp. 165–98, https://doi. org/10.1515/9781501741913–009

Franklin, Jane, (ed.), *The Politics of Risk Society* (London: Polity Press).

Nancy Fraser, and Axel Honneth. *Redistribution or Recognition?: A Political-Philosophical Exchange* (New York: Verso, 2003).

Fukuyama, Francis, *Our Posthuman Future: Consequences of the Biotechnology Revolution* (London: Picador, 2003).

Gabetta, Carlos, 'Argentina: IMF Show State Revolts', *Le Monde diplomatique*, January 2002, https://mondediplo.com/2002/01/12argentina

Gibson-Graham, J. K., Stephen A. Resnick, and Richard D. Wolff (eds), *Class and Its Others*, foreword by Amitava Kumar (Minneapolis: Minnesota University Press, 2000).

Gorky, Maxim, *Lenin* (Oxford: Oxford University Press, 1967).

Gorz, André, *Farewell to the Working Class: An Essay on Post-Industrial Socialism* (London, Pluto Press, 1997).

Graff, Gerald, *Beyond the Culture Wars: How Teaching the Conflicts Can Revitalize American Education* (New York: W. W. Norton & Co., 1993).

— 'Reply', *Profession 2008*, pp. 259–62, https://doi.org/10.1632/prof.2008.2008.1.259

—, and Cathy Birkenstein. *They Say/I Say: The Moves That Matter In Academic Writing* (New York: W. W. Norton & Co., 2014).

Gramsci, Antonio, *Selections from the Prison Notebooks of Antonio Gramsci*, ed. and trans. by Quintin Hoare and Geoffrey Nowell-Smith (London: Lawrence & Wishart, 1971).

'The Green Apple', nar. by Brad Pitt, *e2: The Economies of Being Environmentally Conscious* (PBS, 2006).

Greenspan, Alan, 'Markets and the Judiciary', *Patently-O Blog*, 2 October 2008, https://patentlyo.com/media/docs/2009/03/Greenspan.pdf

Greenwood, Max, 'Trump's Lies Aren't Lies Because "There's No Such Thing" As Facts Anymore, His Surrogate Says', *Huff Post News*, 1 December 2016, https://www.huffpost.com/entry/trump-surrogate-claims-no-facts_n_5840 8f8ee4b0c68e047fd952

Hall, Gary, *New Cultural Studies: Adventures in Theory*, ed. by Clare Birchall (Athens: Georgia University Press, 2007).

Haraway, Donna, *The Companion Species Manifesto: Dogs, People, and Significant Otherness*, (Chicago: Prickly Paradigm Press, 2003).

— *When Species Meet* (Minneapolis: Minnesota University Press, 2008).

Hardt, Michael, 'The Militancy of Theory', *The South Atlantic Quarterly*, 110:1, Winter (2011), pp. 19–35, https://doi.org/10.1215/00382876–2010–020

Harman, Graham, *Object-Oriented Ontology: A New Theory of Everything* (New Orleans: Pelican, 2018).

Hegel, G. W. F., *The Phenomenology of Mind*, trans. by James Black Baillie (New York: Harper & Row Publishers, 1967).

— *Phenomenology of Spirit*, trans. by A.V. Miller (New York: Oxford University Press, 1977).

Hennessy, Rosemary, *Profit and Pleasure: Sexual Identities in Late Capitalism* (London and New York: Routledge, 2000), https://doi.org/10.4324/9781315270142

Hudson, Michael, 'MICHAEL HUDSON on the Economy and Neofeudalism', YouTube, 20 Oct. 2017 https://www.youtube.com/watch?v=7XvWoBhd7X4&ab_channel=RenegadeInc. [accessed 8 June 2024].

Jameson, Fredric, 'Future City', *New Left Review* 21 (2003), pp. 65–79.

— *The Political Unconscious: Narrative as a Socially Symbolic Act* (Ithaca: Cornell University Press, 1981).

Khosla, Alanah, 'Mother causes a storm with rant about her adult children who are struggling to pay the bills', *Daily Mail*, 7 August 2023 https://www.dailymail.co.uk/femail/article-12380023/My-hard-working-children-struggling-pay-bills-Im-tired-feeling-helpless-did-American-dream-Mother-causes-storm-rant-adult-children-struggling-bay-bills.html [accessed 8 June 2024].

Koselleck, Reinhart, 'Crisis', trans. by Michaela W. Richter, *Journal of the History of Ideas*, 67. 2 (April 2006), pp. 357–400, https://doi.org/10.1353/jhi.2006.0013

Krugman, Paul, 'For Richer', *The New York Times*, 20 October 2002, https://www.nytimes.com/2002/10/20/magazine/for-richer.html

Lacan, Jacques, *Écrits: A Selection*, trans. by Alan Sheridan (New York: W. W. Norton & Co., 1977).

Latour, Bruno, 'An Attempt at a "Compositionist Manifesto"', *New Literary History*, 41. 3, (2010), pp. 471–90, https://doi.org/10.1353/nlh.2010.a408295

— 'On Some of the Affects of Capitalism', lecture given at the Royal Academy, Copenhagen, 26 February 2014, http://www.bruno-latour.fr/sites/default/files/136-AFFECTS-OF-K-COPENHAGUE.pdf

— *The Pasteurization of France*, trans. by Alan Sheridan and John Law (Cambridge: Harvard University Press, 1993).

— *Reassembling the Social: An Introduction to Actor-Network-Theory* (Oxford: Oxford University Press, 2005), https://doi.org/10.1093/oso/9780199256044.001.0001

— 'Recomposing the Humanities—with Bruno Latour', Special Issue of *New Literary History*, 47.2–3, Spring & Summer (2016).

— 'Why Has Critique Run out of Steam? From Matters of Fact to Matters of Concern', *Critical Inquiry*, 30.2, Winter (2004), pp. 225–48, https://doi.org/10.2307/1344358

Lenin, V. I., 'Imperialism, The Highest Stage of Capitalism. A Popular Outline', *V. I. Lenin Collected Works*, 45 vols (Moscow: Progress Publishers, 1974), 22, pp. 185–304.

— '"Left-Wing" Communism – An Infantile Disorder', *V. I. Lenin Collected Works*, 45 vols (Moscow: Progress Publishers, 1966), 31, pp. 17–118.

— 'Leo Tolstoy as the Mirror of the Russian Revolution', *V. I. Lenin Collected Works*, 45 vols (Moscow: Progress Publishers, 1977), 15, pp. 202–09.

— 'Liberal and Marxist Conceptions of the Class Struggle', *V. I. Lenin Collected Works*, 45 vols (Moscow: Progress Publishers, 1977), 19, pp. 119–24.

— *Materialism and Empirio-Criticism*, *V. I. Lenin Collected Works*, 45 vols (Moscow: Progress Publishers, 1977), 14, p. 368.

— 'Once Again on the Trade Unions', *V. I. Lenin Collected Works*, 45 vols (Moscow: Progress Publishers, 1974), 32, pp. 70–107.

— 'State and Revolution: The Marxist Theory of the State and the Tasks of the Proletariat in the Revolution', *V. I. Lenin Collected Works*, 45 vols (Moscow: Progress Publishers, 1968), 25, pp. 381–492.

— 'What Is To Be Done?: Burning Questions of Our Movement', *V. I. Lenin Collected Works*, 45 vols (Moscow: Progress Publishers, 1977), 5, pp. 347–529.

Lévinas, Emmanuel, *Nine Talmudic Readings*, trans. by Annette Aronowicz (Bloomington: Indiana University Press, 2019).

Lukács, Georg, *The Destruction of Reason* (London: The Merlin Press, 1980).

— *Lenin: A Study on the Unity of his Thought* (New York: New Left Books, 1970).

— 'Narrate or Describe?', *Writer & Critic and Other Essays* (The Universal Library, 1971), pp. 110–48.

— *The Ontology of Social Being: 3. Labour* (London: Merlin Press, 1978).

Maasik, Sonia and Jack Solomon, *Signs of Life in the USA: Readings On Popular Culture for Writers* (Boston and New York: Bedford St. Martin's, 2015).

Marx, Karl, 'A Contribution to the Critique of Political Economy', *Karl Marx/Frederick Engels: Collected Works*, 50 vols (Moscow: Progress Publishers, 1987), 29, pp. 257–417.

— 'Afterword to the Second German Edition of *Capital*', *Karl Marx/Frederick Engels: Collected Works*, 50 vols (Moscow: Progress Publishers, 1996), 35, pp. 2–20.

— *Capital, A Critique of Political Economy*, vol. I, *Karl Marx/Frederick Engels: Collected Works*, 50 vols (Moscow: Progress Publishers, 1983), 35.

— *Capital, A Critique of Political Economy*, vol. III, *Karl Marx/Frederick Engels: Collected Works*, 50 vols (Moscow: Progress Publishers, 1983), 37.

— *Capital, A Critique of Political Economy, Volume One*, intro. by Ernest Mandel, trans. by Ben Fowkes (London: Penguin Books, 1990).

— 'Civil War in France', Address of the General Council of the International Workingmen's Association, 30 May 1871, *Karl Marx/Frederick Engels: Collected Works*, 50 vols (Moscow: Progress Publishers, 1986), 22, pp. 307–59.

— 'Confidential Communication', *Karl Marx/Frederick Engels: Collected Works*, 50 vols (Moscow: Progress Publishers, 1985), 21, pp. 112–24.

— 'Contribution to the Critique of Hegel's *Philosophy of Law*. Introduction', *Karl Marx/Frederick Engels: Collected Works*, 50 vols (Moscow: Progress Publishers, 1976), 3, pp. 175–87.

— 'Critique of the Gotha Programme', *Karl Marx/Frederick Engels: Collected Works*, 50 vols (Moscow: Progress Publishers, 1984), 24, pp. 75–99.

— 'Economic and Philosophical Manuscripts of 1844', *Karl Marx/Frederick Engels: Collected Works*, 50 vols (Moscow: Progress Publishers, 1975), 3, pp. 229–346.

— 'Economic Manuscripts of 1857–8', *Karl Marx/Frederick Engels: Collected Works*, 50 vols (Moscow: Progress Publishers, 1986), 28, pp. 17–537.

— 'The Eighteenth Brumaire of Louis Bonaparte', *Karl Marx/Frederick Engels: Collected Works*, 50 vols (Moscow: Progress Publishers, 1979), 11, pp. 99–197.

— *Grundrisse: Foundations of the Critique of Political Economy (Rough Draft)* (London: Penguin Books, 1993).

— 'Letter to Sigfrid Meyer and August Vogt', London, 9 April 1870, *Karl Marx/Frederick Engels: Collected Works*, 50 vols (Moscow: Progress Publishers, 1988), 43, pp. 471–76.

— 'Marx to Engels in Manchester', 20 June 1866, *Karl Marx/Frederick Engels: Collected Works*, 50 vols (Moscow: Progress Publishers, 1987), 42, pp. 286–87.

— 'Marx to Ferdinand Domela-Nieuwenhuis in the Hague', 22 February 1881, *Karl Marx/Frederick Engels: Collected Works*, 50 vols (Moscow: Progress Publishers, 1987), 46, pp. 65–67.

— 'Marx to Friedrich Bolte in New York', 23 November 1871, *Karl Marx/Frederick Engels: Collected Works*, 50 vols (Moscow: Progress Publishers, 1989), 44, pp. 251–59.

— 'Marx to Joseph Weydemeyer in New York', 5 March 1852, *Karl Marx/Frederick Engels: Collected Works*, 50 vols (Moscow: Progress Publishers, 1983), 39, pp. 61–66.

— 'Marx to Kugelmann in Hanover', 12 April 1871, *Karl Marx/Frederick Engels: Collected Works*, 50 vols (Moscow: Progress Publishers, 1989), 44, pp. 131–32.

— 'Marx to Paul Lafargue in Madrid', 21 March 1872, *Karl Marx/Frederick Engels:*

Collected Works, 50 vols (Moscow: Progress Publishers, 1989), 44, pp. 346–52.

— 'Marx to Ruge in Kreuznach', September 1843, *Karl Marx/Frederick Engels: Collected Works*, 50 vols (Moscow: Progress Publishers, 1975), 3, pp. 141–45.

— 'Preface' to *A Contribution to the Critique of Political Economy, Karl Marx/ Frederick Engels: Collected Works*, 50 vols (Moscow: Progress Publishers, 1987), 29, pp. 261–65.

— 'Preface to the First German Edition of *Capital*', *Karl Marx/Frederick Engels: Collected Works*, 50 vols (Moscow: Progress Publishers, 1983), 35, pp. 7–11.

— 'Record of Marx's Interview with *The World* Correspondent', 3 July 1871, *Karl Marx/Frederick Engels: Collected Works*, 50 vols (Moscow: Progress Publishers, 1986), 22, pp. 600–06.

— 'Record of Marx's Speech on the Seventh Anniversary of the International', 15 October 1871, *Karl Marx/Frederick Engels: Collected Works*, 50 vols (Moscow: Progress Publishers, 1986), 22, pp. 633–34.

— 'Theses on Feuerbach', *Karl Marx/Frederick Engels: Collected Works*, 50 vols (Moscow: Progress Publishers, 1975), 5, pp. 3–8.

— 'Value, Price and Profit', *Karl Marx/Frederick Engels: Collected Works*, 50 vols (Moscow: Progress Publishers, 1985), 20, pp. 101–49.

— 'Wage Labour and Capital', *Karl Marx/Frederick Engels: Collected Works*, 50 vols (Moscow: Progress Publishers, 1977), 9, pp. 197–228.

—, and Frederick Engels, 'Address of the Central Authority to the League', March 1850, *Karl Marx/Frederick Engels: Collected Works*, 50 vols (Moscow: Progress Publishers, 1978), 10, pp. 277–87.

—, and Frederick Engels, 'Fictitious Splits in the International', Private Circular from the General Council of the International Working Men's Association, January-March 1872, *Karl Marx/Frederick Engels: Collected Works*, 50 vols (Moscow: Progress Publishers, 1988), 23, pp. 79–123.

—, and Frederick Engels, 'The Holy Family, or Critique of Critical Criticism', *Karl Marx/Frederick Engels: Collected Works*, 50 vols (Moscow: Progress Publishers, 1975), 4, pp. 5–211.

—, and Frederick Engels, 'The German Ideology', *Karl Marx/Frederick Engels: Collected Works*, 50 vols (Moscow: Progress Publishers, 1976), 5.

—, and Frederick Engels, 'The Manifesto of the Communist Party', *Karl Marx/ Frederick Engels: Collected Works*, 50 vols (Moscow: Progress Publishers, 1976), 6, pp. 477–519.

—, and Frederick Engels, *The Marx-Engels Reader*, ed. by Robert C. Tucker (New York: Norton, 1978).

—, and Frederick Engels, 'Preface to the 1872 German Edition of the *Manifesto of the Communist Party*', *Karl Marx/Frederick Engels: Collected Works*, 50 vols

(Moscow: Progress Publishers, 1986), 23, pp. 174–75.

Mau, Bruce (perf.), *The 11th Hour*, dir. by Nadia Conners and Leila Conners Petersen (Warner Bros., 2007).

Mazzucato, Mariana, 'Preventing Digital Feudalism', *Project Syndicate*, 2 October 2019.

Meillassoux, Quentin, *After Finitude: An Essay on the Necessity of Contingency*, preface by Alain Badiou, trans. by Ray Brassier (London and New York: Continuum, 2010), https://doi.org/10.5040/9781350252059

Melville, Herman, *Bartleby, the Scrivener: A Story of Wall Street* (New York: HarperCollins e-books, 2009).

Moody, Chris, 'How Republicans are being taught to talk about Occupy Wall Street', *Yahoo News*, 1 December 2011, http://news.yahoo.com/blogs/ticket/ republicans-being-taught-talk-occupy-wall-street-133707949.html

Nancy, Jean-Luc. *The Inoperative Community*, ed. by Peter Connor, trans. by Lisa Garbus et al. (Minneapolis: University of Minnesota Press, 1991).

Negri, Antonio, *Marx Beyond Marx: Lessons on the Grundrisse* (Brooklyn: Autnomedia/Pluto Press, 1991).

—, and Michael Hardt, *Commonwealth* (Cambridge: Belknap Press, 2009), https://doi.org/10.2307/j.ctvjsf48h

—, and Michael Hardt, *Empire* (Cambridge: Harvard University Press, 2000).

—, and Michael Hardt, *Multitude: War and Democracy in the Age of Empire* (London: Penguin Books, 2004).

—, and Raf Valvola Scelsi, Peter Thomas, *Goodbye Mr. Socialism* (New York: Seven Stories Press, 2008).

Nietzsche, Friedrich Wilhelm, *The Will to Power*, trans. by Walter Arnold Kaufmann and R. J. Hollingdale (New York: Random House, 1967).

'99% v 1%: the data behind the Occupy movement, *Guardian* animations', YouTube, 18 November 2011 https://www.youtube.com/watch?v=DxvVZe2fnvI&ab_ channel=TheGuardian [accessed 8 June 2024].

'Not Just China, New York Too Has Over 80 "Wet Markets" That Sell & Slaughter Live Animals', *india.com*, 3 April 2020, https://www.india.com/news/world/ not-just-china-new-york-too-has-over-80-wet-markets-that-sell-slaughter-live-animals-3989281

'Nov. 7, 1917 | Russian Government Overthrown in Bolshevik Revolution', The Learning Network, *The New York Times*, 7 November 2011, https://archive. nytimes.com/learning.blogs.nytimes.com/2011/11/07/nov-7-1917-russian-government-overthrown-in-bolshevik-revolution

'Origin of 2009 H1N1 Flu (Swine Flu): Questions and Answers', *CDC.gov*, 25 November 2009, https://www.cdc.gov/h1n1flu/information_h1n1_virus_ qa.htm

Pape, Robert A, and Keven Ruby, 'The Capitol Rioters Aren't Like Other Extremists', *The Atlantic*, 2 February 2021, https://www.theatlantic. com/ideas/archive/2021/02/the-capitol-rioters-arent-like-other-extremists/617895

Paternotte, David and Mieke Verloo, 'De-democratization and the Politics of Knowledge: Unpacking the Cultural Marxism Narrative', *Social Politics: International Studies in Gender, State & Society*, 28.3 (2021), pp. 556–578, https://doi.org/10.1093/sp/jxab025

Perez, Lorenzo, 'UVA English Professor Lands Large Danish Grant to Explore Literature's Social Use', *UVA Today*, 25 March, 2016, news.virginia. edu/content/uva-english-professor-lands-large-danish-grant-explore-literatures-social-use

Prowse, Michael, 'So you think you make your own choices?', *Financial Times*, 25 November 2000, p. 26.

Quattrocchi-Woisson, Diana, 'Ten Days that Shook the World Bank', *Le Monde diplomatique*, February 2002, https://mondediplo.com/2002/02/08tendays

Rancière, Jacques, *Disagreement* (Minneapolis: Minnesota University Press, 1999).

Reiley, Laura, '2018 saw the most multistate outbreaks of foodborne illness in more than a decade, CDC says', *The Washington Post*, 25 April 2019, https:// www.washingtonpost.com/business/2019/04/25/cdc-releases-its-annual-report-card-foodborne-illness-did-not-have-passing-grade

Riccardi, Nicholas, 'Hey Hey, Ho Ho, Catch Our Anti-Corporate Puppet Show!', *The Los Angeles Times*, 13 August 2000, https://www.latimes.com/archives/ la-xpm-2000-aug-13-tm-3457-story.html

Riding, Alan, 'Pierre Bourdieu, 71, French Thinker and Globalization Critic', *The New York Times*, 25 January 2002, https://www.nytimes.com/2002/01/25/ world/pierre-bourdieu-71-french-thinker-and-globalization-critic.html

Ritvo, Harriet, *The Animal Estate: The English and Other Creatures in the Victorian Age* (Cambridge: Harvard University Press, 1987).

The Road, dir. by John Hilcoat (Dimension Films, 2009).

Roberts, Michael, *The Long Depression: Marxism and the Global Crisis of Capitalism* (Chicago: Haymarket Books, 2016).

Rockhill, Gabriel, 'The CIA Reads French Theory: On the Intellectual Labor of Dismantling the Cultural Left', The Philosophical Salon: A *Los Angeles Review of Books* Channel, 28 February 2017, https://thephilosophicalsalon. com/the-cia-reads-french-theory-on-the-intellectual-labor-of-dismantling-the-cultural-left

Rorty, Richard, *Achieving Our Country: Leftist Thought in Twentieth-Century America* (Cambridge: Harvard University Press, 1998).

— 'Solidarity or Objectivity?', *Objectivity, Relativism, and Truth* (Cambridge: Cambridge University Press, 1991), pp. 21–34.

Roubini, Nouriel, 'Karl Marx Was Right', WSJ/Video, 12 August 2011 https://www.wsj.com/video/nouriel-roubini-karl-marx-was-right/68EE8F89-EC24–42F8–9B9D-47B510E473B0.html [accessed 8 June 2024].

Saunders, Frances Stoner, *The Cultural Cold War: The CIA and the World of Arts and Letters* (New York: The New Press, 2001).

Saussure, Ferdinand de, *Course in General Linguistics*, ed. by Charles Balley and Albert Sechehaye, trans. by Wade Baskin (New York: McGraw Hill, 1966).

Smith, Paul, *Millennial Dreams* (New York: Verso Books, 1997).

Smith, Terry, *The Architecture of Aftermath* (Chicago: Chicago University Press, 2006).

Sprinker, Michael, 'Forum on Teaching Marxism', *Mediations*, Spring (1998), pp. 68–73.

Standing, Guy, *The Precariat: The New Dangerous Class* (London: Bloomsbury Academic, 2011).

Stekloff, G. M., *History of The First International*, Marxists Internet Archive, https://www.marxists.org/archive/steklov/history-first-international/index.htm

Trotsky, Leon, *Terrorism and Communism: A Reply to Karl Kautsky* (Ann Arbor: University of Michigan Press, 1961).

Turkel, Sherry, *Life on the Screen: Identity in the Age of the Internet* (New York: Simon & Schuster, 1997).

Van den Akker, Robin, and Timotheus Vermeulen, 'Periodising the 2000s, or, the Emergence of Metamodernism', *Metamodernism: Historicity, Affect, and Depth After Postmodernism*, ed. by Robin van den Akker, Alison Gibbons, and Timotheus Vermeulen (Washington D.C.: Rowman & Littlefield Publishers, 2017), pp. 1–19.

Varoufakis, Yanis. *Technofeudalism : What Killed Capitalism?* (Brooklyn: Melville House, 2024).

Vološinov, V. N., *Marxism and the Philosophy of Language*, trans. by Ladislav Matejka and I. R. Titunik (Cambridge: Harvard University Press, 1993).

Wark, Mackenzie, *Capital Is Dead: Is This Something Worse?* (New York: Verso, 2019).

Weber, Max, 'Class, Status, Party', *The Inequality Reader: Contemporary and Foundational Readings in Race, Class, and Gender*, ed. by David B. Grusky and Szonja Szelényi (London and New York: Routledge 2011), pp. 64–74, https://doi.org/10.4324/9780429494468–7

Wendy and Lucy, dir. by Kelly Reichardt (Warner Bros., 2008).

Wilkie, Rob, 'In the Case of Gaza', *The Red Critique*, 17, 2024, http://redcritique.

org/WinterSpring2024/inthecaseofgaza.htm

Williams, Casey, 'Has Trump Stolen Philosophy's Critical Tools?', *The New York Times*, 17 April 2017, https://www.nytimes.com/2017/04/17/opinion/has-trump-stolen-philosophys-critical-tools.html

Williamson, Kevin D, 'Chaos in the Family, Chaos in the State: The White Working Class's Dysfunction', *National Review*, 17 March 2016, https://www.nationalreview.com/2016/03/donald-trump-white-working-class-dysfunction-real-opportunity-needed-not-trump

Wolfe, Cary, *What Is Posthumanism?* (Minneapolis: Minnesota University Press, 2010).

'Richard Wolff OWS of WS', YouTube, 25 October 2011 https://www.youtube.com/watch?v=Q261bPJ-sCo&ab_channel=ChristopherBrown [accessed 8 June 2024].

Zavarzadeh, Mas'ud, 'Post-Ality: The (Dis)Simulations of Cybercapitalism', *Transformation 1: Marxist Boundary Work in Theory, Economics, Politics and Culture* (Montreal: Maisonneuve Press, 1995), pp. 1–75.

—, and Donald Morton, *Theory, (Post)Modernity, Opposition* (Montreal: Maisonneuve Press, 1991).

Zito, Salena, 'Taking Trump Seriously, Not Literally', *The Atlantic*, 23 September 2016, www.theatlantic.com/politics/archive/2016/09/trump-makes-his-case-in-pittsburgh/501335

Žižek, Slavoj, 'Ecology — A New Opium for the Masses', *Next Nature*, 16 February 2009, https://nextnature.net/story/2009/ecology-a-new-opium-for-the-masses

— 'An Interview with Slavoj Žižek: "On Divine Self-Limitation and Revolutionary Love"', with Joshua Delpech-Ramey, *Journal of Philosophy and Scripture*, 1.2, Spring (2004), pp. 32–38.

— *First as Tragedy, Then as Farce* (New York: Verso Books, 2009).

— 'Introduction: The Spectre of Ideology', in *Mapping Ideology*, ed. by Slavoj Žižek (New York: Verso Books, 2012).

— 'Jews and Palestinians are both Victims of Western Racism', *Haaretz*, 12 Dec. 2023.

— 'Learn to Live Without Masters', *Naked Punch*, 3 October 2009.

— *Less Than Nothing: Hegel and the Shadow of Dialectical Materialism* (New York: Verso Books, 2012).

— *On Belief* (London and New York: Routledge, 2001).

— 'The Monstrosity of Christ: Paradox or Dialectic?', YouTube, 21 September 2009 https://youtu.be/RqVAiBbSjbI?t=4202 [accessed 8 June 2024].

— *The Parallax View* (Cambridge: MIT Press, 2006), https://doi.org/10.7551/mitpress/5231.001.0001

— 'Preface: Burning The Bridges', *The Žižek Reader*, ed. by Elizabeth Wright and Edmond Wright (Oxford: Blackwell Publishing Ltd., 1999), pp. vii-x.

— *The Puppet and the Dwarf: The Perverse Core of Christianity* (Cambridge: MIT Press, 2003), https://doi.org/10.7551/mitpress/5706.001.0001

— 'Repeating Lenin', *lacanian ink*, 1997/2001, https://www.lacan.com/replenin. htm

— 'Slavoj Zizek at OWS Part 2', YouTube, 9 October 2011 https://www.youtube. com/watch?v=7UpmUly9It4&ab_channel=visitordesign [accessed 8 June 2024].

— 'The Spectre of Ideology', in *Mapping Ideology*, ed. by Slavoj Žižek (New York: Verso Books, 2012), pp. 1–33.

— *The Ticklish Subject: The Absent Centre of Political Ontology* (New York: Verso Books, 1999).

—, and Charlie Nash, 'What I like about coronavirus' by Slavoj Žižek'. *Spectator, USA* (2020).

—, and Costas Douzinas (eds), *The Idea of Communism* (New York: Verso Books, 2010).

—, and V. I. Lenin, 'Afterword: Lenin's Choice', *Revolution at the Gates: The 1917 Writings* (New York: Verso Books, 2014).

—, and Mao Zedong, 'Introduction', *On Practice and Contradiction* (New York: Verso Books, 2007).

Index

value 2–4, 6–9, 14–15, 17, 28–29, 37–40, 47, 50, 54–55, 58, 60, 64–66, 69–70, 72, 74–75, 77, 79–80, 83–86, 88, 90, 92–93, 107, 111–112, 114, 116, 124, 127–129, 131, 140, 142, 149, 151, 174–175, 183, 186, 188, 192, 194–195, 197–198, 200, 209, 212–213, 217–220, 222, 235, 238–240, 243–244, 257, 259, 261, 263, 268, 270
   surplus 3, 65, 128, 142–144
Venezuela 99, 101–104, 113–114, 116, 236
Vološinov, V. N. 49, 241

Wark, McKenzie 3, 72
Weber, Max 64, 187, 205, 220, 258
Wendy and Lucy 90, 92, 94–95

Wilderson, Frank 218
Wilkie, Rob 7
wokeism 137
Wolfe, Cary 46–48, 59
Wolff, Richard 76, 158, 195
writerly 13, 174–175, 177, 225–226, 228, 230, 232–233, 235, 238–243, 245–246, 249–251, 253, 256–257, 260–264, 267, 269–271

Zavarzadeh, Mas'ud 16, 44, 69, 186–187, 190
Žižek, Slavoj 2, 8, 19, 27–30, 32–35, 38, 46, 59–62, 67, 72–84, 87, 140–148, 155, 157, 190, 226, 243, 251, 253–254, 260
Zola, Émile 265

About the Team

Alessandra Tosi was the managing editor for this book.

Elisabeth Pitts proof-read this manuscript.

Anja Pritchard indexed the book and created the Alt-text.

The cover concept is by Stephen Tumino. The cover was designed by Katy Saunders and Jeevanjot Kaur Nagpal, and produced in InDesign using the Fontin and Calibri fonts.

Jeremy Bowman typeset the book in InDesign. The main text font is Tex Gyre Pagella and the heading font is Californian FB. Jeremy also created the EPUB.

Cameron Craig produced the paperback and hardback and the PDF and HTML editions. The conversion was performed with opensource software and other tools freely available on our GitHub page at https://github.com/OpenBookPublishers.

Laura Rodríguez was in charge of marketing.

This book was peer-reviewed by two referees. Experts in their field, these readers give their time freely to help ensure the academic rigour of our books. We are grateful for their generous and invaluable contributions.

This book need not end here...

Share

All our books — including the one you have just read — are free to access online so that students, researchers and members of the public who can't afford a printed edition will have access to the same ideas. This title will be accessed online by hundreds of readers each month across the globe: why not share the link so that someone you know is one of them?

This book and additional content is available at:
https://doi.org/10.11647/OBP.0324

Donate

Open Book Publishers is an award-winning, scholar-led, not-for-profit press making knowledge freely available one book at a time. We don't charge authors to publish with us: instead, our work is supported by our library members and by donations from people who believe that research shouldn't be locked behind paywalls.

Why not join them in freeing knowledge by supporting us:
https://www.openbookpublishers.com/support-us

Follow @OpenBookPublish

Read more at the Open Book Publishers BLOG

You may also be interested in:

Wellbeing, Freedom and Social Justice
The Capability Approach Re-Examined

Ingrid Robeyns

https://doi.org/10.11647/OBP.0130

A Common Good Approach to Development
Collective Dynamics of Development Processes

Mathias Nebel, Oscar Garza-Vázquez & Clemens Sedmak (eds)

https://doi.org/10.11647/OBP.0290

Democracy and Power
The Delhi Lectures

Noam Chomsky (author) Jean Drèze (introduction by)

https://doi.org/10.11647/OBP.0050

Labour and Value
Rethinking Marx's Theory of Exploitation

Ernesto Screpanti

https://doi.org/10.11647/OBP.0182